ica adapting itself to renewal?

What are the problems and prospects for a married clergy?

How much do the demands of personal conscience and ecclesiastical obedience conflict on controversial social and moral problems (race, Vietnam, the poverty program)?

What is the state of human relations and communications between diocesan priests and their religious superiors?

What are the actual working conditions of these priests?

The frank comments of the diocesan priests reveal an overwhelming desire to be treated by their bishops as mature, professional men whose special talents are fostered and used, instead of disregarded and wasted. Their views point up a large current of restlessness among the priests at the lower levels of the diocese, a restlessness stemming not only from the slow pace of *aggiornamento,* but also from questions raised by the clergy even before Vatican II.

The issues raised in this book are discussed in the light of the Council documents. Study and research, says Father Fichter, are ongoing characteristics of the modern world and also of a progressive religious organization. *America's Forgotten Priests* should be of much practical value toward devising programs for action and reform where needed in the Catholic Church in America.

l
h
tl

t
o
3,
pr
rai.
Chu.
the m
these:

To wh.

AMERICA'S FORGOTTEN PRIESTS—
WHAT THEY ARE SAYING

America's Forgotten

HARPER & ROW, PUBLISHERS

NEW YORK
EVANSTON
AND LONDON

Priests-

What They Are Saying

JOSEPH H. FICHTER

HARVARD UNIVERSITY

7219

FIRST EDITION

LIBRARY OF CONGRESS CATALOG CARD NUMBER: 68-11735

M-R

CONTENTS

5

ACKNOWLEDGMENTS

Many people have contributed in various ways to the contents of this book and I express my appreciation to them. Groups of diocesan priests in several parts of the country originated the research project, helped to formulate the general hypotheses as well as the specific questions, and contributed the bulk of the financial assistance. Robert Hoyt and Donald Thorman contributed further financial support. Maida Walker and Rachel Crounse did the preliminary data processing and Jean Blanning cooperated at every phase of the study. The computer work was done by John F. Keller and Norma Batt at Loyola University of the South, and the several versions of the manuscript were typed by Barbara Rhodes at the Harvard University Divinity School. I am especially grateful to the following persons who read the whole manuscript, chapter by chapter, and who helped enormously in the clarification and interpretation of the research findings: Raymond Baumhart, James Blanning, Fortunata Caliri, Thomas Garrett, Edgar Mills, Mary Schniedwind, Edward Stanton, Ernest Wallwork, and Dorothy Willmann.

INTRODUCTION

WHY ASK THE PRIESTS?

One of the remarkable consequences of the Second Vatican Council has been the proliferation of questionnaires. Hardly a week passes without an announcement that some Bishop has decided to make a study of his diocese or that some Provincial Superior has ordered a self-survey of a religious order or congregation. This relatively sudden popularity of opinion polls and factual surveys in the American Catholic Church represents a dramatic shift from pre-Conciliar days when Fitzpatrick could say that "Catholics have a tendency to allow their faith and their philosophy to substitute for knowledge that can be gained only through competent empirical research."[1]

Social science research was going on in the American Catholic Church before Pope John was inspired to convoke the Second Vatican Council, and before the Council itself recommended that the bishops "ought to employ suitable methods, especially social research." It was not a new idea, discovered in Rome by the assembled prelates, that "the forms of the apostolate should be properly adapted to current needs," nor that "religious and social surveys, made through offices of pastoral sociology, contribute greatly to the effective and fruitful attainment of that goal, and they are cordially recommended."[2]

In place of the theoretical discussion which often accompanies the presentation of research findings we are here using the Council documents as a conceptual framework for the analysis of our empirical

11

data. The Council acts also as a model in another way. As Cardinal Shehan remarks, there were "nearly four years of exhaustive preparation" for the opening of the Council.[3] This was then followed by four years (1962–1965) in which the official sessions were held. What was happening, in practical terms, was a world-wide survey through eight years of facts and opinions presented in "working papers" by *periti*, documentary drafts by commissions, interventions by delegates to the Council.

In this sense the Second Vatican Council was in itself an enormous research project, involving some of the best talent in the Church seeking knowledge that would clarify and improve the Church's mission on earth. Study and research are ongoing characteristics of the modern world, particularly of scientific western society, and also of a progressive religious organization. As Pope Paul VI said during the final session of the Council, "From now on *aggiornamento* will signify for us a wisely undertaken quest for a deeper understanding of the spirit of the Council and the faithful application of the norms it has happily and prayerfully provided."[4]

The Conciliar norms at which the delegates arrived were necessarily as broad as the universal Church and were in many instances the fruit of compromise among various points of view of the Council Fathers. This means that the application of the norms, or the implementation of recommendations, requires a flexibility that makes them responsive to the needs of the Church in different nations, regions, and dioceses. It is obvious that the Council recognized social research as an important instrument in the hands of local Churchmen responsible for the needed adaptations.[5] Survey research provides the clergy and laity alike with the data needed for informed judgments about programs for action and reform.

The recent establishment, in 1965, by the American hierarchy of the Center for Applied Research in the Apostolate was a response to Conciliar recommendations and a concrete recognition of the value of empirical research. The American Board of Bishops has already contributed fifty thousand dollars to CARA for a research project on the problem of vocations to the Church. Up to this time, few Catholic organizations, and fewer bishops, have shown a pragmatic readiness to "buy" social science research as a preliminary to decision-making for adaptation and reform.

What about the problem areas for which the Bishops have not commissioned research, or where large research foundations have not seen fit to grant research funds?[6] We have selected only one small area of study. Could we not have put our limited resources of time, money, and talent to work on some of the sophisticated and more pressing questions of theology and sociology? If God is dead, why study the Church? If the Church is really irrelevant, why study the clergy that tries to keep it going? If the whole religious institution is falling into ruins, why bother to poke among those ruins for explanations of the disaster? Why study the priesthood of the clergy if the priesthood of the laity is the giant wave of the religious future? If vocations have declined and priests have lost interest in their work, why not research some of the bigger issues that may have caused this decline and this disinterest?

These questions are not meant to be mere rhetoric. In this post-Conciliar era of anxiety, dissatisfaction, and restlessness one is almost forced to reiterate his belief that the mission of Christ will continue to be carried on by dedicated people in organized social structures. Some of these dedicated people will fill the Bishops' Pastoral Office in the Church; some of them will promote the Apostolate of the Laity; others will be concerned about the Appropriate Renewal of the Religious Life; and still others will be deeply involved in the Ministry and Life of Priests. The Fathers of the Second Vatican Council discussed and voted on these and a dozen other major issues, but did not pretend that they had said the last word about them. This is why they suggested that study and experimentation should take place at the local level.

One may say then that the whole Church in America, as an ongoing socio-cultural system, is available for study by the instruments and methods of social science.[7] One could insist that the hierarchy should be the first target of research because it is the bishops who legislated the new Church at the Council and who are now most responsible in implementing their Vatican decisions. One could argue with vehemence that the laity is now the "new" element in the American Church and that their participation will from now on be the most significant factor in renewal. A case can be made also for the religious orders, especially the Sisters, with their willingness to continue the conventional apostolate as well as to experiment with unconventional ministeries.[8]

There is no question about the importance and need for studying bishops, laity and religious orders, or any subareas within these groups. In this instance, however, we are reporting on a survey of the clergy, but only a segment of these—the diocesan priests who are neither pastors nor monsignors. These rank-and-file priests assist in parochial work or fill a variety of assignments in supraparochial work. Wedged between their high-status superiors and the laity, they have been called the "forgotten men" of the Church. For the most part, these are the men for whom Bishop Leven made an intervention at the final session of Vatican II, when he said that they were forgotten in the Council schema on the Ministry and Life of the Priests.[9] He pointed out that in the larger dioceses they constitute more than half of the clergy, and that they "certainly do more than half the work. Yet the assistant has no juridical status and almost no rights." He felt that the Holy Synod should not pass them over in silence and asked, "Is their place not important, nor their status worthy of correction and examination?"

The selection of these lower-echelon priests as a subject for study does not mean that the rest of the clergy are unimportant or that there is nothing further to learn from and about monsignors and pastors. One curate in his late thirties from a New Jersey diocese wrote, "My pastor, ordained about forty years, feels a bit left out. He wishes that pastors could be polled on these questions and others specifically applicable to them." A priest from a California city says, "I would like to hear good pastors and monsignors express their minds and feelings on these topics and the results sent to a meeting of the hierarchy." A southern priest in his early forties suggested "a similar questionnaire for seminary drop-outs and for those who have left the priesthood—also for ex-religious and ex-sisters." Then a Midwestern curate in his late thirties said "I would like to see a poll of this kind of the bishops of the United States."

Experience in social science research shows that the findings can be more meaningful when one focuses more intensively on a smaller segment of a population than when one attempts to get an extensive view of a total population. There is also value and satisfaction in venturing into hitherto "unexplored" areas and in searching out people who have been the least studied and the most neglected. In an earlier national sample survey of diocesan clergy, we studied both pastors and curates, but omitted monsignors as well as priests in nonparochial specialized work. We shall include some of the findings from the earlier study to supplement the present report.[10]

These lower-echelon priests were mentioned in the Decree on the Bishops' Pastoral Office. After saying that all priests, both diocesan and religious, "participate in and exercise with the bishop the one priesthood of Christ," the Council Fathers say that those in supraparochial work "contribute an exceedingly valuable assistance," and that those in parochial work "make an outstanding and active contribution to the pastoral ministry."[11] One looks in vain for further clarification, recognition, or exposition by the Council on these men. As Bishop Leven remarked, "the Council has said many beautiful things on the status of bishops, auxiliaries, pastors, religious, separated brethren, and non-Christians, but nothing on the role and apostolate of assistants."[12]

Not only were these lower-echelon diocesan clergy ignored by Vatican II. The main reason for focusing our study on them is that these are the men in the Church who are seldom consulted even about matters that concern themselves. No one expressed it better than a curate in his fifties who wrote that "this is the first time in almost thirty years as a priest that anyone in authority asked my opinion about anything. It is about time that we had something to say, since we are the 'shock troops,' the foot soldiers in contact with our parishioners every day. We must have some good ideas, and we are in a better position to fathom our own and the people's needs than a man at a desk or an ivory tower removed from his flock." A much younger priest from Connecticut believes that "getting the opinion of the 'troops' is indeed in order, for there is something about the parish routine that only we in the field can assess and appreciate."

This desire to be heard by his superiors and to be consulted like any professional man is evident throughout the survey findings, and was expressed by many respondents. One curate from New York State wrote, "I have answered these questions with the sincere hope that the information gathered by this survey will be used in a serious and honest effort so that the apostolate of the Church can become more effective and fruitful." A Virginia curate in his early thirties said, "This study is a great step in the right direction. I only hope that its results will be taken seriously by those in authority." A younger priest from Kansas wrote: "Our only hope is that your survey and others like it, plus endeavors in all our respective dioceses, will be eye-openers to our bishops, pastors and people—so that we may all have freedom of expression and action as well as a general and genuine atmosphere of acceptance and understanding."

In a modest way, then, the present study imitates the procedure of the Second Vatican Council by seeking the interventions of concerned and knowledgcable priests. The immediate genesis of the survey was in the spring of 1966 when a group of diocesan clergy determined to raise the necessary funds and engage a social science researcher.[13] They wanted to know more than simply "What's bothering the diocesan clergy?"[14] They sensed a large current of restlessness among their fellow priests at the lower levels of the diocese, stemming mainly from the slow pace of the *aggiornamento*, but going back also to queries that had been raised by the clergy since before Vatican II.

The objective of this research project, therefore, was to investigate in a systematic and scientific manner the status and role of the "men at the bottom," the forgotten men who have little voice and less power to effect changes in either the Church structure or in their own careers. In order to attain this general goal specific areas of investigation had to be staked out, and the manner in which this was done explains why the final questionnaire contains certain items and not others. We asked the sponsoring group to provide a list of the problems and interests that they heard most discussed by diocesan priests and that seemed to be most urgent among them. The large mass of suggestions that emerged from this first stage of inquiry fell into eight general categories, each of which was then subdivided and reformulated in testable and answerable questions. During the summer of 1966 this tentative questionnaire was completely revised five times on the basis of discussion and pre-testing with groups of diocesan priests in Boston, Chicago, Detroit, Los Angeles, Milwaukee, New Orleans, New York, and St. Louis.

It seems important to emphasize that the eight major categories of questions did not come from any "arm-chair" sociologist or from any "ivory tower" Church administrator. These questions emerged from the hard-core experiences of the diocesan clergy in the day-by-day pursuit of their priestly assignments. Dedicated to their own vocation and devoted to the mission of Christ in society, they wanted to know what their fellow diocesan priests could report and suggest about the following general problems of the Church and the priesthood:

(a) To what extent is the Church in America adapting itself in some of the obvious practices that require renewal?

(b) What is the state of human relations and communication between the diocesan priests and their ecclesiastical authorities?

(c) What are the important facts about seminary training and its relationship to the professional life of the clergy?

(d) In what ways can the priest continue his education after the seminary and keep up with the demands of his calling?

(e) What are and should be the actual working conditions in the assignments in which these priests have been placed?

(f) To what extent does a career pattern develop during the working lifetime of the diocesan clergy?

(g) What are the problems and prospects of a married clergy among those who are ordained for the dioceses of the Latin rite?

(h) How is a priest to form and follow his conscience on some of the important social and moral problems he encounters?

Each specific question proposed under each of these eight headings was repeatedly tested, re-formulated and re-tested in the "field," that is, among the working priests of the several urban dioceses. We had to make sure that the meaning of the question was unambiguous and that it was applicable to the actual situation of the respondent. The wording of each item was carefully tested and revised so that the whole range of opinion from affirmative to negative, or from liberal to conservative, could be registered in the answers.

Not everyone was satisfied with the questionnaire schedule that resulted from these months of consultation and discussion. Survey research by mailed questionnaire has certain limitations as well as certain advantages.[15] Unlike personal interviewing, for example, a survey questionnaire cannot probe deeply for explanations (unless it includes many uncodable open-end items). The diocesan priests who inaugurated and financed this survey felt that they could not afford the much higher cost of the interview method of research. They were convinced that a mailed questionnaire would reach a larger sample of the priests and would adequately supply the kind of information they were seeking. No questionnaire can ask everything; and the lengthier the questionnaire, the lower will be the rate of returns.[16] We asked the respondents to make suggestions about other important items that should be included in a survey of priests. We shall list and discuss these added interventions in Appendix C.

It should be clear, then, that this project was not conceived as "pure" research or that its findings would be published only in one of the journals devoted to the behavorial sciences. It is the nearly unanimous opinion of both the promoters and the respondents that the findings of this survey can be of practical utility to the Church in America and that the results should be widely circulated. One New York curate in his early forties wrote that "self-evaluation is an effective technique in the business world. How the Church has kept itself immune from this therapeutic technique is a mystery to me. How effective it could be on all levels—from parish societies to deaneries and dioceses."

The Fathers of the Second Vatican Council declared that "the wished for renewal of the whole Church depends in large measure on a ministry of priests which is vitalized by the spirit of Christ."[17] Part of this revitalization must come from the experienced voices of the "forgotten" clergy, for these too are full-time professionals in the Church whose ministry and life need study and appraisal. As Bishop Leven said at the Council, the almost universal system of inefficient utilization of personnel in the Church prevents these lower-echelon priests "from exercising their charismata now and unfits them to do so when and if they become pastors."

NOTES

1. Joseph P. Fitzpatrick, "Catholic Responsibilities in Sociology," *Thought*, Vol. 26, Autumn 1951, p. 389.
2. *Bishops' Pastoral Office in the Church*, Articles 16, 17.
3. Lawrence Cardinal Shehan, "Introduction," p. xv in Walter Abbott, ed., *The Documents of Vatican II* (New York: Angelus Books, 1966), from which all quotations used in the present report are taken.
4. Quoted *ibid.*, p. xviii.
5. "The forms of the apostolate should be properly adapted to current needs not only in terms of spiritual and moral conditions, but also of social, demographic and economic ones." *Bishops' Pastoral Office in the Church*, Article 17. The Council's *Decree on Ecumenism*, Article 6, tells us that "Christ summons the Church, as she goes her pilgrim way, to that continual reformation of which she always has need, insofar as she is an institution of men here on earth." Deficiencies should be "appropriately rectified at the proper moment."
6. It should be pointed out that the two large research projects on Catholic education conducted by the University of Notre Dame and the National Opinion Research Center of the University of Chicago were funded by grants from the Carnegie Foundation and not by "Catholic money."
7. For a series of research projects that focused on the urban Catholic parish, see the following books by Joseph H. Fichter, *Southern Parish: Dynamics of a City Church* (Chicago: University of Chicago Press, 1951); *Social Relations in the Urban Parish* (Chicago: University of Chicago Press, 1954), especially the Appendix, "Utility of Social Science for Religion," pp. 235–48; *Soziologie der Pfarrgruppen* (Münster, Germany: Aschendorff Verlag, 1957); *Parochial School, A Sociological Study* (Notre Dame, Ind.: University of Notre Dame Press, 1958).
8. A survey questionnaire of 649 items was distributed to 160,000 Sisters in April, 1967, by the Research Committee of the Conference of Major Religious Superiors of Women's Institutes in the United States.
9. Reported from Rome on October 16, 1965, by the Divine Word News Service. The Bishop said also: "Let no one deny that the trauma of frustrated assistants is serious in the Church . . . Would modern technology and industry spend so much time and energy and money to train men and use them so poorly?"
10. Some of the results of that survey are contained in Joseph H. Fichter, *Priest and People* (New York: Sheed and Ward, 1965), a misleading title for a book about the "Friends of Priests" who were studied in a companion survey in 1960, and not to be confused with the work of Conor K. Ward, *Priests and People* (Liverpool, England: University of Liverpool Press, 1961).
11. *Bishops' Pastoral Office in the Church*, Articles 29 and 30. Of course, the generalizations made about the clergy in the decrees on *Priestly Formation* and on the *Ministry and Life of Priests* are applicable to the parochial assistants and to those in specialized diocesan work.
12. Philip A. Hamilton, "Sociologist Looks at the Pastor–Assistant Structure,"

The Catholic Messenger, August 4, 1966, p. 5, points out that the editor of The Documents of Vatican II had 119 index references on the bishop, twenty-six on the pastor, and two on the assistant, both of which refer to the same page.

13. About two thirds of the cost of this survey came from the voluntary contributions of 283 secular priests, mainly from the larger dioceses, and the remainder from Catholic lay people, notably the National Catholic Reporter, which enjoyed an "exclusive" for the first press release of the findings. See the report and description, Vol. 3, No. 8, December 14, 1966.

14. Under the general heading, "What's Bothering Priests Today?" America, Vol. 115, April 23, 1966, published three articles by Francis Canavan, James Kavanaugh and Mary Perkins Ryan, pp. 582–88, foreshadowing many of the questions raised in this survey.

15. Any standard textbook on social science research methods makes this point. For a thoughtful essay see Frank W. Neff, "Survey Research," pp. 23–28, in Alvin W. Gouldner and S. M. Miller, eds., Applied Sociology (New York: The Free Press, 1965).

16. We found this to be the case in a survey of college graduates. The longer questionnaire sent to Negro colleges had a much lower rate of returns than that sent to the white colleges. See Joseph H. Fichter, 1964 Graduates of Predominantly Negro Colleges (Washington: U. S. Government Printing Office, 1967).

17. Opening words of the Preface to the decree on Priestly Formation.

AMERICA'S FORGOTTEN PRIESTS—
WHAT THEY ARE SAYING

WHO ARE THESE PRIESTS?

According to the statistics in the 1966 edition of Kenedy's official *Catholic Directory* there were in the United States 17,814 diocesan priests who were neither pastors nor monsignors. Experts in the art of opinion polling have long since learned that it is not necessary, or even useful, to reach everybody in a given population in order to obtain reliable information about their attitudes.[1] For some purposes the U.S. Census Bureau is satisfied to take a sample of only 5 per cent of the population it wants to study. The best-known and most reliable public opinion polls are able to achieve quite accurate results by taking a representative sample of less than three thousand adults out of the many millions of the American population.[2]

In order to reach a representative cross-section of the lower-echelon diocesan priests for this survey we employed a strict interval one-third sample, which is extraordinarily large for a study of this kind. From the list of diocesan priests who are not pastors, a listing which the publishers of Kenedy's official *Catholic Directory* guarantee to be "ninety-eight per cent accurate," every third name was mechanically selected. From the resultant addressed envelopes we manually removed the names of monsignors, as well as those of the "two per cent error" which consisted mainly of religious order priests who had somehow slipped into the Kenedy listing. We then mailed the survey questionnaire to 5,938 priests.

About one half (51%) of this selected sample answered the questionnaire before the "cut-off date," which was ninety days after the forms had been sent out in early September. In order to guarantee anonymity to the responding priests, we did not preserve their names and addresses. For this reason, but also mainly because of limited research funds, we did not send a follow-up schedule to those who did not respond. A follow-up would undoubtedly have increased the rate of returns but it is doubtful if it would have changed the nature of the responses.[3] The original size of the sample, one third of the potential universe, was already an unusually high proportion, as compared to that employed in most survey sampling.

Can we say then that the actual rate and distribution of the responses are satisfactory for our purposes? Any survey of a national sample of a selected segment of the diocesan clergy must attempt to obtain a regional distribution that is proportionate to the numbers and location of these priests throughout the country. Since we asked the priests to identify the diocese to which they belong we were able to make a comparison between their residential distribution and the actual regional distribution of respondents. Table 1.1 lists the regions of the United States as established by the Census Bureau and as used also for the statistics of the *Catholic Directory*. The data in the first three columns are derived from the later source, showing the distribution of all Catholic clergy in the United States, of all diocesan clergy, and of all diocesan nonpastors and nonmonsignors. The final column, comparable only with the third column, gives the regional distribution of our respondents.

We must remember that the total number of 58,651 American priests of the Latin rite include 22,693 men who belong to religious orders and congregations.[4] This survey provides no information about these four out of ten (38.7%) priests, whom we excluded because their life and ministry differ in some ways from that of the diocesan clergy. A further analysis of the statistics reveals that these two types of priests are not proportionately distributed throughout the country. The religious order clergy are in highest proportions (54.5%) in the South Atlantic States (Delaware, Maryland, District of Columbia, Virginia, West Virginia, North and South Carolina, Georgia, Florida) and they are in lowest proportions (31.9%) in the West North

Central States (Minnesota, Iowa, Missouri, North and South Dakota, Nebraska, Kansas).

Table 1.1 reveals that half (49.5%) of all American diocesan priests belong in the lower echelon that we are studying; that is, they are neither monsignors nor pastors of parishes. We have no statistical information on the distribution of monsignors throughout the coun-

Table 1.1 Regional distribution of all clergy, diocesan priests, nonpastors and nonmonsignors, and current survey respondents

	All priests	Diocesan clergy	Not pastors or monsignors	Respondents to this survey
New England States	11.7%	12.2%	13.4%	14.4%
Middle Atlantic	25.4	27.6	31.8	29.7
South Atlantic	6.4	4.8	5.2	4.6
East North Central	24.2	24.0	23.0	26.0
East South Central	2.7	2.8	2.7	2.7
West North Central	11.5	12.7	8.8	9.6
West South Central	6.0	5.3	4.5	4.1
Mountain States	3.1	3.1	2.5	2.5
Pacific States	9.0	7.5	8.1	6.4
(Total Number)	(58,651)	(35,958)	(17,814)	(3,048)

try but are aware of the fact that episcopal "policy" in the recommendation of priests for this honor differs from diocese to diocese.[5] It should be expected, however, as shown in the comparison between the second and third columns of Table 1.1, that the proportion of nonpastors will be high in areas where the Catholic population is large and where the priest must wait thirty years or more after ordination before being promoted to a pastorate. For example, although these lower-echelon priests constitute half of all diocesan priests in the country, they are in much higher proportions (57.2%) in the Middle Atlantic States (New York, New Jersey, Pennsylvania) than they are in the West North Central States (34.4%).

To what extent then does the sample of priests we have reached in this survey represent the actual regional distribution of diocesan nonpastors and nonmonsignors? The answer lies in the comparison between the third and fourth columns of Table 1.1. We find there, that while the statistical differences are not great, the East North Central States (Ohio, Indiana, Illinois, Michigan, Wisconsin) are somewhat over-represented, and that the Middle Atlantic States are somewhat under-represented in our sample.

Since we are making occasional reference in this report to the findings of our 1960 survey of diocesan curates and pastors (excluding monsignors), it seems of some importance to compare the regional distribution of that study with the present survey. The statistics in Table 1.2 help us to recognize the maldistribution of "career opportunities" for the diocesan clergy.

Table 1.2   Regional distribution of 1960 survey, by pastors and curates, and of current survey, by nonparochial and parochial assignments

	1960 Survey		Current Survey	
	Pastors	Curates	Non-curates	Curates
New England States	7.8%	15.1%	10.0%	16.0%
Middle Atlantic	16.6	28.5	30.1	29.5
South Atlantic	3.1	4.6	3.4	4.9
East North Central	28.8	26.1	27.3	25.6
East South Central	3.8	2.8	4.2	2.2
West North Central	22.3	10.2	13.0	8.5
West South Central	5.7	4.5	3.6	4.3
Mountain States	5.7	1.7	2.4	2.5
Pacific States	6.2	6.5	6.0	6.5
(Number of respondents)	(944)	(1,239)	(761)	(2,287)

It should be stated again that we are not striving for a national representative sample of all Latin rite clergy (since we excluded religious order priests), or of all diocesan priests (since we excluded pastors and monsignors). What is of most significance to our question whether we are using a representative sample is the close proportional similarity between the second and fourth columns in Table 1.2. In a sense the curates are the only strictly comparable categories in the two surveys since the earlier survey excluded the men who are engaged in specialized, nonparochial work.

A priest in the Brooklyn diocese may have to wait more than thirty years before he is promoted to the pastorate, while a priest in Grand

Island (Nebraska) may become a pastor five or six years after ordination. The difference of opportunity for "career promotion" is dramatically revealed in the first two columns of Table 1.2, which show the relative location of pastors and curates who responded to our 1960 survey. For the purposes of that study, every seventh name of the diocesan parish priests (excluding monsignors) was selected from the 1959 edition of Kenedy's *Catholic Directory*. Since some pastors are monsignors, this procedure lowered the percentage of pastors who were questioned, but the generalization is still valid when we say that curates outnumber pastors in the New England and Middle Atlantic regions, and pastors outnumber curates in the West North Central and Mountain regions. What happened then in the selective sample of curates in both surveys was that dioceses where the Catholic population is small, and where diocesan priests become pastors at a fairly young age, have proportionately fewer representatives among the respondents than do the more populous dioceses.

Another way of checking whether these survey samples are representative of the priests we were trying to reach is to study their proportional age categories. Unlike the statistics on place of residence, however, there is no available Church census which provides the true age distribution of the Catholic clergy in the United States. The best we can do here is to conjecture that the samples we took in 1960 and 1966 approximate a representative age distribution of the categories studied. Table 1.3 shows the comparison between the two surveys.

Table 1.3 Age distribution in 1960 survey, by pastors and curates, and in current survey, by nonparochial and parochial assignments

| | 1960 Survey | | Current Survey | |
	Pastors	Curates	Non-curates	Curates
Under 30 years	1%	26%	10%	26%
30–34 years	5	30	25	28
35–39	10	18	29	24
40–44	17	14	16	11
45–49	19	8	9	6
50–54	19	3	5	3
55 and older	29	1	6	2
(Number of respondents)	(944)	(1,239)	(761)	(2,287)

Table 1.3 shows the expected age disparity of the earlier survey in the fact that two thirds (67%) of the pastors were forty-five years of age and older, while almost nine out of ten (88%) of the curates were less than forty-five years old. The more interesting comparison, however, is between the statistics in columns two and four of the Table. We find here a remarkable similarity in the age groupings when we combine the curates into three categories: those under thirty-five (56% to 54%), thirty-five to forty-nine years (40% to 41%), fifty years of age and older (4% to 5%). Table 1.3 reveals also that the men in specialized assignments include a smaller proportion under thirty-five than do the parish priests (35% to 54%) and a larger proportion who are forty-five and over (20% to 11%) but we can make no comparison with the earlier survey, which excluded the men in specialized work.

What can be said then in response to the young curate in Nevada who thinks that all American clergy, or at least all diocesan priests, should have an opportunity to answer a survey of this kind? One may well agree with this laudable suggestion, but not with the complaint he makes that "this survey is unjust because it does not present a true picture of the clergy in this country. It is unfair in excluding all pastors and all prelates, and this makes the whole purpose of the study worthless." Nevertheless, he said, he answered the questionnaire because he wanted us to know that not all young priests are in favor of the "new ideas" in the Church. "I want my voice to be counted against a one-sided survey like this."

After discussing the sample distribution by region and age, let us see whether there is another possible source of bias among the priests who actually answered the questionnaire. Some of the more conservative priests who responded opined that there was an "obviously liberal slant" to this survey, and one young curate from Indiana asked, "Is your sampling loaded with likely liberal priests? Only such received the questionnaire in this diocese." The mechanical selection of every third name clearly prevented the deliberate selection of only liberals, or only conservatives, even if we knew which diocesan priests in America belong in these two groupings.

If there was not a liberal bias in the original selection of respondents, could there be a bias of this kind among the priests who chose to answer the survey? This kind of question is prompted by the possibility that the survey would most likely be answered by the overeager, the liberals and the malcontents among the diocesan clergy, and would be ignored by those who are satisfied with things as they are. Although we have no way of knowing the mind of the nonrespondents, we are able in Table 1.4 to test the assumption that those who answered immediately and eagerly would differ considerably in their opinions from those who delayed their response.

Table 1.4 Comparative answers to selected questions by earliest and latest respondents

	First 800 question-naires	Last 600 question-naires
Approve a diocesan "grievance committee"	88.8%	90.1%
(Number of respondents)	(793)	(589)
Dispense with title of monsignor	74.0	74.1
(Number of respondents)	(800)	(599)
Approve voluntary resignation from priesthood	65.4	63.8
(Number of respondents)	(796)	(594)
Approve freedom of choice to marry	60.6	63.9
(Number of respondents)	(780)	(577)
Approve choice of separate residence for curates	29.9	32.8
(Number of respondents)	(799)	(597)
Approve clergy's wearing civilian suits	20.0	19.4
(Number of respondents)	(800)	(596)

If the discontented liberals among these priests rushed to register their complaints by answering the questionnaire as soon as they received it, the first column in Table 1.4 should show them to be much more liberal and dissatisfied than the men who took their time to answer. The Table reveals clearly that there is hardly any statistical difference in the proportional responses of these two groups. We shall see later that the two key issues for the disgruntled clergy in this sample concern a voluntary resignation, or "honorable discharge" from the priesthood, and the freedom of choice to marry on the part of the diocesan clergy. On these two matters the earliest and the latest respondents balance each other.

The most important conclusion that we can draw from the comparative statistics of Table 1.4 is the confident prediction that succeeding "batches" of questionnaires from those who did not answer the questionnaire would not have differed substantially from the findings of this report. Under normal conditions and with similar surveys, research scholars who have expensively searched out nonrespondents have found also that they do not differ significantly from the respondents. In the present instance we have no hesitation in claiming that our findings represent the attitudes and opinions of American rank-and-file diocesan priests.

The fact that these priestly respondents are "so young" raises the question of whether their opinions are worth listening to. Bishop Leven says that these men are spoken of as though they were children; "but they are not children; they are mature men." In the larger dioceses they are promoted to the pastorate "only after their years of vigor and energy have passed." Are these the kind of men who can intelligently and honestly make judgments about themselves, their work, and the diocese and Church they serve? It is apparent that Archbishop Vagnozzi does not think so. In a press conference arranged by Washington female news reporters he belittled the priests who responded to this survey. The exclusion of monsignors and pastors from the study meant that "the group was composed of older priests who had not been promoted—possibly for good reason—and of young rather immature clerics."[6]

Returns reveal that half (49%) of the respondents to this study are under thirty-five years of age and are presumably the "rather immature" clergy of the reference. These men are the products of the Church's seminary system which is supposed to foster in them a "solid maturity of personality" and train them to "act on their own initiative and energetically."[7] They are working under the direction of episcopal administration. These are the men whom the bishop should regard as his "brothers and friends," and also as "necessary counselors and helpers in the ministry."[8] If they are still immature during the decade following their ordination, one may well ask serious questions of both the seminary system and the episcopal administration.

The small proportion of "older priests" (those over forty-five) who had not, "possibly for good reason," been promoted either as monsignor or pastor, are almost exclusively from the large American dioceses where priests do not become pastors until they have been ordained at least twenty years. Many of them are noncurates doing specialized diocesan work (chancery office, chaplains, seminary teaching, etc.). In most dioceses the clergy selected for such assignment are specially trained and trustworthy. The diocesan clergy, at various age levels, who are in supra-parochial work constitute one fourth of the respondents to the present study. Their opinions seem well worthy of attention.[9]

When we look at the type of employment in which these diocesan priests are engaged, we find that most of them (55%) are full-time parochial curates, or assistant pastors; one out of five has been appointed to assist the pastor but also does a significant amount of nonparish work; one out of four is a "specialist," on a nonparish assignment in the diocese. Table 1.5 demonstrates that these priestly roles are not distributed with regularity throughout the country.

Table 1.5 Regional distribution of current survey by assignment: full-time curate, part-time curate, noncurate and total

	Full-time curate	Part-time curate	Non-curate	All respondents
New England States	17.7%	10.8%	10.0%	14.4%
Middle Atlantic	31.3	24.4	30.1	29.9
South Atlantic	4.4	6.5	3.4	4.5
East North Central	23.3	32.2	27.3	26.0
East South Central	1.9	3.0	4.2	2.7
West North Central	8.1	9.5	13.0	9.6
West South Central	3.9	5.7	3.6	4.1
Mountain States	2.3	3.2	2.4	2.4
Pacific States	7.1	4.7	6.0	6.4
(Number of respondents)	(1,688)	(599)	(761)	(3,048)

We have already seen in Tables 1.1 and 1.2 that the proportion of nonpastors to pastors is highest in those areas where the Catholic population is largest. Table 1.5 gives us the opportunity to compare the distribution of the three categories of priests, defined by their type of employment. The noncurates who are occupied full-time in the various non-parochial ministeries of the diocese are in smaller proportions in the New England States, and in higher proportions in the midwest (including both the East North Central and the West North Central States) than are the full-time assistants in the parish. It so happens that both New England and the Midwest have large concentrations of Catholic population. It appears then that population concentration is not the main explanation for the presence or absence of extra-parochial specialists in a diocese.

The same observation seems to be appropriate when we look at the location of part-time curates, who have one foot in the parish and one in some specialized diocesan employment. These men are not simply "moonlighting" by choice, but have usually been assigned by superiors to high school teaching, chaplaincies in hospitals, prisons, or on college campuses, or to a variety of other apostolic tasks. In some dioceses it seems to be the policy of the Bishop that many priests should have "two jobs," and in other places, like Alabama, Mississippi and Tennessee, it may be accounted for by a local shortage of priests. There is also the probability, which we do not investigate here, that religious order priests perform more of the specialized than of the parochial type of work.[10]

In summary of these findings we can say that the priests who answered this survey are representative, or "typical," of the rank-and-file diocesan clergy of the United States. If we were to attempt a rough statistical "profile" of them, we would say that they are urban-ites mainly from the large dioceses where promotions are slow, and that most of them are doing parish work. Their average age is 35.9 years; on the average they have been ordained 9.6 years; and their average age at entrance to the seminary was 17.7 years. This means that they have spent about half of their lives (an average of 18.2 years) under the supervision of the Church, either in preparation for their life work or in the actual functions of the diocesan priesthood.

NOTES

1. For example, Louis Harris and Associates interviewed only 993 adult Roman Catholics for the widely publicized *Newsweek* Poll, "How U.S. Catholics View Their Church," March 20, 1967, pp. 68–75.

2. The construction of a small representative sample is a highly technical and complicated procedure. For a sophisticated discussion of the problems involved see Matilda W. Riley, *Sociological Research* (New York: Harcourt, Brace & World, 1963), Unit Six, "Some Sampling Methods," pp. 256–305.

3. A study was made of those who refused to answer the survey of Samuel A. Stouffer, *Communism, Conformity, and Civil Liberties* (New York: Doubleday, 1955), Appendix A. "Some extraordinary pains were taken to discover whether the failure to get such cases would introduce a serious bias in our analysis. Our considered conclusion is that it would not."

4. The total priests recorded in Kenedy's *Catholic Directory* for 1966 numbered 59,193, but among these were the Eastern rite clergy: 461 diocesan and 81 religious order priests.

5. There appears to be no regular pattern in the designation and "elevation" of monsignors since the granting of this honorific title is mainly the decision of the Bishop Ordinary. See below, Table 7.9, where the priests think the title is given to those with the "best connections."

6. These remarks were attributed to the Apostolic Delegate, Archbishop Egidio Vagnozzi, at his Washington press conference on December 21, 1966 and were released to the news services the following day.

7. Decree of Vatican II on *Priestly Formation*, Article 11.

8. Decree on the *Ministry and Life of Priests*, Article 7.

9. For a discussion of other comments on the press release of the preliminary report of this survey, see Joseph H. Fichter, "That 'Celibacy' Survey," *America*, January 21, 1967, pp. 92–94.

10. For example, almost all 309 Catholic colleges and universities in the United States are operated by religious orders. In the academic year 1966–1967, only twelve of them were conducted by the diocesan clergy.

THE PACE OF DIOCESAN CHANGE

A time of transition is a time of tension and turmoil, especially within religious structures where the tendency is to maintain order and to conserve traditional values. When Pius XII recommended adaptation and John XXIII urged an up-dating, they recognized that change cannot be introduced without disturbance and an element of risk. The Council document on the Church in the Modern World remarks that "today, the human race is passing through a new stage of its history. Profound and rapid changes are spreading by degrees around the whole world." Many people are "burdened down with uneasiness" because they are "buffeted between hope and anxiety and pressing one another with questions about the present course of events."[1]

Some priests who answered this survey made anxious reference to both the pace and kind of change occurring in the Church. One Massachusetts curate in his early fifties complained that "this state of change we're going through is a state of confusion. How can we preach the life-long Christian doctrine as absolute Gospel when so many new problems and possible inferences are being declared? Yesterday's answers are no longer answers but fallacies. As the saying goes: give me the old time religion."[2] An Indiana priest in his early thirties says that "what is difficult for priests over thirty is the fact that the Church we are now in is a different Church from the one we anticipated in the seminary. Doctrinal change in the Church is a disturbing element to me. It is something that the seminary never hinted at; and now everything is under question."

Since the Church is an association of human beings there never was a time when all its members agreed on everything. Historically, it was impossible to record the extent of this disagreement because there was no scientific procedure for reaching the opinions of the rank-and-file clergy or laity. The Council has encouraged communication at all levels of the Church and this may account for the current "considerable disarray" that some observers discuss. "When Pope John XXIII decided to open the ecclesiastical windows he had no notion that he might be letting in a minor hurricane."[3]

At any rate, one should now expect to find that attitudes on renewal and change differ by age and position of respondents, as well as by geographical regions and dioceses. This is an expected consequence of the spirit of flexibility that emerged from the Council. Yet there are priests who want to fix regulataions that bind Catholics universally. A Massachusetts curate writes that "I feel as though my diocese has been dragging its feet, and as a result confusion and individualism have sprung up from one parish to another. The diocese has not laid out specific norms, and as a result extremes in both traditionalism and modernism have arisen among the clergy, and the laity have become very confused. While change is needed and welcome, it should be uniform throughout the diocese, if not throughout the entire country, so that the people will be able to recognize and accept the universal Church to which they had long been accustomed. These variations lead to confusion, and confusion leads to indifference, which is intolerable in this day when a strong united Church is so necessary."[4]

It is apparently difficult for many Catholics to accept a "new" interpretation of the fortress Church which since the Reformation has withstood "assaults" of secularism and modernism, schism and heresy. The Fathers of the Council had themselves to wrestle with the concepts of continuity and change, with the acknowledgment that the truths of Christianity could be clarified and developed even while they remain essentially the same.[5] Much of the arguments of the so-called "conservatives" in the Council rested precisely on the point that the Church had always been right, that the Holy Spirit protected it from error through the centuries, that its whole doctrinal position would be forever shaken if the Fathers admitted the need for reform and renewal.

The fact is that the conservatives and traditionalists lost the debate on every important point of discussion, but the problem of the justification of change in the unchanging Church still bothers many of the clergy. Yet the changes have been introduced and approved, and the empirical question now becomes this: How long will it take for the spirit of renewal to permeate the Church? How soon will the *aggiornamento* be implemented in the various dioceses, parishes and other structures of the Church? Karl Rahner believes that "it will certainly be a long time before the Church which has been given the Second Vatican Council will be the Church of the Second Vatican Council, just as it took a number of generations after the close of the Council of Trent before she became the Church of Reform of Trent."[6] This kind of comparative prediction ignores the impatient temper of modern man and the fact that the pace of twentieth-century change is almost incredibly swifter than that of the sixteenth century.

WHAT IS CHANGING?

One cannot logically discuss change without specifying that which is expected to change. Even here, in this limited survey of clergy opinion we obviously could not ask about "everything" that is changing in the American Church or that the Council recommended for renewal. Experimentation and progress, in whatever ways these are defined, are now almost endemic to the American sociocultural system, and they could hardly be strange concepts to the priests who are products of that system. American priests are generally known as activists and they are not likely to presume that the Holy Spirit alone will perform the task of Church renewal, or that change will certainly "happen" if patience and forbearance are exercised.[7]

There is indeed recognized movement in some dioceses of the country. A young curate from New Jersey says that "your question-naire hits our diocese just as we are in the process of change; for example, the clergy senate is just getting under way, and this is true also of other dioceses." In some items of this survey we asked about changes that have occurred, and in others about changes the respondents would like to see occur. At this point, however, we are concerned only about the rate of change, whether the priests think it is taking place too fast, too slowly, or about right. We selected some of the more obvious phenomena in which American Catholics are involved and asked the priests to rate them. Our double hypothesis, to be tested against the data, is that (a) some of these phenomena are seen as changing more rapidly than others and that (b) the younger clergy are in general more favorably disposed to change than are the older.

The data in Table 2.1 afford an immediate demonstration that, in the opinion of these respondents, the pace of change differs significantly according to the activities observed. The two areas of Church life in which the potential involvement of the laity is greatest, are at opposite ends of the scale. While three out of ten feel that liturgical adaptations are going too slowly in their dioceses, the highest proportion of all (65%) think that the pace in this area is about right.[8] One young priest from Texas thinks that the liturgy "still needs revamping," while his counterpart from Indiana says he fears "we are falling into a new formalism in our liturgical renewal." It is true, of course, that the liturgical movement was well under way before the opening of the Second Vatican Council, and also that the first document promulgated by the Council dealt with the liturgy.

It seems significant to note that the greatest dissatisfaction about the rate of diocesan change focuses on the participation of the laity in "parish planning." While approximately one fifth (22%) are satisfied with their own diocese in this regard, three quarters of them (76%) think that this is coming about too slowly. The Council said that "the laity ought to collaborate energetically in every apostolic and missionary undertaking sponsored by their local parish."[9] Although parish councils are recommended—and have been introduced in some American dioceses—the delicate question of pastoral and episcopal authority is raised when the laity are invited to participate in the administration and planning of the parish. A New England curate in his late forties remarks bluntly that "in this diocese mistrust of the laity is deep-rooted."

Table 2.1 Distribution of opinion concerning diocesan rate of change in specified Church activities

	About right	Too fast	Too slowly	(Number of Respondents)
Liturgical adaptations	65%	5%	30%	(3,037)
Inter-faith dialogue	53	5	42	(3,014)
Rules for mixed marriage	53	3	44	(3,008)
Change of seminary routine	49	9	42	(2,640)
Racial apostolate	43	3	54	(2,940)
Laity in parish planning	22	2	76	(3,014)

We shall see that a substantial minority (about one out of five on some issues) of the priests who are fifty years of age or older feel that changes occur too fast in their dioceses. Table 2.1, however, reveals clearly that only a small proportion of all respondents take this view. It is obvious from the statistics, as well as from their comments, that these priests are not extremists who want to "change everything" and want to do it radically and rapidly. Their general attitude seems to be best expressed by a young curate from Brooklyn who writes: "There should be a change in those conditions that we all admit were very unsuitable for the apostolate, but it would be lamentable if we changed so much as to go to the other extreme."

The Council's Pastoral Constitution on the Church in the Modern World points out that "the institutions, laws, and modes of thinking and feeling as handed down from previous generations do not always seem to be well adapted to the contemporary state of affairs. Hence arises an upheaval in the manner and even the norms of behavior."[10] The opinions expressed by most of these lower-echelon diocesan priests hardly reflect an "upheaval" in their manner and norms of behavior. They unquestionably want change and renewal, but they also recognize and appreciate it when and where it occurs.

LITURGY AND INTER-FAITH DIALOGUE

We saw previously (Table 1.3) that half (49%) of the respondents are below thirty-five years of age, and that only 7 percent are fifty years of age or older. We have hypothesized that age makes a difference in the attitudes these men have concerning the pace of change, and specifically that the younger clergy is more favorable than the older to quick change. This hypothesis will be tested in the following series of Tables and discussion on each of the Church activities involving diocesan change. Invariably, it will be seen, more of the oldest than of the youngest—though always a minority of both—check off "too fast," and more of the youngest than of the oldest check off "too slowly" in estimating the rate of change.

Table 2.1 showed that two thirds (65%) of them in all age categories are satisfied that the liturgy is changing at about the right rate of speed in their dioceses. The second and third lines of Table 2.2, however, show where the dissatisfactions lie according to the age of the respondents. They show that the younger men are much more likely than the older to say that adaptations are occurring too slowly (36% to 15%) while the older men are much more likely to say that the liturgy is changing too fast (20% to 2%). One of the oldest curates from New England gives a special reason for his own dissatisfaction. "The new liturgy in my diocese was used as an instrument to kill off national parishes. We were ordered to do the liturgy in English, and it took almost two years of insistent and repeated requests before we were reluctantly allowed to use the national language."[11]

Table 2.2 Distribution by age categories of opinion concerning diocesan rate of liturgical adaptations

	Under 35 years	35 to 49 years	50 years and over
About right	62%	68%	65%
Too fast	2	7	20
Too slowly	36	25	15
(Number of respondents)	(1,518)	(1,316)	(203)

If we look at the comments of the younger men who feel that the liturgy is changing too slowly in their dioceses, we find a kind of echo of the Council Fathers who said that "a change in attitudes and in human structures frequently calls accepted values into question. This is especially true of young people, who have grown impatient on more than one occasion, and indeed become rebels in their distress."[12] One of the youngest priests from a western diocese finds a reluctance on the part of the older clergy to change their attitudes on the liturgy. "Bishops, older pastors and the diocesan curia really stifle any initiative even in trying to execute what Rome permits. No altars *versus populum*, no offertory processions, are allowed here. Liturgical adaptation is simply in a retarded stage."[13]

Diocesan changes in ecumenism, with particular reference to inter-faith dialogue, elicit a clear split of opinion among the younger clergy, with about half evidencing satisfaction and half saying it is going too slowly. In this instance, in Table 2.3, the oldest priests show the most satisfaction (60%) with the rate of change, but here again they present a substantially larger minority (17%) who think that the change is occurring too rapidly. Strangely enough, hardly any priests wrote comments about this aspect of the survey. This seems to mean that they think the changes are bound to be introduced everywhere.

Table 2.3 Distribution by age categories of opinion concerning rate of diocesan change in *inter-faith* dialogue

	Under 35 years	35 to 49 years	50 years and over
About right	49%	57%	60%
Too fast	2	6	17
Too slowly	49	37	23
(Number of respondents)	(1,504)	(1,310)	(200)

Unlike the liturgy, which is largely a "domestic" problem, the movement for ecumenical encounter requires "outside" participation. The fact that the older men evince more satisfaction with the rate at which inter-faith dialogue is proceeding in their diocese does not necessarily mean that they are personally involved in it. A Pennsylvania curate in his early thirties who says that he is deeply involved in ecumenical relations, claims that in his large city "inter-faith dialogue is an exercise in futility. Maybe it is good publicity, but it is not getting at the grass roots."

As in other issues discuseed in this study there is unquestionably a range of difference in ecumenical activities from diocese to diocese.

Indeed, the Council's Decree of Ecumenism advises that "the practical course to be adopted, after due regard has been given to all the circumstances of time, place, and personage, is left to the prudent decision of the local episcopal authority, unless the Bishops' Conference according to its own statutes, or the Holy See, has determined otherwise."[14] In 1965, the American Bishops did provide a statement on "interim guidelines" to be followed in certain ecumenical practices.[15]

MIXED MARRIAGES AND SEMINARY ROUTINE

During the recent past the Catholic Church has relaxed considerably its regulations for the marriage of a Catholic to a non-Catholic. There is a startling contrast between the earlier period, when such marriages were performed in the parish rectory with a minimum of liturgical ceremony, and the present time, when the non-Catholic party may receive Communion and the non-Catholic clergyman may be there to bless the couple.[16] Whether or not such changes can be introduced at mixed marriages depends mainly on the permission of the local bishop. Table 2.4 demonstrates again

Table 2.4 Distribution by age categories of opinion concerning rate of diocesan change on the rules for mixed marriages

	Under 35 years	35 to 49 years	50 years and over
About right	51%	55%	60%
Too fast	1	4	11
Too slowly	48	41	29
(Number of respondents)	(1,504)	(1,306)	(198)

that the youngest priests are much more ready (48%) than the oldest (29%) to say that the rules in this regard are changing too slowly in their diocese. One of the youngest curates from Connecticut comments "the policy of the Church at large is changing too slowly, and this question should really be put to Rome, or to the National Conference of Bishops, rather than to the dioceses."

Toward the end of the third session (November 21, 1964) of the

Council, the Decree on Eastern Catholic Churches mentioned the marriages of Catholics and Orthodox. It was not until several months after the fourth and final session that a document of instructions on mixed marriage was released over the signature of Cardinal Ottaviani. This document has been called "unecumenical" since the whole question of mixed religious marriages involves certain aspects of the ecumenical movement. The agreement that the children of such unions must be raised as Catholics, the validity of the marriage itself if it is witnessed by a Protestant clergyman, and the Christian status of baptized non-Catholic—all of these are involved as "sources of friction" between the Catholic Church and other Churches.[17]

We have seen in Table 2.1 that the statistics of response are very similar on the two questions concerning inter-faith dialogue and inter-faith marriage. The age breakdown of respondents also reveals relatively little difference of opinion on these two matters. Although both issues are ecumenical, they deal with two differnt contexts of human relations. Diocesan patterns or "rules" for interdenominational contacts govern many more people, who come together for a variety of reasons, than do the rules for mixed marriage.

We have seen earlier, in Table 2.1, that about four hundred of these priests did not answer the question concerning changes in the seminary. The reason is that many dioceses do not maintain a seminary, but send their students to other parts of the country for seminary training.[18] About half (49%) of all respondents are satisfied with the pace of seminary change, and there is not a great difference of opinion at this level among the age categories. Again, however, the age differences show up in the fact that the youngest priests, who were most recently in the seminary, are much more ready than the oldest priests to say that the changes are occurring too slowly.

In a later chapter we shall discuss in more detail the whole matter of seminary training, as seen by these diocesan priests. On the question of change, however, one Minnesota curate in his early thirties suggests that "if students for the priesthood were free to attend the seminary of their choice, seminaries would reform much faster." This means that the major seminaries preparing men for the priesthood would become competitive, vie for better faculties and facilities, offer a more attractive curriculum, and open themselves to the appraisal of prospective students and of educators in general.

Many of the respondents to this study exhibit a genuine interest and concern about seminary education. A curate in his late thirties

Table 2.5 Distribution by age categories of opinion concerning rate of diocesan change in seminary routine

	Under 35 years	35 to 49 years	50 years and over
About right	48%	50%	54%
Too fast	5	12	19
Too slowly	47	38	27
(Number of respondents)	(1,318)	(1,153)	(169)

from Pennsylvania believes that "the seminary course could be improved if there were better dialogue between seminary professors and students for the priesthood." An older curate, in his late forties, from the same state, thinks that the spiritual quality of prospective students should be stressed. "There should be a revision of standards of admission. We must seek solidity of character in preference to brilliance of intellect in the students."[19]

RACIAL APOSTOLATE AND LAY PARTICIPATION

The Second Vatican Council, following Pope John's directives, was not given to condemnations, but it found "racial and religious discrimination too disturbing not to condemn."[20] In its brief declaration on non-Christian religions, it stated that "the Church rejects as foreign to the mind of Christ, any discrimination against men or harassment of them because of their race, color, condition of life, or religion."[21] The question we asked in the survey dealt with diocesan practice rather than with doctrinal principles. More than half (54%) of all respondents think that their diocese is moving too slowly in this work. The Catholic position on race relations has been stated clearly and vigorously by the American hierarchy as a group, but with more vehemence by some bishops than by others. The responses then, in Table 2.6, reflect the degree of compliance with

Table 2.6 Distribution by age categories of opinion concerning rate of diocesan change in the racial apostolate

	Under 35 years	35 to 49 years	50 years and over
About right	38%	46%	61%
Too fast	2	4	8
Too slowly	60	50	31
(Number of respondents)	(1,467)	(1,282)	(191)

the doctrine of both the Vatican Council and the American hierarchy.

Approximately one hundred priests did not answer this question, most of them from dioceses in the west and northwest where they said there exists no serious race problem. It is probable also that there is a regional difference of opinion among these men since the Church, like other American institutions, tends to exhibit different regional approaches to the solution. The attitudes and directives of the local bishop also vary considerably from diocese to diocese even within the same geographical region. Nevertheless, Table 2.6 demonstrates a dramatic age contrast of opinion, with six out of ten of the youngest men complaining that the diocese is moving too slowly in race relations, while six out of ten of the oldest men declare themselves satisfied with the pace of change in this regard.

One Michigan curate in his early thirties is apparently expressing the impatience of young men when he complains that "assistant priests in the parishes are frequently not allowed to preach the Gospel of Jesus Christ on this particular point. Both priests and laity must learn that the word Catholic means universal, that the Church is for all men—not just the white man. Apparently very few priests and bishops have either the conviction or the courage to preach this basic Christian doctrine."[22] This may appear to be a harsh judgment of his fellow priests, but there is no question that the difference of approach to the racial apostolate has exhibited one of the sharpest cleavages in both attitude and practice between the younger and older clergy.

The survey question on the admission of the laity to parish planning is the only one on which more than half of the priests in all three age groups think that change is occurring too slowly. One reads occasional accounts of parochial experiments which involve cooperation and planning by lay people, but this survey indicates that such experiments are relatively rare and slow moving.[23] One curate in his late forties from the West Coast says that "my pastor has such a distrust of lay people that I cannot even invite them into the rectory to do the work of the parish. The result is that I am working harder doing things which could be done easier and better by lay persons."

Table 2.7 Distribution by age categories of opinion concerning rate of diocesan change in participation of laity in parish planning

	Under 35 years	35 to 49 years	50 years and over
About right	17%	24%	38%
Too fast	1	2	11
Too slowly	82	74	51
(Number of respondents)	(1,512)	(1,309)	(193)

The laity's "proper and indispensable role in the mission of the Church" is mentioned in eight out of sixteen documents of the Second Vatican Council.[24] Among these the Constitution on the Church made the following recommendation: "Let sacred pastors recognize and promote the dignity as well as the responsibility of the layman in the Church. Let them willingly make use of his prudent advice. Let them confidently assign duties to him in the service of the Church, allowing him freedom and room for action. Further, let them encourage the layman so that he may undertake tasks on his own initiative. Attentively in Christ, let them consider with fatherly love the projects, suggestions, and desires proposed by the laity."[25]

RESISTANCE TO CHANGE

It should be clear that in the foregoing Tables only those who check off the answer, "about right," are satisfied with the pace of change in these several diocesan activities. Those who are dissatisfied are of two kinds and maintain opposite points of view. Where there is an age difference, it is the younger men who want more rapid adaptation and the older men who want slower change, if any. We have seen that opinions differ, not only according to age, but also according to the subject under consideration. We shall see further that these "forgotten men" among the diocesan clergy, like the Fathers of Vatican II, do not want to "change everything." To exemplify the fact that there is also resistance to change among these priests we have chosen two examples from the data: one concerning clerical attire and the other clerical friendships.

Table 2.8 Distribution by age categories on suggestion that priests wear ordinary civilian suits as street wear

	Under 35 years	35 to 49 years	50 years and over	All respondents
Agree	21%	17%	19%	19%
Disagree	53	62	68	58
Neutral	16	14	10	15
Don't know	10	7	3	8
(Number of respondents)	(1,519)	(1,318)	(204)	(3,041)

Table 2.8 reveals that only one out of five (19%) agrees with the proposition that "it would be better if the Catholic clergy in America wore regular 'civilian' suits on the street, instead of the black suit and Roman collar." The minority agreement on this suggestion is not significantly affected by the age of the respondents, but the youngest men are more hesitant (26% "neutral" and "don't know") than the oldest men (13%) about the matter, and the latter are much more (68%) in disagreement than the former (53%).

Clerical street wear obviously provides a symbolic distinction of status between clergy and laity, and it is interesting that among some Protestant clergymen there appears to be a growing custom of imitating the clerical garb of Catholic priests. Meanwhile, some of our respondents feel that a less formal mode of attire would help to lessen the status differential and would allow priests to associate more successfully—and comfortably—with the laity. The older priests probably recall that the cassock is street wear in some places and that only in recent years Quebec Church authorities ordered them not to wear the cassock in public. In Chile we found that the majority of both clergy and laity favor a gradual change from cassock to suit, while in Tasmania the clergy conference, with the approval of Archbishop Young, voted to replace the clergy jacket with a grey shirt with crosses on the lapel during the summer.[26]

The next question we asked was not put precisely in terms of change, but in it we attempted to discover whether the traditional seminary advice concerning personal friendships was acceptable to these priests. From an old seminary notebook provided by one of our discussants we took the statement that "it would be better if priests restrict their close friendships to fellow priests and deal with the laity only on a professional, impersonal basis." The notion that the clergy should find their best and closest friends among fellow priests has often been urged as a means of mutual support and fraternal charity. Table 2.9 reveals that three quarters of all respondents disagree with the suggestion, but that in the minority opinion the oldest men are more than four times more likely (35%) than the youngest men (8%) to agree with it. The implication in the statistics on disagreement seems to be that the youngest men (83%) have a broader acquaintance with the laity, while the oldest men (46%) are more likely to seek their close friendships among the clergy.

Table 2.9 Distribution by age categories on suggestion that clergy restrict close personal friendships to fellow priests

	Under 35 years	35 to 49 years	50 years and over	All respondents
Agree	8%	17%	35%	14%
Disagree	83	70	46	75
Neutral	6	10	13	8
Don't know	3	3	6	3
(Number of respondents)	(1,516)	(1,306)	(203)	(3,025)

Some of the respondents found fault with the wording of the question and felt that it should have been asked in two separate parts. They thought that the priest should indeed deal with the laity on a professional level, but that "the laity are persons and we should

not be impersonal with them." Many of them think that it is
"better" to have close friendships with priests than with lay people,
and that the whole question of the status and role of the laity in the
Church should be further researched. We have seen in Table 2.7
that the laity is being incorporated much too slowly in parish planning. There can be no doubt that the majority of these lower-
echelon priests agree with the recommendation of the Council decree
on the Pastoral Office of Bishops which says that the clergy should so
act that "the individual parishioners and the parish communities will
really feel that they are members of the diocese and of the universal
Church."[27]

SUMMARY

To summarize these research findings concerning priests' attitudes
on the rate of change: there is a clear demonstration that their view
varies considerably in the several issues about which we questioned
them. The polar cases, as listed at the top and bottom of Table 2.1,
show general satisfaction with the rate of liturgical adaptation, but
general dissatisfaction with the extent to which lay people are allowed to participate in parish planning. More than half (53%)
think that the pace is adequate in inter-faith dialogue and the regulations for mixed marriage, but more than half (54%) also feel that
their diocese is moving too slowly in the racial apostolate. The
pragmatic importance of these findings is the recognition that some
things are easier to change than others, that there is a range of attitudes and practices from readiness to resistance, as well as a range
of technical "know-how" in promoting adaptation and renewal.

Our second hypothesis was that the youngest priests are more
favorable to change than are the oldest. Every item we have tested,
from Table 2.2 to Table 2.7 shows consistently that a significantly
higher proportion of the youngest priests think that things are moving too slowly in their diocese. We cannot avoid the implication
that there is an inter-generational contrast of attitudes toward the
rate of change but we do not have direct evidence of a "conflict" between the priestly generations. As a young French priest recently
commented: "It would certainly be regrettable if the senior members

of the clergy looked down their noses, so to speak, at the junior clergy and treated them as altar boys. It would be equally regrettable if the members of the junior clergy believed that they had nothing to learn from their elders and considered them behind the times."[28]

Expert American psychologists, however, have noted the "increasingly difficult communication between the generations." Older clergy complain that "the young priests ignore our views and resent our directives." The younger clerical generation says "the older priests don't understand us."[29] It appears, however, that age difference is only one of the factors to be considered, and that difference of status within the diocese is an even more important factor. We are dealing here with the "forgotten men" of the priesthood, the men at the bottom of the diocesan structure who most often do not seem to have the conservative outlook that characterizes many of the pastors and monsignors.

There is a corollary to these data—and we shall note this further —that these priests are not anxious to change "everything right away." This is demonstrated in Table 2.8 on the change of clerical street wear; it is shown in the proportions who think that the pace of change is "about right" in many areas; and it will be seen in the numbers who express uncertainty about various proposals for change.

NOTES

1. *The Church in the Modern World*, Article 4.
2. Psychological experiences of "changes in religious attitudes" are discussed in Chapter 10 and 11 of Hervé Carrier, *The Sociology of Religious Belonging* (New York: Herder and Herder, 1965), pp. 228–90.
3. See Dom Aelred Graham, "A Dissenting View of Vatican II," *Jubilee*, Vol. 13, No. 10, February 1966, p. 36.
4. This is, of course, the recurring ecclesiastical dilemma of institutionalization and charisma, of freedom and authority. One of the "dynamic developments" of the Council was the decision to allow latitude to individual bishops and to regional and national conferences of bishops. See the remarks of Walter Abbott, ed., *The Documents of Vatican II* (New York: Angelus Books, 1966), p. 428, footnote 73.
5. Xavier Rynne, *The Second Session* (New York: Farrar, Straus & Giroux, 1964), pp. 223–34, reports the historic statement of Bishop de Smet on religious liberty, but especially the explanation how "this doctrinal change took place according to a two-fold law." This is the law of continuity and progress.

When we talk of progress or development, we must distinguish on the one hand between false ideologies and the institutions to which they gave rise, and on the other hand, between error and the persons who err in good faith. In another context, *On the Sacred Liturgy*, Article 21, we are told that "the liturgy is made up of unchangeable elements divinely instituted, and elements subject to change."

6. Karl Rahner, *The Church After the Council* (New York: Herder and Herder, 1966), p. 28.

7. The technological aspects of social change are handled by various contributors to Warren Bennis, Kenneth Benne and Robert Chin, eds., *The Planning of Change* (New York: Holt, Rinehart & Winston, 1961).

8. A recent survey of subscribers to the *National Catholic Reporter* showed that more of the clergy (59%) than of the laity (55%) say that liturgical adaptations are going too slowly in America.

9. *Apostolate of the Laity*, Article 10. There is a remarkable statistical similarity in the *National Catholic Reporter* survey, where a majority of both clergy (73%) and laity (77%) think that the Church is too slow in admitting the laity to decision-making. See the pre-Conciliar work by Gerard Philips, *The Role of the Laity in the Church* (Cork, Ireland: Mercier Press, 1956), Chapter 6, "The Laity and Church Government," pp. 83–111.

10. *The Church in the Modern World*, Article 7.

11. The switch to the vernacular liturgy does not always mean a change to the English language in the United States. "Provision should be made for the faithful of different language groups, either through priests or parishes of the same language, or through an episcopal vicar well versed in the language." *Bishop's Pastoral Office in the Church*, Article 23.

12. *The Church in the Modern World*, Article 7.

13. Bishops who were interviewed at the Council by Rock Caporale felt that the foremost problem would be "the need to interpret the Council to the masses in general so as to stimulate in them the same experience and eventual change that took place in the bishops. . . . But the primary responsibility for the implementation of the Council would rest with the bishops, and at the diocesan level." *Vatican II: Last of the Councils* (Baltimore: Helicon, 1964), p. 145.

14. *Decree on Ecumenism*, Article 8.

15. See the statement of June 18, 1965, by the Bishops' Commission on Ecumenical Affairs, "Interim Guidelines for Prayer in Common and Communicatio in Sacris," *The Catholic Mind*, October 1965, pp. 57–64.

16. News reports of the marriage ceremony in Italy in 1966 when the Presbyterian bride was permitted to receive Communion indicate that this was a most exceptional and "confidential" permission.

17. See the *Decree on Eastern Catholic Churches*, Article 18. In his syndicated column, *Sum and Substance*, April 15, 1966, John Sheerin discusses some of the confusion and disappointment that greeted this "puzzling" document on mixed marriage. The *National Catholic Reporter* survey finds that six out of ten clergy (58%) and laity (61%) think that the Church is moving

"too slowly" on the rules for mixed marriage, but that less than half of the clergy (45%) and more than half of the laity (54%) think this about changes in inter-faith dialogue.

18. "Where individual dioceses are not equal to establishing an adequate seminary of their own, seminaries serving several dioceses, a whole national section, or a nation itself should be set up and fostered. The decree on *Priestly Formation*, Article 7, is at this point speaking specifically about the necessity for major seminaries. The item in the survey asked simply about "change of seminary routine."

19. *Ibid.*, Article 8, says that "spiritual formation should be closely linked with doctrinal and pastoral training."

20. Abbott, *op. cit.*, p. 668, footnote 31.

21. *Relationship of the Church to Non-Christian Religions*, Article 5.

22. The Civil Rights Movement has involved priests and Sisters in demonstrations and marches, a practice which elicited contrasting statements from various Catholic bishops, although all are said to "agree in principle." How can a zealous priest "follow his conscience" when prohibited from doing so by his cautious pastor or bishop? We shall discuss this problem below in Chapter 9.

23. There does not seem to be any national program of systematic observation and appraisal of these experiments, but the editors of *America* did a survey, "Diocesan Post-Conciliar Programs," and published the results in three parts, Vol. 115, June 11, 1966, pp. 825–27; July 9, 1966, pp. 28–30; August 6, 1966, pp. 136–38.

24. Abbott, *op cit.*, p. 489, footnote 3 to the decree on *The Apostolate of the Laity*, lists the references to these eight documents.

25. Constitution *On the Church*, Article 37.

26. For the Chilean survey see Joseph H. Fichter, *Cambio Social en Chile* (Santiago, Chile: Editorial Universidad Catolica, 1962), *passim*. On Archbishop Young, see "Electing Bishops," *The Priest*, Vol. 22, No. 10, October 1966, p. 810. A doctoral dissertation was written on this subject by Bernard J. Gantner, *Clerical Attire* (Washington, Catholic University Press, 1955). See also C. Walter Weiss, "Clerical Attire," *The Priest*, Vol. 22, No. 1, January 1966, pp. 53–58.

27. *Bishops' Pastoral Office in the Church*, Article 28. For the layman's point of view see Daniel Callahan, *The Mind of the Catholic Layman* (New York: Scribner's, 1963), Chapter 6, "Concord and Conflict: Clergy and Laity."

28. See A. M. Charue, *The Diocesan Clergy* (New York: Desclee, 1963), pp. 218–19. On the other hand, "Certainly, there is restlessness among the clergy, particularly the younger clergy, but it is a restlessness which exists in many other quarters in the world." Henry J. Yannone, "Needs and Problems of the Modern Parish," pp. 137–47, in Eugene J. Weitzel, ed., *Pastoral Ministry* (Milwaukee: Bruce, 1966).

29. George Hagmaier and Eugene Kennedy, "Psychological Aspects of Seminary Life," pp. 254–85 in James Lee and Louis Putz, eds., *Seminary Education in a Time of Change* (Notre Dame, Ind.: Fides, 1965).

THE PRIEST–BISHOP RELATIONSHIP

The bishops of the universal Church who attended the Second Vatican Council seemed more intent on their pastoral and apostolic role than on their administrative and juridical role. They proposed an episcopal model when they said that "in exercising his office of father and pastor, a bishop should stand in the midst of his people as one who serves. Let him be a good shepherd who knows his sheep and whose sheep know him." They paid special attention to the relationship between the bishop and his clergy, saying: "A bishop should always welcome priests with a special love since they assume in part the bishop's duties and cares and carry the weight of them day by day so zealously. He should regard his priests as sons and friends. Thus by his readiness to listen to them and by his trusting familiarity, a bishop can work to promote the whole pastoral work of the entire diocese."[1]

One of the most important aspects of the present survey is the manner in which the status and role of the rank-and-file diocesan clergyman depend upon his relationship and communication with the bishop. Is he always an obscure, neglected, and "forgotten" man because of his lowly position in the diocese? Are there variables in the diocesan structure that may alleviate or change this position? In questions asked of these priests concerning the Council recommendations we received a wide spectrum of responses. They indicated that bishops vary considerably in personality, as well as in age and experience. In 1966 there were one hundred and fifty episcopal sees in the United States, and there were great dissimilarities among the Ordinaries of these sees. The problems of communication between priests and bishop are greater in some places than in others because of distance, as well as both the kind and number of clergymen involved.

FACTORS IN COMMUNICATION

The Council decree said that the size of a diocese and the number of inhabitants should generally be such that the bishop can "be especially well-acquainted with his priests and with the religious and laity who have some part in diocesan enterprises."[2] How can this occur in a place like the archdiocese of Newark which has fourteen hundred priests and a million and a half Catholics crowded into 541 square miles, or even in the archdiocese of Denver with 327 priests and a quarter of a million Catholics spread out over 54,679 square miles? One young curate from Indiana wrote sympathetically that "the lack of dialogue with the bishop comes more from the unwieldly size of everything than from bad will. How can the bishop have free and open communication when he has more than five hundred priests?"[3]

We dealt with this question of "bigness" in the 1960 survey of diocesan clergy, where we asked the same question about the bishop's personal and friendly interest in his priests. We tested there the sociological assumption that the larger an organization becomes the more likely it is to develop a bureaucratic structure. "This implies that procedures are routinized, traditions take on a sacred character, relationships become more formalized, and the social distance from top to bottom is increased."[4] We compared the responses of the priests from the twenty-four smallest dioceses with those from the twenty-four largest dioceses, and found that the former were much more likely (44%) than the latter (17%) to say that their bishop took a positive and personal interest in them.

The data distributed in Table 3.1 are in answer to the question:

"In general, during the past year, has it been your experience that the Bishop Ordinary of the diocese takes a positive and personal interest in you?" From this Table, as well as from Table 3.2, one can conclude that the size of the diocese, either geographically or demographically, is not a complete and exclusive explanation for the type of personal relationship existing between the bishop and his priests. Pastors are obviously in closer communication with the bishop since they are twice as likely (34%) as the curates (17%) to answer "very much so" or "quite a bit" to this question.

Table 3.1 Degree of bishop's personal interest in pastors and curates (1960 survey)

	Pastors	Curates	All respondents
Very much so	14%	7%	10%
Quite a bit	20	10	14
More or less	37	28	32
Hardly at all	20	25	23
Not at all	9	30	21
(Number of respondents)	(935)	(1,231)	(2,166)

If we compare the last column in these two tables we find that a smaller proportion (44%) of all priests in the earlier survey than in the current survey (61%) gave a negative answer, "hardly at all" or "not at all," to the question. There seems to be more than one reason for this. The current survey has a greater representation from the larger dioceses where social distance between bishop and priest is greatest. Furthermore, there are marked differences by age level in the bishop's personal interest in the respondent. Most of the men aged fifty and over in the earlier study were pastors, and this combination of age and position helps to explain why only one third of them, compared to one half of the men under thirty-five, gave a negative judgment of the bishop's interest. In the current survey, position is a more important factor than age.[5]

Table 3.2 is a dramatic demonstration that the "lowly" curate feels himself furthest removed from the bishop, while the priests who are in supra-parochial assignments are closest to him. Almost seven

Table 3.2 Degree of bishop's personal interest by type of emploment of priest (current survey)

	Full-time curate	Part-time curate	Non-curate	All respondents
Very much so	6%	7%	14%	8%
Quite a bit	8	11	16	10
More or less	18	26	23	21
Hardly at all	25	23	22	24
Not at all	43	33	25	37
(Number of respondents)	(1,681)	(598)	(759)	(3,038)

out of ten (68%) of the former, and less than half (47%) of the latter give a negative appraisal of their bishop's personal interest in them. A New Jersey curate in his early forties says: "My bishop is not approachable. The majority of his time is spent in the Chancery, where he surrounds himself only with those who agree with his own definite and fixed ideas. He does not have real knowledge of either the priests or the people. Items which demand his personal attention are shifted off to a chancery official who usually handles even extremely personal affairs over the phone."

In contrast, a noncurate from a small Midwestern diocese says "We have good communication with our bishop. Any priest or layman can make an appointment and be sure to see him within twenty-four hours. He does not listen too well and he has a high opinion of his own judgment. Perhaps this is why he prefers the priests to make their own decisions, but always to keep him informed of what is going on. I think most of us do not use the freedom he has allowed and are too dependent on him even in things where we know he has no competence." This kind of self-revelation implies a childlike dependence of the subject on his superior and raises serious questions about the training for mature professionalism that some of these priests have had.

The question responded to in Table 3.3 is not directed at the immediate personal relationship between the respondent and his bishop but to the general situation in the diocese. We wanted his opinion about the degree to which communication with the bishop follows the suggestion of Vatican II that "there be free and open two-way communication between superiors and subordinate in the Church."[6] Here again the answers vary according to the position the priest holds in the diocese, with the full-time parish assistants giving less favorable responses than those in supra-parochial assignments.

Table 3.3   Extent to which free and open two-way communication exists with the bishop, by type of employment

	Full-time curate	Part-time curate	Non-curate	All respondents
Very much so	6%	7%	9%	7%
Quite a bit	11	14	17	13
More or less	22	29	29	25
Hardly at all	32	32	29	31
Not at all	29	18	17	24
(Number of respondents)	(1,668)	(598)	(751)	(3,017)

Up to now we have looked at the bishop's personal interest in his priests and at the general openness of communication between the bishop and his clergy. In Table 3.2 we saw that six out of every ten (61%) gave a negative appraisal of the bishop's interest in them, and in Table 3.3 that almost as many (55%) were negative about open communication between bishop and clergy in the diocese. In analyzing the answers more closely, and especially the comments that were volunteered, we found some situations in which the priests think the bishop has a personal interest in them, but does not communicate well, and some situations in which the reverse was true.

ALIENATION AND ACCEPTANCE

We felt that the contrast between "good" and "bad" bishop–priest relations in the diocese could be clarified if we combined the answers in these two Tables. We therefore selected two polar categories of respondents and compared them on certain key items of diocesan organization and communication. The men who feel "accepted" by the bishop, are closest to him, and have the best relations with him are all those who answered "very much so" on both bishop's personal interest and open communication with him. Those who are "alienated" from the bishop, are most distant from him, and suffer from lack of communication are all those who answered "not at all" on *both* bishop's interest and communication.[7] Let us look first at their age distribution.

Table 3.4 Distribution in three age categories of priests who have close and distant relations with Bishop

	Close to Bishop	Distant	All respondents
Under 35 years of age	40%	51%	50%
35 to 49 years old	44	42	43
50 years and older	16	7	7
(Number of respondents)	(109)	(563)	(3,048)

We hypothesized that both age level and type of assignment of the respondents were somehow associated with the judgment they made concerning bishop–clergy relations in their diocese. In other words, the younger the priest, the more alienated and further away he is from his bishop. Second, the full-time parish curate is more distant and alienated than the priest with a supra-parochial job. We have already seen, however, in Table 1.2 that non-curates are proportionately older than full-time curates, and we may assume that the type of employment is a factor of age, that probably special diocesan assignments are given to the most promising men; hence the bishop is more willing to communicate with them and to have a higher opinion of their views. Let us look now at how the accepted and the alienated compare in their work assignments.

The comparative data in Tables 3.4 and 3.5 tend to confirm the

Table 3.5 Distribution in three role categories of priests who have close and distant relations with Bishop

	Close to Bishop	Distant	All respondents
Full-time	42%	68%	55%
Part-time curate	19	16	20
Noncurate	39	16	25
(Number of respondents)	(109)	(563)	(3,048)

hypothesis that type of employment is more important than age as an explanation of why some priests are close to their bishop and others are distant. We see indeed that a higher proportion of those close to the bishop (16%) than of those distant from him (7%) are fifty years of age or older, and that more of the former (39%) than of the latter (16%) are exclusively engaged in nonparochial work. A more dramatic contrast lies in the fact that half of those who are distant from their bishop are under thirty-five years of age, but almost seven out of ten (68%) are in full-time parish work. Furthermore, the age distribution of those who see "bad" relations in the diocese is approximately the same as that of the total respondents, but their role distribution, as seen in Table 3.4 is significantly different from that of the total respondents.

COMMUNICATION IN THE DIOCESE

Let us now broaden the scope of our diocesan vision through the eyes of these two sets of priests and at the same time see how all of the priests look at diocesan communications and relations. Most of the priests feel that the Catholic diocese should not be a "one-man show" with all decisions and directions in the hand of the bishop. A New Jersey part-time curate in his late thirties says, "It is shocking the number of priests who are discouraged and aggravated by the lack of communication with the bishop."[8] An Ohio non-curate in the same age bracket praises his bishop as "most dynamic" but complains that the diocese is "made up of cliques." A part-time curate in New York says that "the spirit of priestly fraternity and unity is lacking in this diocese because a man belongs either to the in-group or the out-group."

The data in Table 3.6 indicate a general appraisal of the extent to which the total diocese is following the suggestion of Vatican II concerning free and open two-way communication between Church superiors and subordinates. Only two out of ten (19%) of all respondents are willing to give a positive appraisal, while more than half (53%) make a negative judgment. The general opinion then is that there is a serious lack of open communication within American dioceses, but the specific opinion in the first and second columns of

Table 3.6 points directly at the influence of the bishop. In other words, wherever the bishop takes a personal interest in his men and also has the reputation of communicating well with them, there is also likely to be free and open communication throughout the whole diocese.[9]

Table 3.6 Comparative responses of those with close and distant relations concerning open communication in the total diocesan structure

	Close to Bishop	Distant	All respondents
Very much so	50%	0%	5%
Quite a bit	31	1	14
More or less	13	6	28
Hardly at all	3	35	36
Not at all	3	58	17
(Number of respondents)	(108)	(561)	(3,003)

The contrast between the two categories of priests is not only statistically significant but spectacular. Eight out of ten (81%) of those who see good bishop–clergy relations in their diocese also see good communication throughout the diocese. On the other hand, the overwhelming majority (93%) of the men who recognize poor bishop–clergy relations in their diocese also make a negative judgment about communication in the total structure. A young curate in Kansas quotes Rahner's statement[10] that priests should exercise the right to express their opinions, but says that "we are stifled and often defeated by the system. It kills our zeal to try new ways and ideas. Our greatest present hope is for freedom of expression and action, and we need more men like Bishop Reed of Oklahoma to help realize that hope."

The fact is, of course, that there are other "leaders" besides the bishop in every large diocese, and that the total diocesan structure is composed of many substructures, both formal and informal. One of the oldest curates in a Pennsylvania diocese complains about the influence of "youngster monsignori," and also about the "usual Cathedral clique of priests who put great pressure on episcopal judgments and changes. The clique surrounds the Ordinary ever and always and manages to manipulate changes in favor of their clergy friends throughout the diocese." A young noncurate in a California diocese says that "we are making progress in many areas, but the junior clergy are firmly convinced that this progress comes in spite of poor leadership and in spite of cliques and dissension."

THE CHANCERY OFFICE

We have seen that free communication is a problem at all levels of the diocese. Aside from territorial parishes, traditional deaneries and the more recently established vicariates, the Catholic diocese embraces a large variety of functional offices and commissions.[11] As is the case with the Vatican Curia the local bishop operates an administrative bureau with numerous officials like the Vicar-General, Chancellor, Consultants and their various assistants. The whole diocesan curia is meant to be an "instrument of the bishop," not only for administrative purposes but also to promote the complex and multiple apostolate of the diocese.[12] The lower-echelon diocesan priest may have intermittent dealings with any of these various officials, but he will deal more often with the Chancery Office than with any other diocesan bureau. We posed the following statement and question: "Every priest deals with the Chancery Office of the diocese, and looks for both efficiency and humaneness in this dealing. How would you rate your Chancery Office?"

We assumed here that the bureaucrats in the Chancery would reflect the attitudes and patterns of the bishop. Where there are good bishop–clergy relations there would also be chancery officials who deal humanely and efficiently with the priests.[13] The last column in Table 3.7 shows that all of the respondents to this survey are much more likely to perceive efficiency (82%) than humaneness (42%) in the diocesan chancery office. The first column, representing good relations between bishop and clergy, shows higher proportions for both efficiency (90%) and humaneness (83%), while the second column, representing distant clergy–priest relations, shows lower percentages in both efficiency (75%) and humaneness (19%). It is this last statistic which seems to be the key to an understanding why these priests feel alienated from the diocesan authorities.

Table 3.7 Comparative responses of those with close and distant relations concerning efficiency and humaneness of their Chancery Office

	Close to Bishop	Distant	All respondents
High in both efficiency and humaneness	77%	17%	37%
More efficient than humane	13	58	45
More humane than efficient	6	2	5
Poor in both efficiency and humaneness	4	23	13
(Number of respondents)	(108)	(558)	(2,988)

Priests who commented on this question seem to feel that the humane quality of the Chancery Office is best expressed by officials who treat the clergy like mature, responsible persons. A remark that is typical of the lower clergy is made by a Texas curate: "There is less concern and care about the persons who are priests than there is about the good order in which the priests work." The problem is not that of "over-efficiency" nor the presence of a middle-management group between the bishop and his priests. In fact, many of the clergy think that these intermediary structures should be multiplied. What they see is a double defect: First, "The bishops surround themselves with men who have a vested interest in bolstering the episcopal ego" and second, "As a result, many of these bishops who are excellent men are alarmingly out of contact with the real world of their diocese." These remarks were made by a Missouri curate in his early forties who feels that "the system is only as good as the functionaries who operate it."

This analysis of the two carefully selected qualities about which we asked the priests should emphasive the fact that efficiency is characteristic of the administrative functions of bishops and chanceries, while humaneness is characteristic of the pastoral functions which the Council Fathers recommended so strongly. What these lower diocesan clergy are telling us then is that the administrative aspect is still much more in evidence in American dioceses than is the pastoral aspect. The Council Fathers tell us that pastoral work is more effective when there is mutual love and understanding. "The relationship between the bishop and his diocesan priests should rest above all upon the bonds of supernatural charity so that the harmony

of the will of the priests with that of their bishop will render their
pastoral activity more fruitful."[14]

THE SENATE OF CLERGY

The judgments that these diocesan priests make about local conditions of communication are in a sense an empirical confirmation
of the concern shown by the Council Fathers about the bishop–
clergy relationship. We incorporated into this survey several questions
which emerged from the Council itself or from various American
experiments and suggestions since the Council. Three of these are
matters of diocesan organizations: the senate of clergy, the personnel
committee for priests, and the intermediary grievance committee for
priests who have complaints to make. We asked them not only if
these things exist in their diocese but also whether or not they approve of them.

One of the recommendations by the Council Fathers most frequently cited among these respondents is found in the Decree on the
Ministry and Life of Priests. The bishop should gladly listen to his
priests; indeed, he should "consult them and have discussions with
them about those matters which concern the necessities of pastoral
work and the welfare of the diocese. In order to put these ideals into
effect, a group or senate of priests representing the presbytery should
be established. It is to operate in a manner adapted to modern
circumstances and needs and have a form and norms to be determined
by law. By its counsel, this body will be able to give effective assistance to the bishop in his government of the diocese."[15]

The questionnaire for this survey was distributed one year after
the fourth and final session of the Second Vatican Council was held,
but only three out of ten (29%) of all respondents said that the
senate of clergy had been, or was being, established in their diocese.[16]
As is clear from the answers recorded in Table 3.8 the overwhelming
majority (94%) of these rank-and-file diocesan clergy give approval
to the idea of a clergy senate, and this approval is about in the same
proportion whether there are close bishop–priest relations (92%) or
distant relations (96%). The sharpest contrast appears, however, in
the fact that those who report poor communication with the bishop

are much less likely (15%) than those who have good communication (40%) to be in a place that has established the clergy senate.

This does not necessarily mean that the establishment of a clergy senate automatically improved relations between the bishop and his priests. It probably means that the dioceses that have begun to implement the Council recommendation in this regard were already in the

Table 3.8 Comparative responses of those with close and distant relations concerning existence and approval of senate of clergy

	Close to Bishop	Distant	All respondents
Don't have one, but I approve it	53%	83%	67%
Do have one, and I approve it	38	13	27
Do have one, but I disapprove of it	2	2	2
Don't have one and I disapprove of it	7	2	4
(Number of respondents)	(107)	(558)	(3,001)

hands of progressive and adaptive bishops. Some of the respondents, however, who are in places where there is a senate and who approve it, express some question whether the bishop will adapt himself to the new structure. One experienced curate in a New England diocese says: "I wonder whether the senate will ever do anything. I think it may be only window dressing in a place like this where no one, except the Ordinary, is really in charge of anything." A nonparochial priest in his early forties from a Missouri diocese, who expresses admiration for his bishop, says, "We have just elected a senate of the priests. I favor it, but its function and effectiveness are yet to be shown."

CLERGY PERSONNEL COMMITTEE

In the American occupational system, particularly in large-scale industrial organizations, the personnel office has become a necessary instrument for the improvement of human relations. The personnel committee is prevalent as a means of helping people who have problems. The Vatican Council says that "priests should realize that they have special obligations toward priests who labor under certain difficulties. They should give them timely help."[17] In another place we read that "with active mercy a bishop should attend upon priests who are in any sort of danger or who have failed in some respect."[18] At any rate, there is a recognition here that priests sometimes need help with their problems.

The question that is answered in Table 3.9 was worded as follows: "Some suggest that a full-time personnel committee made up of experienced and qualified priests should work with priests who have problems. Does your diocese have such a committee, and what do you think of it?" Hardly any of these priests (7%) live in a diocese which has a personnel committee of the kind described, yet they are almost unanimous (96%) in their approval of the suggestion. There is obviously a widely felt need among them for an arrangement of this kind, and one wonders why this need has escaped the attention of so many bishops in our times. Perhaps the reason lies in the opinion of a curate in his late thirties from a New York diocese who says that "most of the bishops, I suspect, would not even dream of asking the questions you are asking, let alone listen to the answers. I hope the results of this survey will be made available to them."

Table 3.9 Comparative responses of those with close and distant relations concerning existence and approval of clergy personnel committee

	Close to Bishop	Distant	All respondents
Don't have one, but I approve it	71%	95%	89%
Do have one, and I approve it	21	2	7
Do have one, but I disapprove of it	1	1	*
Don't have one, and I disapprove of it	7	2	4
(Number of respondents)	(108)	(588)	(3,011)

Although relatively few priests have experience with a diocesan personnel committee, it seems significant that a much higher proportion (22%) of those who experience good bishop–clergy relations than of those who have poor bishop–clergy relations (3%) live in a place where such a committee exists. One older curate in a large eastern city wants the members of the personnel committee to be elected from the several age levels of the diocesan clergy and to be put under the "seal" of confessional secrecy concerning the problems they deal with. "If possible," he adds, "each ordination class should have a member on the committee."

The function of a personnel committee is probably as narrow or as wide as the bishop permits, but those that are now in formation throughout the country seem to be designed mainly to help in the manpower utilization of the diocese. We shall see that the great majority (86%) agree that a diocesan personnel office should work out priests' assignments, and also (83%) that curates should be interviewed before receiving their appointments.[19] Whether or not there is a personnel office, the Council advises that "for the sake of greater service to souls let the bishop engage in discussion with his priests, even collectively, especially about pastoral matters. This he should do not only occasionally but, as far as possible, at fixed intervals."[20]

A young Southern curate thinks that if the bishop were a pastor "serving the diocese instead of an administrator ruling the diocese, if he were a priest's priest himself, there would not be so much clamor among the clergy for intermediate committees." An Illinois curate in his late thirties says, "Our bishop does not show a fatherly interest in us; a priest with a problem of any kind would be very reluctant to approach him." A young curate from Minnesota says, "We definitely need a personnel committee. I feel so uneasy with the bishop that I avoid contact with him and would just as soon that he not take a personal interest in me."

CLERGY GRIEVANCE COMMITTEE

The responses distributed in Table 3.10 are to this question on the survey: "Some think there should also be an intermediary 'grievance committee,' elected by the priests themselves, to which priests can bring their complaints. Does your diocese have such a committee, and what do you think of it?" Nine out of ten (89%) respondents say that there is no grievance committee of this kind in their diocese, but the same proportion (90%) express approval of the idea. There is an interesting contrast within the category of priests who have good relations with their bishop. About one out of five (22%) says that this committee does exist in his diocese and he approves it; but the same proportion (21%) says that it does not exist and also disapproves the idea. We can only surmise that those who are not favorable to the establishment of an elected grievance committee are satisfied that the bishop can handle such problems by himself.

A young curate in a large West Coast diocese thinks that the curates themselves need a separate kind of representation for their complaints. "I would favor some kind of diocesan body elected by

Table 3.10 Comparative responses of those with close and distant relations concerning the existence and approval of a clergy grievance committee

	Close to Bishop	Distant	All respondents
Don't have one, but I approve it	55%	91%	80%
Do have one, and I approve it	22	3	10
Do have one, but I disapprove of it	2	1	1
Don't have one, and I disapprove of it	21	5	9
(Number of respondents)	(107)	(562)	(3,005)

the assistant pastors which would represent them and would spell out their grievances."[21] From the other end of the country a young New England curate feels that "priests should be free to go right to the source of the grievance they have, discuss it freely and openly and get matters straightened out in an adult way."

While this survey was being conducted, many priests heard about the grass roots organization of the clergy in the Chicago archdiocese and commented upon its prospects.[22] One Midwestern respondent in his early thirties wrote: "Personally I have high hopes for it. Even if it is crushed or ignored by higher authority, I still have high hopes for it and think it is a great idea. Perhaps these years are meant to be a testing of our priesthood." Another priest in his late thirties from the same area hopes that the Chicago organization "will be a main breakthrough to a more humane and intelligent direction of diocesan affairs. It is my considered judgment that if something like this does not succeed, the human wreckage among priests in the diocese will be enough to produce either more defections or a kind of clerical revolution."

SUMMARY

The research findings in this section of the survey may come as a disappointment to those Ordinaries in the largest dioceses who are genuinely attempting to carry out the promptings of the Second Vatican Council. They are faced with a task that has become patterned in an administrative mold and are concerned about the proposed transition to a more pastoral episcopal role. They participated in the formulation of the Council documents and, like their lower clergy, have studied them carefully. They will remember that they and their priests are engaged in a common task. "On account of this sharing in his priesthood and mission, let priests sincerely look upon the bishop as their father, and reverently obey him. And let the bishop regard his priests, who are his co-workers, as sons and friends, just as Jesus called His disciples no longer servants but friends."[23]

The first pertinent finding here is the reported lack of accessibility to the bishop by his priests. More than half of these lower-echelon clergy express a negative opinion on the three important tests of bishop—clergy relations: the personal interest of the bishop, his communication with them, and the free and open communication that exists in the diocesan structure as a whole. More than half of the diocesan curates in the 1960 survey also said their bishop showed little or no personal interest in them. The data show quite clearly that social distance between bishop and priest is more a function of the job the priest has than of his age. Episcopal communication is least with the full-time curate and most with those in special assignments outside the parish.

When we suggested three organizational arrangements that would help to improve the communication relation between the hierarchy and lower clergy, we found the priests overwhelmingly in favor of a diocesan senate of clergy, a personnel committee to handle the problems of priests, and an elected grievance committee to which the clergy could bring their complaints. On all these areas we compared the responses of the "alienated" and the "accepted," of those who felt close to the bishop (109) and those who felt far removed from him (653). These priests live and work in two contrasting social situations and their attitudes are greatly affected by this fact.

We hypothesized that other diocesan aspects of superior–subordinate relations would elicit widely different responses from these two polar sets of priests. The two groups differ considerably in their opinions about communication in the total diocesan structure, and about the chancery office, especially in the "humaneness" of its officials. These comparisons suggest quite definitely not only the overwhelming approval of a clergy senate, a personnel committee, and a grievance committee, but also that good communication with authorities is likely to exist in dioceses where these structures are effectively established.

NOTES

1. *Bishops' Pastoral Office in the Church*, Article 16.
2. *Ibid.*, Article 23.
3. *Ibid.*, Articles 22–24 provide the norms for a "fitting revision of diocesan boundaries." In strong language the Council "decrees" this and says it is a "mandate." The 1967 edition of Kenedy's *Official Catholic Directory* lists twenty-seven dioceses with more than five hundred priests (diocesan and religious) and eighteen with fewer than one hundred priests. Territorial size makes a difference; e.g., the State of Rhode Island with one diocese has 609 priests, the State of Alaska with three dioceses has a total of seventy-five priests.
4. Joseph H. Fichter, *Priest and People* (New York: Sheed and Ward, 1965), Chapter 10, "Growth of Bureaucracy" pp. 163–81.
5. The position of pastor is especially significant in attitudes on communication with the bishop. This is demonstrable on the following age breakdowns on the question of the bishop's positive interest in the respondent, as seen in the 1960 survey where we included pastors, and the current survey where we excluded them.

1960 survey of clergy	Under 35 years	35 to 49 years	50 years and over
Very much so, quite a bit	21%	24%	31%
More or less	29	31	36
Hardly at all, not at all	50	45	33
(Number of respondents)	(736)	(935)	(495)
Current survey			
Very much so, quite a bit	18%	18%	27%
More or less	21	22	15
Hardly at all, not at all	61	60	58
(Number of respondents)	(1,515)	(1,319)	(204)

6. The Council recognized and approved modern "advances in the development and organization of the means by which men communicate with one another," *The Church in the Modern World*, Article 54, and it is expected that these "means" are useful also within the Church.

7. The alienation of the lower-echelon clergy implies much more than the absence of personal and familial ties with the bishop. It means that he sees the whole system as remote, complex, meaningless, impersonal, and unrewarding. This perspective seems to be a basic ingredient of the discontent vaguely expressed by many priests. See Robert A. Nisbet, *The Sociological Tradition* (New York: Basic Books, 1966), "Alienation," pp. 264–312.

8. "Clerical Freedom," an editorial in *Commonweal*, Vol. 78, No. 4, April 19, 1963, p. 87, raises the question of clerical freedom of speech, and says that "the priest is so rarely free to raise a public voice in his own behalf." In a survey of subscribers of the *National Catholic Reporter*, the majority of both laity (72%) and of clergy and Sisters (63%) think that the Church is moving "too slowly" on the question of the rights of priests.

9. The bishop who regards his priests as "sons and friends" can promote the whole pastoral work of the entire diocese "by his readiness to listen to them and by his trusting familiarity." *Bishops' Pastoral Office in the Church*, Article 16.

10. See Karl Rahner, *Free Speech in the Church* (New York: Sheed and Ward, 1959), p. 36.

11. Deaneries are territorial subdivisions of a diocese which seem most useful in rural places where the parishes are widly scattered. Vicariates are territories that have not yet been formed in dioceses. The Council introduced a new term: "episcopal vicars empowered by the bishop with the authority of a vicar general, but only for a certain part of the diocese, for a determined type of activity, or for the faithful of a particular rite." Abbott, *op. cit.*, p. 416, footnote 58. It should be noted that the Military Vicariate, or Ordinariate, is supra-diocesan, and is the model for a proposed Vicariate, or Ordinariate, for married clergy in the Latin rite, suggested by the National Association for Pastoral Renewal. The term is used in still another context by Joseph Mastrangelo, "Needed: A Vicar for Priests," *The Priest*, Vol. 22, No. 9, September, 1966, pp. 717–20.

12. *Bishops' Pastoral Office in the Church*, Article 27, where the administrative staff of the diocese is described and the statement made that "the most important office in the diocesan curia is that of vicar general." See also Joseph O'Donoghue, "Those Faceless Chanceries," *Commonweal*, April 28, 1967, pp. 167–71.

13. In the 1960 survey of diocesan pastors and curates we did not ask about the humaneness of the Chancery office, but found that three quarters of the respondents appraise its efficiency as "excellent" (pastors 51%, curates 44%) or "pretty good" (pastors 26%, curates 32%). It should be pointed out, of course, that efficiency is not synonymous with effectiveness in all cases, a discovery made long ago by industrial sociologists.

14. *Bishops' Pastoral Office in the Church*, Article 28.

15. *Ministry and Life of Priests*, Article 7. This clergy senate is not to be con-

fused with the pastoral council, or commission, to be established in each diocese, in which the laity, as well as priests and religious, will participate. *Bishops' Pastoral Office in the Church*, Article 27.

16. The Decree was promulgated on December 7, 1965, but was followed by an announcement of *vacatio legis*, which allowed the bishops until June 29, 1966, when the laws contained in the Decree were to become effective. Our survey questionnaire was "in the field" from early September to early December, 1966. It would be important to investigate with what degree of "prompt obedience" the American hierarchy implemented the decree.

17. *Ministry and Life of Priests*, Article 8.

18. *Bishops' Pastoral Office in the Church*, Article 16.

19. In the 1960 survey we inquired how the priests received their current assignment. More than one third (36%) of the pastors but only three per cent of the assistants said that either the Bishop or the Chancellor asked them if they were willing to take it. See the discussion below, Chapter 7, "Facets of the Career."

20. *Bishops' Pastoral Office in the Church*, Article 28.

21. "There is need for immediate access to grievance machinery and court hearings for all church members," writes William H. DuBay, *The Human Church* (Garden City: Doubleday, 1966), p. 165. In October 1966, he organized the American Federation of Priests, open only to men in non-management positions. A pastor in a large eastern diocese has proposed a management association of supervisory clergy to negotiate with the representatives of the priests' union. On this matter see also James F. Cunningham, "Mediation Boards for the Clergy," *The Priest*, Vol. 22, No. 8, August 1966, pp. 614–17.

22. As a matter of fact, some of the questions on this survey were derived from the preliminary documents of the Chicago Clergy Conference, which has since been renamed the Association of Chicago Priests. See Daniel L. Flaherty, "Chicago Priests Organize," *America*, Vol. 116, November 5, 1966, pp. 540–43. At a significant meeting on May 8, 1967, the ACP expanded its interests to include the social problems of the general community. See the editorial, "A New Witness," *Commonweal*, May 26, 1967, p. 277.

23. *Constitution on the Church*, Article 28, where we read also that "they constitute one priesthood with their bishop." They are "associated with their bishop in a spirit of trust and generosity," and they take upon themselves "his duties and concerns."

SEMINARY TRAINING

One of the bishops who commented on the Vatican Council's decree on Priestly Formation, said that "A seminary is not a lumber mill or a smelter. It cannot take a raw youth and, after subjecting him to a few approved processes, turn out a neatly fashioned or keenly honed priest."[1] Educators in all fields have recognized that there are no automatic devices that guarantee successful training and preparation for any professional career. Yet in the case of the Catholic clergy the Council recommended an improved system of training "in the spirit of renewal." At the same time, "it urgently entreats those who are readying themselves for the priestly ministry to realize clearly that the hope of the Church and the salvation of souls are being entrusted to them."[2]

Every diocesan priest who responded to this survey has had seminary training in preparation for his ordination and for his life work in the ministry. One of them remarked that "we were all subjects of the exact same curriculum in the seminary with the result that we were turned out like so many copies from a mimeograph machine." Yet this is surely overstating the case because, while the academic curriculum may have a certain similiarity among all the major seminaries, there are also significant differences in the general operation of seminaries. There is also a difference in the length of time that these men spent under seminary direction—less than three out of ten

71

had all of their high school education in a minor seminary while one out of six did not enter the seminary until graduation from college.[3]

WHEN TO BEGIN TRAINING?

We asked these priests at what age they had begun their studies for the priesthood and then asked them at what age they would enter if they had the chance to do it over again. The Council Fathers gave no direct recommendation on this matter, but they do seem to favor a delay in the age of ordination and say that bishops may decide "that the age currently required by general law for holy orders be raised," and also to consider that men who have completed their theological studies "exercise the dioconate for an appropriate length of time before being advanced to the priesthood."[4]

In answering the question about the best time to start preparing for the priesthood, D'Arcy and Kennedy say that "most priests seem to advocate the way they did it themselves. There are many mature and fully functioning priests who started their preparation for the priesthood after the eighth grade. It is a misconception that a young man could not possibly mature in the minor seminary. What is clear is that there are varying states of readiness for this vocational decision. It is unfortunate if a person is forced to make the decision too soon, just as it is unfortunate if a person who is ready to make a solid vocational choice is delayed."[5]

The data of the present survey provide information about the actual age of entrance to the seminary and allow us to test the hypothesis that they would "advocate the way they did it themselves." Table 4.1 shows that among the youngest men, three out of ten did all their high school studies in the minor seminary, having entered at age thirteen or fourteen, while only one out of ten started his studies at age twenty-one or older. Among the oldest men, about one out of five (22%) did high school in the minor seminary, but one third (34%) entered the seminary at age twenty-one or older.

These comparative statistics must be interpreted with some caution. The age differences of response do not necessarily mean here a trend toward earlier entrance to the seminary. Many of the "delayed" vocations do not show up in the youngest age category, especially of men who entered the seminary in their late twenties and are not yet ordained. The large proportion of the oldest category, men who were ordained a quarter-century or more ago, who delayed their entrance to the seminary may be partly accounted for by the problems of the Great Depression and of the Second World War.[6]

Table 4.1 Actual age at entrance to seminary compared with present preference, by three age categories and totals

Actual age at entrance:	Under 35 years	35 to 49 years	50 years and over	All respondents
13–14 years old	30%	25%	22%	27%
15–16	10	9	13	10
17–18	38	28	18	32
19–20	12	16	13	14
21 or older	10	22	34	17
(Number of respondents)	(1,521)	(1,322)	(205)	(3,048)
Present preference:				
13–14 years old	12%	13%	13%	13%
15–16	2	3	8	3
17–18	34	30	21	31
19–20	14	13	19	14
21 or older	27	26	23	26
Hesitate to enter at all	11	15	16	13
(Number of respondents)	(1,484)	(1,294)	(199)	(2,977)

The spread of opinion in the last column of Table 4.1 reveals the difference of current attitudes about entering the seminary. While almost four out of ten (37%) had actually entered the minor seminary before the age of seventeen, a much smaller proportion (16%) would now do so if they had the chance to decide again. A Louisiana curate in his late thirties wrote that "I do not regret the fact that I entered the seminary after eighth grade. I think personally it helped me in my vocation, but times have changed and the question of high school minor seminaries is to me very debatable." A Wisconsin priest in his early thirties confesses that "I myself would hesitate to enter at all. As far as others are concerned, I think they should not enter till they have completed college."

The general tendency in all three age brackets seems to be a preference to avoid early entrance to the seminary if they could do it
over again. This preference is strongest among the men under thirty-
five years of age among whom 22 per cent actually entered at age
nineteen or over, but 41 per cent would now choose to do so. The
contrast is somewhat different among the men of fifty or older,
among whom almost half (47%) report that they entered the seminary at age nineteen or older, but a smaller percentage (42%) say
they would now do so. This may be partly explained by the fact
that a larger proportion of the oldest category (16%) than of the
youngest (11%) say that they would now hesitate to enter the seminary at all.

Table 4.2 Proportions of priests who would enter younger, the same age, older,
or hesitate to enter at all, according to age at which they began
studies

Age at entrance	Enter younger	Enter at same age	Enter older	Hesitate to enter	(Number of respondents)
13–14 years old	—	38%	49	13	(811)
15–16	8%	23	59	10	(283)
17–18	2%	50	35	13	(965)
19–20	13%	39	32	16	(418)
21 or older	20%	64	—	16	(500)
All respondents	7%	45	35	13	(2,977)

In Table 4.2 we ignored their present age and pursued further the
question whether these priests would do the same thing over again.
In this approach we measured their response against their actual age
at entrance and found that less than half (45%) of all respondents
would enter at the same age if they were doing it over again. Table
4.2 shows that one half (49%) of those who had all their high school
education in a minor seminary would now start their studies later,
while about one out of eight (13%) would hesitate to enter the
seminary at all. At the other end of the age range, among those who
began studies at age twenty-one or older, one fifth feel that they
would now enter younger, while about one out of six (16%) says
that he would hesitate about going to the seminary at all. The bottom

line of the Table reports on all respondents and reveals that the priests in general are five times as likely (35%) to say that they would enter older than they actually did, than they are to say that they would enter younger (7%) than they did.

THE MINOR SEMINARY

There is apparently a range of opinion concerning the advisability of maintaining the minor, or high school, seminary. A strong argument is made against it by a Catholic educator, James Michael Lee, who gives five "cogent reasons for the abolition of all seminaries below the theologate."[7] These reasons are as follows: (1) the excessive dropout rate; (2) many minor seminaries are educationally inferior; (3) normal family life should be experienced during adolescence; (4) the experience of life in the world makes for a more effective priest; (5) boys should interact dynamically with their peers. On the other hand, it may be argued that the minor seminary protects a boy against the temptations of the world, brings him closer to God, preserves his vocation, and introduces him sooner to the subculture of the Church profession which he will follow. Most of the arguments on both sides of this question are unsupported by empirical data and untested by scientific instruments of research.

In the 1960 survey of diocesan priests we asked what advice concerning seminary entrance they would give to a thirteen-year-old boy just finishing the eighth grade and who wants to be a priest. Table 4.3 shows that those who had graduated from a minor seminary high school were twice as likely (76%) as those who graduated from other secondary schools (37%) to say that the boy should enter the minor seminary right after elementary school. This finding supports the notion that the clergy tend to think that others should do as they had done in this regard. Comparative responses are given also in the Table from a companion survey of the lay friends of priests, and from a larger study of the opinions of Catholic parents in the Peoria diocese.[8]

One may suggest, of course, that the priest who did not attend a minor seminary high school is not in a position to make the kind of informed judgment about it that can be made by the priest

Table 4.3   Advice on minor seminary to 13-year-old boy, by priest graduates and nongraduates of minor seminary high school, by Catholic laity and Catholic parents

	Minor seminary high	Other high schools	Catholic laity	Catholic parents
Enter minor seminary now	76%	37%	40%	16%
Attend other high school	20	56	52	68
Go to college first	1	4	4	13
Other advice	3	3	4	3
(Number of respondents)	(888)	(1,284)	(2,212)	(8,639)

graduate of such a school. This is even more true of lay people who are friends of the clergy and of whom only four out of ten would advise the youngster to enter the minor seminary. When the question is put to parents who have children under eighteen years of age the matter becomes much more personal. Here we find that only about one out of six (16%) is willing to advise the young boy to attend high school in the minor seminary. If diocesan officials intend to maintain and promote secondary schooling in the seminary it appears that they must devise ways of overcoming the opposition of Catholic parents.[9]

While we did not ask the respondents to the current survey to make a judgment for or against the minor seminary high school, we have already seen in Table 4.1 that only a minority of them would like to make all, or part, of their secondary studies in a seminary. Some are for it; some are against it. A young curate in an Oregon diocese believes that " a priest living in a diocese where there is a high school seminary would be interfering with God's providence if he discouraged a young boy from going there." Differing from him, an Indiana curate in his late forties says, "I cannot in conscience encourage grammar school boys to enter the junior seminary. I believe that they should be at home during these formative years, and no seminary can substitute for his parents."

The Fathers of the Second Vatican Council did not attempt to settle the controversy concerning the advisability of minor seminaries.[10] They said that these schools "are built to nurture the seeds of a vocation," and then advise that "under the fatherly guidance of superiors and with appropriate cooperation of parents, the students should lead a life which is suited to the age, mentality, and developmental stage of young men, and which fully conforms to the laws of a healthy psychology. The students should be suitably involved in normal human activities, and have frequent contact with their own families."[11] Many American dioceses do not conduct minor seminaries, and opinions about them seem to stem from the circumstance under which they are conducted. One of the priests who said that he would "hesitate to enter" complained that the biggest problem in his minor seminary was the discord between the day students and the resident students. Others said they would be hesitant to enter because the seminary has not yet conformed to the recommendations of the Second Vatican Council nor introduced the modern approaches of educational psychology.

PROMOTING VOCATIONS

The Council Decree on Priestly Formation recommends that "to the greatest possible extent every priest should manifest the zeal of an apostle in fostering vocations. Let him attract the hearts of young people to the priesthood by his own humble and energetic life, joyfully pursued, and by love for his fellow priests and brotherly collaboration with them."[12] This appears to be the attitude of one young Midwestern priest, who says that he does not use high pressure methods. "I am very much involved but not in the direct sell. I try to be 'real' and 'happy' and so present an attractive vocation to the youngsters. I would prefer to have entered at twenty-one, but in my special circumstances it was expedient and necessary at age thirteen, so I feel that I should continue to be available to the kids."

We may logically make the assumption that a man who believes in his profession and finds satisfaction in it would want to share that belief and satisfaction with potential recruits. We asked these men the extent to which they are personally involved in attempting to interest boys in the priestly vocation and found that less than one quarter (23%) of them confess that they are "hardly at all" or "not at all" involved in recruiting seminarians. Not every priest can be an officially appointed vocation recruiter, but most of them seem to be interested in increasing the number of aspirants to the priesthood, and at the same time they try to be realistic about the image they present to youth. "At present I feel that we diocesan priests are about as exciting, romantic, and attractive to dynamic outer-directed boys as the neighborhood paper boy. I would certainly go to the seminary again, but it would be because of what I feel the priesthood could and should be, and not because of the drab, faceless role we curates play."

As a priest gets older, does he lose his zeal for promoting vocations and for talking to boys about the seminary and the priesthood? We asked the priests to what degree they are "personally involved in attempting to interest boys in the priestly vocation." Table 4.4 reveals a progressive decline from youngest to oldest in this involvement. We thought that this youthful enthusiasm could be explained

Table 4.4 Distribution of personal attempts to interest boys in the priestly vocation, by age categories

	Under 35 years	35 to 49 years	50 years and over	All respondents
Very much so	17%	15%	12%	15%
Quite a bit	28	23	20	25
More or less	37	36	38	37
Hardly at all	15	20	17	18
Not at all	3	6	13	5
(Number of respondents)	(1,509)	(1,320)	(203)	(3,032)

Table 4.5 Distribution of personal attempts to interest boys in the priestly vocation, by type of employment

	Full-time curates	Part-time curates	Non-curates
Very much so	12%	15%	23%
Quite a bit	25	28	24
More or less	41	37	28
Hardly at all	17	15	20
Not at all	5	5	5
(Number of respondents)	(1,678)	(598)	(756)

by the fact that the younger priests are more often in full-time parish work and have broader contacts with youth. This hypothesis did not test out. We found that the full-time curates are less likely (37%) than those in specialized diocesan work (47%) to say that they are "very much" or "quite a bit" involved in this apostolate. Many of the latter are engaged in high school teaching and have more frequent contact with prospective candidates for the seminary.

We have seen in these two Tables that the older a priest becomes the less interest he shows in trying to promote vocations to the priesthood, and that the type of employment he has in the diocese seems to be a factor in this interest. We may take this query a step further by assuming that the satisfaction a man feels in being a priest would also be an influence on his attitudes toward bringing more boys into the seminary. In this survey we may measure satisfaction by the answer to the question whether the respondent would again enter the seminary and at the same age at which he had previously entered.[13] Using this norm we find that the satisfied are somewhat more likely (49%) than the dissatisfied (43%) to be under thirty-five years of age, and also more likely (27% to 21%) to be in specialized non-parochial work. The difference between satisfied and dissatisfied respondents is revealed in Table 4.6.

The implications of these findings seem of tremendous importance to the whole clerical profession. A happy and satisfied priest will try to attract more boys to the seminary. The conditions of the clerical life and the elements that account for happiness and satisfaction in the priestly calling are therefore an important consideration in the

Table 4.6 Distribution of personal attempts to interest boys in the priestly vocation, by satisfied and dissatisfied priests, and all others

	Satis-fied	Dissat-isfied	All others
Very much so	20%	5%	13%
Quite a bit	30	8	26
More or less	36	30	40
Hardly at all	11	39	18
Not at all	3	18	3
(Number of respondents)	(1,335)	(399)	(1,298)

whole vocation apostolate. In various parts of this survey we are able
to discern what these conditions are for the lower clergy in the
American dioceses.

WHAT KEEPS BOYS OUT OF SEMINARIES?

We attempted to probe further into the thinking of these diocesan
clergymen concerning the reasons for the so-called vocation shortage
and for the reasons why so many young men are apparently not at-
tracted to the priestly calling. Most of their comments seem to
reflect the manner in which the priests themselves relate to prospective seminarians. In this area of inquiry a recurring theme is that the
parish priests are themselves "unsure" of their own role.[14] One young
curate in a Connecticut diocese says that "Many boys hesitate to
enter the seminary because of the uncertainty of priests as to their
role in the New Church." A Kansas curate in his late forties writes
that he used to "talk up" vocations very frequently but has ceased
doing so because of the "confused state of seminary training and the
confused role of the parish priest today." A Nebraska noncurate in
his early thirties says that the young men who think about entering
the seminary "have trouble understanding just what the role and
purpose of the priest is, and what they do understand does not present
much of a challenge to them."

The distribution of responses in Table 4.7 reveals the interesting
opinion that seven out of ten of these diocesan priests think that
feelings of unworthiness on the part of young men are hardly a
serious reason for their reluctance to enter the seminary. At the other
end of the scale only one out of nine (11%) believes that the attraction of other occupations is not a serious deterrent to the priestly
vocation. It appears then that the youths who are known to these
diocesan clergy are quite confident about their own worthiness and
abilities for the priestly role, but they also recognize in the American
society many other attractive avenues for a life career.[15]

For the most part, the men who commented on this question seem
to have a fairly high estimate of modern American youth. "Many
Catholic young people do have an ideal of service, but they seem
to think that there is a greater and more rewarding opportunity to

Table 4.7 Proportions estimating the degree of seriousness of several reasons that keep boys from the seminary

	Very serious	Moderately serious	Hardly serious	(Number of respondents)
Unwillingness to lead single life	53%	36	11	(2,963)
Lack of encouragement from parents	39%	41	20	(2,948)
Lack of contact with priests	37%	46	17	(2,941)
Feelings of unworthiness	28%	46	26	(2,903)
Attraction of other occupations	5%	25	70	(2,874)

serve others by joining the Peace Corps or going into social work or other programs where they can be more helpful to others." One recently ordained young priest seems to show his disillusionment when he goes so far as to say: "I could not in conscience encourage any young man to enter the seminary and the priesthood. It seems to me that he could do more good for others in social work or teaching." A similar remark is made by a priest from a rural diocese: "A foremost cause for lack of vocations is that the diocesan clergy has lost its challenge for young American men."

It is an interesting fact that few comments were made concerning the role of parents in fostering vocations. One curate thinks that parents too often "push their kids" into occupations where they can make high income; and another feels that there is too much emphasis on "pleasure and materialism" in the American family. More than one third (37%) of them think that lack of encouragement from parents is a "very serious" reason why boys hesitate to enter the seminary. In the Dogmatic Constitution on the Church the Fathers at the Council wrote that "the family is, so to speak, the domestic Church. In it parents should, by their word and example, be the first preachers of the faith to their children. They should encourage them in the vocation that is proper to each of them, fostering with special care any religious vocation."[16]

We have no way of knowing whether, or to what extent, the prospect of a married diocesan clergy would increase the potential number of aspirants to the priesthood. Four out of ten (39%) of our respondents think that the boy's unwillingness to lead a single life is a "very serious" reason for not entering the seminary.[17] Father

Bier has written about "the psychological demands made by this way of life which unquestionably are greater than those of the lay state. With ordination, the priest renounces the compensations which cushion frustrations for the average layman, namely, the joys and mutual comfort of wedlock, the pride and sense of purpose in family and possessions, and finally, the autonomy of generally, at least, plotting one's own course. The Church herself seems to be giving recognition to these factors, among others, in the significant change in Church discipline approved by the Second Vatican Council which would make a limited provision for married deacons."[18]

Studies of seminarians have shown that the strongest influence on their vocation has come from a priest. Studies of Catholic laymen have revealed that those who have seriously considered entering the seminary were men who have had the most contact with priests. In the present survey, however, less than three out of ten (28%) of the diocesan clergy think that lack of contact with priests is a "very serious" reason why boys hesitate to enter the seminary. This answer does not necessarily underestimate the importance of such contact but probably suggests that priests do have sufficient contact with Catholic youth. D'Arcy and Kennedy remark that "the priesthood in general and the priests with whom the young man comes into personal contact in either the parish or school are some of the potent sources of his image of the priesthood. Candidates for the priesthood say that the strongest influence on their vocation came from a priest they knew."[19]

In the 1960 survey we asked both clergy and laity whether they thought parish priests were encouraging boys to go to the seminary. Table 4.8 shows that the priest respondents, when making a judgment about other parish priests, were less likely (42%) than the laity (68%) to say that this was being done "very much" or "quite a bit." In that survey we found generally that the parishioners had a higher opinion of the clergy than the clergy had of themselves, but it is probable that the clergy opinion is more accurate since they are more immediately concerned with the situation.[20] In the Peoria vocation study we found that among the parents who had attended Catholic schools, almost half (47%) said that there is now more promotion of vocation than when they went to school, and only about one out of six (16%) thought that there is less now, while the remainder (37%) felt that there is about the same amount. At any rate, it appears that the Catholic laity does not see any diminution of the Church's efforts to recruit vocations.

Table 4.8 Comparative opinions of clergy and laity in 1960 survey on extent to which they think parish priests are encouraging priestly vocations

	Clergy	Laity
Very much so	20%	38%
Quite a bit	22	30
More or less	22	25
Hardly at all	23	5
Not at all	13	2
(Number of respondents)	(2,177)	(2,166)

We have seen in Table 4.6 that the satisfied priests are much more likely (50%) than the dissatisfied (13%) to report positively that they are personally involved in attempting to interest boys in the priestly vocation. It seems probable that a man's feelings toward his own priestly career will color his opinions about the reasons why young men do not follow the same career. This assumption may also be reversed in that the reasons for a man's own dissatisfaction with the priesthood may be those he sees as a hindrance to entrance to the priesthood by others. The data in Table 4.9 show a curious

Table 4.9 Proportions of satisfied and dissatisfied priests who consider "very serious" several reasons that keep boys from the seminary

	Satis- fied	Dissat- isfied	All others
Attraction of other occupations	50%	61%	53%
(Number of respondents)	(1,308)	(382)	(1,273)
Unwillingness to lead single life	32	60	40
(Number of respondents)	(1,294)	(386)	(1,270)
Lack of encouragement from parents	40	30	36
(Number of respondents)	(1,303)	(374)	(1,264)
Lack of contact with priests	29	20	29
(Number of respondents)	(1,281)	(368)	(1,254)
Feelings of unworthiness	5	5	5
(Number of respondents)	(1,269)	(365)	(1,240)

contrast of opinion between the satisfied and the dissatisfied. The latter are more likely to say that the attraction of other occupations and the attraction of marriage are "very serious" hindrances; while the satisfied priests are more likely to say that lack of encouragement from parents and lack of contact with priests are "very serious."

DID THE SEMINARY PREPARE THEM?

In reflecting about their own seminary training, some of the priests —even those who are fairly young—say that many changes have occurred since "their day" in the seminary, but that parallel changes have not occurred among the parish priests themselves. "Our seminary has undergone some radical changes since I attended and my objections are not to the seminary as such. Yet there is a certain anomaly in having seminarians trained in this new way and then enter into a priesthood that has not really undergone much reevaluation at all. I think that I too would hesitate to become a priest if I felt that there would be little possibility that the diocesan priesthood would be affected by the spirit and decrees of Vatican II."

The manner in which the clergy differentially appraise the several effects of their own training in the major seminary is clearly demonstrated in Table 4.10. They have a fairly high regard for the spiritual and academic training they received in the major seminary, with only a small minority (15%) saying that they were helped "hardly at all" or "not at all" to lead a holy life, and another minority (21%) giving this negative opinion about training to lead an intellectual life. On the other hand, two thirds (65%) of them give a negative estimate about their seminary training on how to deal with lay people, and seven out of ten are negative about their preparation in the handling of practical parish problems.[21]

The comparative statistics in Table 4.10 between the earlier and the current survey suggests at first sight that the seminary is getting "worse" in preparing men for their role as priests. The respondents to the 1960 survey gave a higher appraisal on each of the four items on which we questioned them. We must remember, however, that the earlier study reached only parish priests and excluded those in

Table 4.10 Proportions estimating degree to which major seminary prepared them for following things, current survey and 1960 survey

Current Survey:	Lead a holy life	Lead an intellectual life	Deal with the lay people	Handle parish problems
Very much so	21%	15%	4%	3%
Quite a bit	33	30	9	7
More or less	31	34	22	20
Hardly at all	12	17	41	42
Not at all	3	4	24	28
(Number of respondents)	(3,032)	(3,019)	(3,020)	(3,017)
1960 Survey:				
Very much so	39%	29%	13%	10%
Quite a bit	35	33	19	14
More or less	21	28	28	27
Hardly at all	4	8	31	33
Not at all	1	2	9	16
(Number of respondents)	(2,178)	(2,161)	(2,150)	(2,173)

non-parochial assignments, while the current survey excludes pastors but reaches a large number of diocesan priests who are not in full-time parish work. The greater proportion of older men (especially pastors) tend to give a higher appraisal of their seminary training.

This age differential of opinion shows up again in both surveys when we contrast the three age categories as in Table 4.11. In every case and in both studies the youngest men give a lower estimate than do the oldest men. In other words, the priests who were most recently in the seminary think less of their training than do the priests who were more remotely there. Do these contrasting estimates mean merely that the younger men are more critical and the older men more tolerant? Do they mean rather that the major seminaries have not kept abreast of the changing needs of the times and are therefore relatively less successful than they used to be in preparing men for the priestly life?

The fact is, of course, that there has been steady and demonstrable improvement in American Catholic seminaries, beginning long before the convocation of Vatican II. Their faculties are better educated than ever with more doctoral degrees; their courses of study have been broadened and improved. These changes have been noted and discussed in innumerable journals, institutes, and educational conventions.[22] The seminaries have not become conservative in recent years. The problem is one of relative expectations on the part of the world, the Church, and its priests and laity. The Council has underscored the needs of the Church and the great tasks it confronts, and

Table 4.11   Proportions answering "very much" or "quite a bit" as extent of seminary preparation for following things, by age categories, current survey and 1960 survey

Current survey:	Under 35 years	35 to 49 years	50 years and over	All respondents
Lead a holy life	48%	59%	67%	54%
(Number of respondents)	(1,516)	(1,313)	(203)	(3,032)
Lead an intellectual life	44	45	54	45
(Number of respondents)	(1,514)	(1,309)	(196)	(3,019)
Deal with the lay people	11	13	25	13
(Number of respondents)	(1,515)	(1,312)	(193)	(3,020)
Handle parish problems	9	11	22	10
(Number of respondents)	(1,516)	(1,308)	(193)	(3,017)
1960 survey:				
Lead a holy life	75%	71%	79%	74%
(Number of respondents)	(741)	(939)	(498)	(2,178)
Lead an intellectual life	59	63	67	62
(Number of respondents)	(739)	(937)	(485)	(2,161)
Deal with the lay people	31	30	37	32
(Number of respondents)	(735)	(927)	(488)	(2,150)
Handle parish problems	21	25	29	24
(Number of respondents)	(737)	(936)	(490)	(2,173)

as a result the attitudes of priests and people have changed more rapidly than the seminaries. This seems to be the explanation for the contrasting opinions revealed in Table 4.11, where we see higher appraisals in the earlier study and lower appraisals among the youngest respondents in both surveys.

There is a mixture of both appreciation and disappointment in some of the remarks made by the respondents. "Our spiritual training would have been fine," writes one young curate from Missouri, "if we could live in the shadow of the seminary for the duration of our lives. We learned to love God and to be devoted to Him only in the ideal conditions of the seminary, but little thought was given to the fact that a daily schedule, spiritual or otherwise, becomes a thing of the past in any really active parish.[23] As a result, I am definitely incompetent as a professional parish priest."

The suggestions were made that the course in pastoral theology should include some form of field education or pre-service training, and several respondents made reference to the Vatican Decree on Priestly Formation. "Seminarians need to learn the art of exercising the apostolate not only in theory but also in practice. They have to be able to pursue their assignments both on their own initiative and in concert with others. Hence, even during their course of studies, and also during holidays, they should be introduced into pastoral practice by appropriate undertakings. Depending on the age of the seminarians and the local conditions, and given the prudent approval of their bishops, such programs should be pursued in a methodical way and under the guidance of men experienced in pastoral matters."[24]

CHANGE AND COMMUNICATION

We must remember that the opinions expressed by these priests refer for the most part to seminary training as it used to be. Some of the clergy from several large dioceses report that large-scale changes were introduced into their seminaries as recently as a year or so before this survey was taken.[24] Even those who were ordained three years or less had not had the full benefit of the "reformed" and renewed major seminaries. We have already seen in Table 2.1 that half of the respondents thinks that the pace of change in their seminary is "about right" but that the younger men are much more ready to complain that it is moving too slowly (Table 2.5). Let us see how the satisfied and dissatisfied priests react to this question.

One of the dissatisfied priests, a Southern curate in his early thirties, says that his seminary teachers were "wholly inadequate in their handling of pastoral theology. This was particularly true in the area of pastoral counseling. We simply did not get any training along these lines. I would like to see a major overhaul of the cur-

Table 4.12   Distribution of opinion of satisfied and dissatisfied priests concerning rate of change in seminary routine

	Satis-fied	Dissat-isfied	All others
About right	53%	37%	49%
Too fast	11	9	8
Too slowly	36	54	43
(Number of respondents)	(1,127)	(351)	(1,162)

riculum and the useful employment of the men in both minor and major orders. In other words, give them an opportunity to serve in the parishes, an idea of what they are getting into, some practical application of the things they learn from books and lectures."

We tried to obtain a contemporary appraisal of one facet of seminary life by asking the priests to what extent the major seminary of their diocese currently exhibits free and open communication between the students and the administration. Unlike the previous questions, this one does not refer to the past experience which they themselves have had, but is a test of the reputation that the major seminary currently enjoys in the diocese. Many of the smaller dioceses do not maintain a major seminary, and for this reason approximately 40 per cent of the priests did not answer this question.

Table 4.13   Proportions estimating the degree to which the major seminary currently has open communication between students and administration, by age categories

	Under 35 years	35 to 49 years	50 years and over	All respondents
Very much so, quite a bit	33%	35%	29%	33%
More or less	29	26	28	28
Hardly at all, not at all	38	39	43	39
(Number of respondents)	(881)	(811)	(109)	(1,801)

The close similarity of opinion among the three age categories in Table 4.13 indicates that it is not only the younger clergy who keep a sharp eye on the seminary, or who are generally more critical than the older men. As a matter of fact, a somewhat higher percentage

(43%) of the oldest group than of the youngest (38%) are negative about the extent to which there is free and open two-way communication between the students and the superiors in the major seminary. In the last column of Table 4.13 there is a spread of opinion among all respondents, with almost as many answering positively (33%) as negatively (39%), and this probably reflects significant differences from diocese to diocese. We have no intention of singling out particular diocesan major seminaries for comment here even though the spotlight of publicity has been directed to some specific instances of the breakdown of communication in the recent past.

The manner in which communication occurs in the seminary is probably a reflection also of the manner in which the lines of communication are open, or closed, within the total diocesan structure and between the bishop and his priests. It has not been easy for either superiors or subordinates in the Church to follow the recommendations of the Second Vatican Council in revising the long-term authoritative system in which a "one-way" system of directives from the top down was in effect. This subject is dealt with in more detail in other sections of this research report.[25]

In several instances the people at the seminary are praised but the "system" is condemned. "Several priests at the seminary personally stimulated many of us intellectually, spiritually, apostolically, but the system was deadening. My own contacts with inspiring priests and also with lay people who were involved in social action helped me the most." When they talked about the seminary "system" the reference is to the daily routine, the regulations of behavior, as well as to the curriculum and class schedule. They feel that there is a certain standardization that tends to "repress" their individuality. "It is difficult to be oneself and to develop one's singular personality and talents in the system."[26]

The obvious need, recognized by progressive seminary rectors, is to align more clearly the training with the demands of the profession. A young priest in an eastern city writes: "I feel that my seminary training was almost completely unrealistic and ambiguous about the priestly life I have assumed. My thinking and my ideals have changed greatly in the year and a half since my ordination." A Rhode Island curate who was ordained a decade ago reflects that "in the seminary the priesthood was presented as an ideal, a challenge, something noble and sacrificial. But after ordination it becomes something very concrete, earthy and human."

SUMMARY

What we have found in this chapter is a confirmation of previous information that a majority of the diocesan clergy did not attend a minor seminary high school and that a greater majority would not do so if they could decide again. Statistically, however, there appears to be a trend toward younger entrance to the seminary although the laity, and especially parents, do not favor a boy entering the seminary immediately after grammar school. If they could do it over again, a larger proportion of the oldest priests than of the youngest would hesitate to enter the seminary.

The younger men are more involved than the older in promoting vocations to the priesthood, and those in specialized work more than the full-time parish curates, but satisfaction with the priestly role is the most important factor why a priest tries to interest boys in going to the seminary. It is the priests' belief that young men are not hindered from entering the seminary by feelings of unworthiness, and they think that the attraction of alternative occupations is a more serious hindrance than celibacy or the attitudes of parents and priests. The laity thinks that the clergy promotes vocations to the seminary more than the clergy actually does. The dissatisfied priests feel that unwillingness to lead a single life keeps boys out of the seminary.

There is general agreement among the respondents that the major seminary prepared them much better to lead a holy and intellectual life than to deal with people and to handle practical parish problems. Comparisons between the earlier and the current survey and between the youngest and the oldest respondents indicate that the renewal programs of the major seminaries are not proceeding fast enough to keep up with the expectations of the clergy and the needs of the Church. There is some evidence, however, that the expectations of the younger priests were raised in the seminary but are not being fulfilled in the slowly changing Church in which they are now working.

In making a judgment about the rate of contemporary changes in seminary routine, the satisfied priests think it is about right while the dissatisfied think it is going too slowly. In appraising the current system of communication between superiors and students in their own diocesan major seminaries, more of the respondents give a negative (39%) than a positive judgment (33%) but in this case the younger priests are not significantly more critical than the older.

NOTES

1. Canadian Bishop Alexander Carter discussing the *Decree on Priestly Formation* in Abbott, *op. cit.*, p. 436. Cardinal Ritter says that "there must be an *aggiornamento* in seminary education. Certainly one of the most imperative tasks confronting the Church today is a reconstruction of methods by which its priests are educated for the ministry," in Lee and Putz, *op cit.*, Foreword, p. v.

2. *Priestly Formation*, conclusion. Cardinal Suenens pointed out that the hopes of the Council for the renovation of the Church were closely linked with the renovation in priests' education and training. See Douglas Horton, *Vatican Diary 1964* (Philadephia: United Church Press, 1965), pp. 160–61.

3. See the summary of several research studies on this question in Joseph H. Fichter, *Religion as an Occupation* (Notre Dame, Ind.: University of Notre Dame Press, 1961), pp. 27–33.

4. *Priestly Formation*, Article 12.

5. Paul F. D'Arcy and Eugene C. Kennedy, *The Genius of the Apostolate* (New York: Sheed and Ward, 1965), p. 36. See also the differences of opinion concerning the "Age of Decision" in *Religion as an Occupation*, pp. 15–20.

6. See Walter D. Wagoner, *The Seminary Protestant and Catholic* (New York: Sheed and Ward, 1966), Chapter 7, "Whence Cometh Melchizedek?"

7. James M. Lee and Louis J. Putz, eds., *Seminary Education in a Time of Change* (Notre Dame, Ind.: Fides Publishers, 1965), Chapter 4, "Overview of Educational Problems in Seminaries," pp. 130 ff. See also Stafford Poole, *Seminary in Crisis* (New York: Herder and Herder, 1965), *passim*.

8. The lower-class lay friends of priests are twice as likely as the upper-class friends to approve a boy's entrance to the minor seminary. See Joseph H. Fichter, *Priest and People* (New York: Sheed and Ward, 1965), p. 56; also *Catholic Parents and the Church Vocation* (Washington: Center for Applied Research in the Apostolate, 1967).

9. "The task of fostering vocations develops on the whole Christian community, which should do so in the first place by living in a fully Christian way." *Priestly Formation*, Article 2.

10. See the comments by Abbott, *op. cit.*, p. 441, footnote 11.

11. *Priestly Formation*, Article 3.

12. *Ibid.*, Article 2.

13. For other comparisons between the satisfied and the dissatisfied priests, see below, Chapter 7, "Facets of the Career."

14. D'Arcy and Kennedy, op. cit., p. 228, discuss this confusion. "The aggiornamento has brought to priests not peace but a sword. Within the last year, as trumpets of new hope have been heard throughout the world, many priests have experienced deep and seering conflicts. Paradoxically, as unparalleled opportunities seem about to open for the Church, her priests have tasted a bitter harvest of self-doubt and frustration. This suffering is complex, and the finest priests, because of their sensitivity, have felt it most keenly."

15. In our survey of Catholic parents in Peoria pp. 14–15, the most frequently mentioned hindrance to vocation for boys was the attraction of other occupations, and for girls the attraction of the opposite sex. They thought that lack of contact with clergy and religious was much more important than negative attitudes of parents.

16. On the Church, Article 11. An indirect effect of the Council decree on the Apostolate of the Laity may be a higher appreciation of secular, or non-Church, occupations. Lay people "share in the priestly, prophetic and royal office of Christ and therefore have their own role to play" (Article 2). The "upgrading" of secular occupations as lay vocations may increase the problem of recruiting men to the priesthood.

17. The respondents who favor freedom of choice to marry and who say they might do so if the rules change rank the "very serious" obstacles to seminary entrance as follows: Unwillingness to lead a single life 72%, attraction of other occupations 53%, lack of encouragement from parents 29%, lack of contact with priests 22%, feelings of unworthiness 5%. For further discussion of these attitudes, see below, Chapter 8, "Married Clergy."

18. See William C. Bier, "Selection of Seminarians," in Lee and Putz, op. cit., pp. 170–204.

19. D'Arcy and Kennedy, op. cit., p. 38. Research surveys show also that the greatest encouragement to the convent comes from religious Sisters, and to the Brotherhood from religious Brothers. See Religion as an Occupation, p. 22. Also for the Protestant ministry, Keith Bridston and Dwight Culver, Pre-seminary Education (Minneapolis: Augsburg, 1965), Table 44, found that pastor and mother are most important influences toward the ministry.

20. The lay friends of priests in the 1960 survey were not a representative sample of American Catholic adult laity. See Joseph Fichter, Priest and People, Chapter 1, "The Closest Friends," pp. 3–21. James Didier's study of role expectations of Baptist ministers showed also that laymen tend to judge their ministers more generously than ministers do (Doctoral dissertation, Michigan State University Library, 1966).

21. For a "speculative" view of pastoral theology see the final chapter, pp. 418–37, by the editor, Eugene G. Weitzel, Pastoral Ministry in a Time of Change (Milwaukee: Bruce, 1966). See also H. Richard Niebuhr, The Purpose of the Church and its Ministry (New York: Harper & Row, 1956), p. 83, who writes, "It is significant that when ministers reflect on their theological education they are likely to regret more than any other deficiency in it the failure of the school to prepare them for the administra-

SEMINARY TRAINING 93

tion of such a church." In the Spring of 1966, the Midwest Association of Theological Schools surveyed priests who had been ordained from thirty-two seminaries during the previous fifteen years. Preliminary findings from 5,350 respondents show that these priests got their best preparation in canon law and moral theology, but that they consider canon law the "least valuable" course they had in the seminary. They say their poorest preparation was in pastoral counseling and in modern social problems.

22. See the discussions by the departments of seminary in the annual *Bulletin* of the National Catholic Educational Association. Also Walter Wagoner, *op. cit.*, Chapter 4, "Pipings in Academe," and especially his fanciful description of "St. Optimus Seminary," pp. 185–88, which foreshadows a cooperative program now in the planning stages.

23. In our 1960 survey of diocesan priests we found that almost two thirds (64%) do not have a daily work schedule, and the proportions were the same for pastors and curates. We found also that the parishioners are almost twice as likely (48%) as the clergy (25%) to favor definite office hours for the parish priest.

24. Decree on *Priestly Formation*, Article 21.

25. See above, Chapter 3, "Bishop–Priest Relations," and below, Chapter 6, "Local Working Conditions."

26. In a speech delivered at Cincinnati, Monsignor John R. Gorman, rector of Chicago's St. Mary of the Lake Seminary, said that today's seminarians want to be known as individual persons, and that "trust, loyalty and respect are characteristic of the responses given to leaders, not to mere officials; the awakening of such attitudes is a more fundamental objective of the exercise of authority than mere conformity to regulations."

CONTINUING EDUCATION

Professional men who hope to succeed in their careers realize that their education has not been completed with the academic diploma. This is ideally the case also among the diocesan clergy with ordination to the priesthood. It was already stated in the Code of Canon Law (#129) that the clergy should not give up their pursuit of learning, especially in the sacred sciences, after they are ordained. Pope Pius XI had addressed these words to the clergy: "The priest must be graced by no less knowledge and culture than is usual among well-bred and well-educated people of his day. This is to say that he must be healthily modern, as is the Church, which is at home in all times and all places, and adapts itself to all."[1]

The need for modernization, renewal, and continual adaptation was in the minds of the Fathers of the Second Vatican Council and they re-emphasized this recommendation for further professional training of the clergy. "Especially because of the circumstances of modern society, priestly training should be pursued and perfected even after the seminary course of studies has been completed."[2] They indicated that it is a collective obligation of episcopal conferences and not the duty only of a local bishop to employ "effective means" for this purpose. They recommended pastoral institutes, conferences, and projects "designed to afford the younger clergy a gradual introduction into the priestly life and apostolic activity under their spiritual, intellectual, and pastoral aspect, and calculated to help young priests renew and develop this life and activity more intensely every day."

The clergy has been historically among the learned professions, and Harvard was not the only American college that was established for the perpetuation of a learned clergy.[3] The level of formal academic schooling has been consistently higher among Catholic priests than among Protestant ministers in the United States. The fundamentalist sects still look with suspicion on highly educated clergymen and would prefer that their ministers teach from the heart rather than from the head.[4] On the other hand, the institutional members of the American Association of Theological Schools have been constantly raising the educational standards for the professional ministry. The concept of sabbaticals and refresher courses and the movement for continuing education have also been largely promoted by the more sophisticated Protestant churches and divinity schools.

RISING LEVEL OF EDUCATION

The increasing educational demands on the clergy reflect what is happening in other American occupations and professions The level of schooling in the general population, as well as among the American Catholic laity, has been constantly rising. While the Catholic clergy has consistently been more educated than their Protestant counterparts, there is now dependable research evidence that the Catholic laity is no less "intellectual" than their Protestant fellow citizens.[5] Nevertheless, the education of priests must be continuously reappraised if the clergy are to have the kind of knowledge and culture that is "usual" among modern well-bred and well-educated people.[6]

In this chapter we are asking not only whether there is a rising level of formal schooling among these diocesan priests, as measured by their academic degrees, but also whether they are continuing their education after ordination. Given the developments of seminary accreditation and the modernization of academic programs, our assumption is that the younger priests are more likely than the older to have earned academic degrees. The distribution of responses in

Table 5.1 shows both academic achievement and intention, and indicates that these are not a function of age alone.

The changes that have occurred in academic achievement of Catholic clergy during more than a quarter-century point to a rising level of accredited formal schooling among these diocesan priests, with

Table 5.1 Distribution of academic degrees and academic intentions by age categories

	Under 35 years	35 to 49 years	50 years and over	All respondents
Have no academic degree				
Will not get one	8%	13%	28%	11%
Intend to get one	4	2	1	3
Have Bachelor's degree				
Will not get Master's	41	42	36	41
Intend to get Master's	22	11	3	16
Have Master's degree				
Will not get doctorate	18	22	18	20
Intend to get doctorate	6	5	2	5
Hold the doctorate	1	5	12	4
(Number of respondents)	(1,509)	(1,312)	(204)	(3,025)

the oldest more than twice as likely (29%) as the youngest (12%) to report that they have no academic degree at all. This finding must be interpreted, however, with some caution, particularly if one is interested in "learning achievement" as well as in "degree attainment." The standard course for all these priests was eight years of study beyond high school graduation, so that the men without a degree did not necessarily have fewer years of formal education than did those who possess the Bachelor's, or even the Master's degree. In most cases it probably means that they studied at a seminary without official academic accreditation. As late as 1966, only thirty-five out of the eighty-nine Catholic seminaries at the college and professional level had regional accreditation.[7]

Aside from the question of accredited major seminaries and the fact that diocesan priests normally spend eight years in collegiate and professional study before ordination, the higher degrees at the Master's and Doctor's level are usually earned after ordination. This is noted in the comparison that more of the men in the middle and oldest age categories (32%) than in the youngest (25%) obtained these graduate degrees. Table 5.1 bears this out also in the "intentions" expressed by the respondents. Only a small proportion (6%) of the oldest men still hope to earn a degree, and a larger percentage of the youngest group (32%) than of the middle group (18%) still have intentions of doing so.

Whether or not these intentions for further professional training and formal graduate study are ever realized does not depend exclusively on the wishes of the individual priest. As one young curate from Pennsylvania pointed out, the word "intend" may mean "would like to." He remarks that the problem in his diocese "is whether one has the opportunity to get to graduate school and also has the approval of the bishop to do so, even if he has the ambition and the money required to pursue further study." He can hope that the urgings of the Council Fathers will be heard in his diocese. "Bishops should see that young men suitably fitted by temperament, virtue, and talent are sent to special schools, colleges, or universities, so that there will be a supply of priests versed in the higher scientific method of sacred sciences and other sciences which may appear serviceable. Such priests will be able to meet the various needs of the apostolate."[8]

EDUCATION AND TYPE OF EMPLOYMENT

Although the Council recommended continuing education for all the clergy, we hypothesized that the parish priests are not so interested in higher degrees and further studies as are those priests who are in specialized and nonparochial assignments. This assumption is based on the analogy that in every profession the general practioner is hardly ever as highly trained as the specialist. The responses here provide a clear-cut demonstration that the priests in specialized nonparochial work are better educated and intend to get more education than is the case with the full-time parish curates.

Table 5.2 reveals that the men in special assignments are more than three times (56%) as likely as those in full-time parish work (17%) to have a graduate academic degree. It shows also that a larger proportion of them (32% to 18%) intend to continue their formal academic study. There are several reasons why full-time parish curates do not seek higher degrees. One of them in his early forties from Michigan writes, "I have tried to earn a Master's degree, but with only one day off a week I could not accomplish it. Pastors can roam around wherever and whenever they like, but the assistant has to stay put in the parish." Another in the same age bracket and from Ohio says, "I am too old to go back to school, but I regret that more opportunity is not given in this diocese so that younger priests can get graduate degrees."

Table 5.2 Distribution of academic degrees and academic intentions by type of employment

	Full-time curate	Part-time	Non-curate	All respondents
Have no academic degree				
Will not get one	15%	9%	6%	11%
Intend to get one	3	3	1	3
Have Bachelor's degree				
Will not get Master's	52	39	18	41
Intend to get Master's	13	20	19	16
Have Master's degree				
Will not get doctorate	14	20	32	20
Intend to get doctorate	2	7	12	5
Hold the doctorate	1	2	12	4
(Number or respondents)	(1,676)	(596)	(753)	(3,025)

In some instances the full-time parish curates exhibit a resistance to, and even a disdain for, further professional and academic training.[9] One man in his early thirties from Illinois says he had no degree and does not intend to get one "because I am not engaged in any specialized field and it would be superfluous for me to take time off, even on a limited basis, to work toward a degree." Another young curate from New York insists that "the diocesan priest is ordained to serve in the parish. Therefore, his desire to specialize is an indication of his dissatisfaction with the life of a diocesan priest.[10] Let him get released from the diocese and join a religious order that does specialized work." Also from New York a part-time curate in his late thirties complains that "the priestly fraternity is split asunder by the separation of those in special work and those in parish work."

While the younger priests are expected to go into parish work immediately after ordination, they are expected also in many dioceses to perform some concurrent nonparochial task, usually in high school teaching. This becomes evident in Table 5.3 where more than six out of ten (62%) of those who report that they are part-time assistants in their parish are in the youngest age bracket.[11] A Connecticut man in his early thirties who is doing two jobs complains that "the pastor assigns you to the hospital and you become a hospital chaplain with no training. Or he tells you you're in charge of the grammar school and you become a school principal without knowing anything about it."

Table 5.3 Age distribution of respondents by type of employment

	Full-time curate	Part-time	Non-curate	All respondents
Under 35 years	52%	62%	36%	50%
35 to 49 years	42	35	53	43
50 years and over	6	3	11	7
(Number of respondents)	(1,688)	(599)	(761)	(3,048)

It has been traditional in most dioceses that every newly ordained priest be assigned at least for a while to full-time parish work. We have seen that one quarter of the respondents to this survey are currently in full-time nonparochial assignments, but most probably all of them had at one time been assigned to parish work. We have only slight evidence of a kind of career pattern in which these men advanced through three stages from full-time to part-time curate and then to full-time specialist. There is evidence, however, that the weight of "two jobs" becomes burdensome as a man grows older. An Illinois curate in his late forties says that "the boss has announced a new policy that every man must have two jobs. That may be all right for the younger priests, but you get to a point in your life when you want to concentrate on the thing you can do best. For instance, I don't think a chancery official should be a pastor, or that a pastor should also be superintendent of education."

The functions of priests are manifold and essentially pastoral in the sense that priests represent Christ, the Shepherd, and "are collaborators with the order of bishops in that threefold sacred task which by its very nature bears on the mission of the Church."[12] The Council Fathers did not teach that all priestly functions are parochial or that every priest must do some parish work, or that continuing education is only for those who are not working in the parish.[13] In this survey we find that some of the priests who are in the parish and who intend to spend the rest of their lives in exclusively parochial duties do not feel the need of further training or specialized study. A curate from Ohio in his late forties opines that "every priest, including those in religious orders, should spend at least two years doing nothing but pastoral and parochial work. Then and only then should he go into specialized work or be considered for any promotion or even eventually allowed to become a bishop."

The peculiar notion that only parochial and sacramental duties are genuine priestly work is seen in Lee's remark that "the current multi-purpose role of the American seminary is doubtless reflective of the 'modern' conception of the priesthood. To be sure, the priesthood is becoming a side-line occupation for many priests, something to be squeezed in when not performing other, more important non-sacerdotal activities. Not a few priests might be said to be 'moonlighting' when they engage in sacramental or sacerdotal functions. Indeed, the priesthood seems to be interfering with the regular work of some priests."[14]

TRAINING THE SPECIALISTS

Whatever negative criticism there may be about the "multi-purpose" training of priests there can be no doubt about the attitude of the respondents to this survey. The answers in Table 5.4 tell us that the overwhelming majority (87%) of them agree to the statement that "curates who want to prepare for specialized work should be encouraged to do so." The understanding is, of course, that this encouragement should come from the seminary faculty, diocesan officials, and bishops. The remarkable similarity of response across the current occupational lines shows that this favorable attitude is not restricted only to those who are already in specialized work. The great majority (84%) of the oldest priests also concur on this suggestion.

This question was included in the survey at the suggestion of priests who said that in their diocese the man who asked permission to take graduate work or specialized training was usually looked upon with suspicion as a "nonconformist" or even as a "status-seeker." This problem hits at the heart of our main concern in this study: the nature of communication between superiors and subordinates in the diocese. Priests are supposed to be trained, while seminarians, in the

Table 5.4 Opinions, by type of employment, on statement that "curates who want to prepare for specialized work should be encouraged to do so"

	Full-time curate	Part-time	Non-curate	All respondents
Agree	86%	88%	85%	87%
Disagree	4	3	4	3
Not sure	10	9	11	10
(Number of respondents)	(1,686)	(598)	(755)	(3,039)

ability to make considered decisions, to pass judgments and "to act on their own initiative and energetically."[15] Yet, in many dioceses they are discouraged from taking initiative concerning their own talents and career potentials and are expected to wait passively and obediently until they are "selected" for further training and special assignments.

A New York curate in his late thirties tells us that "the special interests and abilities of the men are not considered or encouraged, and there is no diocesan program for further training after ordination." A part-time curate in his late twenties from Wisconsin points out another problem of "mismanagement" when he says that "some men have been prepared, and with degrees, for work that they never got the opportunity to do." On the other hand there is a kind of suspicion on the part of some parish priests that the man who wants special training is trying to escape regular priestly duties. A curate from South Dakota warns that "you have to be sure that he is not just running away from the demands of parish work and life." A part-time curate in his late thirties from a Texas diocese says he favors the idea of graduate work and professional training, "but you have to watch out for prima donnas among the specialists."

A young noncurate from one of the New York dioceses said that he and a few other priests had been discussing the following question: "Should some diocesan priests hold regular jobs, like teaching or social work, thus supporting themselves, and then practice their parish ministry in the evenings? Most of the 'action' in the priesthood is in the evenings. In many parishes the priests are occupied during the day with nonpriestly work, or are not occupied at all." A part-time curate in his early fifties from a Pennsylvania diocese says that men with twenty years experience in parish work are being "shanghaied" into teaching even though they have no experience and less interest in school work. "Most of the men entering the diocesan priesthood have done so to work in the parishes, and this unwanted switch from the parish tends to frustrate and sour them."

We have no way of knowing from the present data how widespread is this practice of shifting diocesan priests into roles for which they have not been prepared. One priest in his late forties from a Pennsylvania diocese, who calls himself an "institutional chaplain," says that "my only specialized training was obtained after I got the assignment and at my own time and expense. Certainly nothing in the seminary prepares you for this kind of work. The institutional population is tremendous (armed forces, schools, hospitals, delinquents, prisoners, etc.). About the only contact these people have with religion is the chaplain. Too often, the chaplains assigned for the work are misfits, the ill, the aged, the problem priests. If done properly, this is a highly specialized type of ministry. Priests should be assigned who have a liking for this type of work and they should be given adequate training for the job."

SABBATICALS AND INSTITUTES

In probing further the attitudes of these diocesan priests we asked them whether "diocesan priests should have periodical sabbatical leaves to take refresher courses in the work and problems of the ministry." Here again, the overwhelming agreement in Table 5.5 shows that the full-time parish assistants are as favorable as the others to this kind of continuing education. As may be expected, the age of the respondents makes a considerable difference in the proportional answers. While the majority of all priests are in favor of sabbaticals, the youngest men are much more ready (90%) than the oldest (69%) to give agreement to the statement. The Council Fathers themselves put the accent on the younger clergy, saying that the refresher courses "should be held at set times, especially a few years after ordination. By these and other appropriate helps newly appointed pastors and those who are assigned to new pastoral activity can be assisted with special care."[16]

A curate in his early thirties in a New Jersey diocese is very much in favor of the sabbatical for every diocesan priest but feels that it is "impractical in most places because of the shortage of priests." A hospital chaplain in an Iowa diocese who has had no special training for this work says, "I feel so ignorant about so many things I should know: alcoholism, psychotics, counseling, the new moral theology,

Table 5.5 Opinions, by type of employment, on statement that "diocesan priests should have periodical sabbatical leaves to take refresher courses in the work and problems of the ministry"

	Full-time curate	Part-time	Non-curate	All re-spondents
Agree	86%	88%	86%	86%
Disagree	5	2	3	4
Neutral	7	7	8	7
Don't know	2	3	3	3
(Number of respondents)	(1,684)	(599)	(758)	(3,041)

Scripture, and other important fields. Sure, I can read; but try to read when you are tired, nervous, and swamped with work. Perhaps periodic seminars are the answer. The one I attended this summer was very good, but it lasted only five days and when I got back I had to work day and night to catch up on my duties."

The concept of the sabbatical leave, or periodical refresher course, in the active ministry is not the same as the apostolic internship, which is also mentioned by the Vatican Council but which had been introduced some years before the convocation of the Council.

The earlier program, recommended by Pius XII in 1949, was for newly ordained priests in the religious orders and congregations.[17] It is fashioned according to the functional needs and prospective roles of each group, lasts for approximately an academic year, and is usually called by various terms: tertianship, second novitiate, apostolic novitiate, year of perfection, *schola affectus.* This special apprenticeship is not prescribed for the diocesan clergy, except while they are still in the seminary.[18] The Council says that bishops should "consider the opportuneness of deciding on a certain interruption of studies or arranging for a suitable pastoral apprenticeship so that a more rounded test can be made of priestly candidates."[19]

It is one thing to have favorable attitudes toward specialized study and sabbatical leaves, but it is quite another thing to take the opportunity for continuing education. The test of a diocesan priest's realistic interest in such opportunity is, at least in part, his attendance at summer institutes, study weeks, and similar programs that are widely available throughout the country.[20] The measure of their interest in such programs by the pastors and diocesan officials is the extent to which they provide opportunities, and especially time off, for the lower-echelon priests to attend them. A Kentucky curate in his late thirties remarked: "I planned to attend an institute at Notre Dame but because of circumstances beyond the control of the pastor I could not get permission to attend."

The question answered in Table 5.6 refers specifically to the summer immediately preceding the distribution of the survey, and it shows that almost half (48%) of the men in specialized work, as compared to only three out of ten of the parish assistants, attended a summer institute or study week. It seems significant that those in nonparish work were twice as likely (33%) as the curates (17%) to report that they were able to get time off without sacrificing their annual vacation.[21] A part-time parish assistant in his late thirties from Virginia thinks that "many priests become stalemated because it becomes almost impossible for them to take a few weeks off each year for summer courses and institutes." It should be noted, however, that men under thirty-five were more than twice as likely (43%) as the oldest group (18%) to say that they attended such a summer course, a comparison which indicates that interest and the willingness to take such opportunities wane with the years.

The "opportune aids" recommended by the Vatican Council logically imply that time will be made available for priests to continue their education. "That priests may more easily pursue their studies and learn methods of evangelization and of the apostolate to better effect, every care should be taken to provide them with op-

Table 5.6 Distribution by type of employment of attendance at summer institute or study week

	Full-time curate	Part-time	Non-curate	All respondents
Yes, did it on my vacation	13%	21%	15%	15%
Yes, given time off for it	17	24	33	22
No, did not attend any	70	55	52	63
(Number of respondents)	(1,665)	(592)	(753)	(3,010)

portune aids. Such would be the instituting of courses or of congresses, according to the conditions of each region, the establishment of centers dedicated to pastoral studies, the setting up of libraries, and appropriate programs of study conducted by suitable persons."[22]

One cannot help but notice the contrast between the large proportion—more than eight out of ten—who favor opportunities for continuing education, and the small proportion (15%) who used their vacation, or were given time off (22%) to take such opportunities. One California priest who is a school teacher says, "I am lucky that I have the chance for summer study, but the men in parish work find it difficult to get away." A Massachusetts curate in his early thirties says that "in the light of the pressing problems of the modern world, the bishop should not only permit, but should make compulsory, these institutes and courses. Very few of us are keeping abreast of modern trends, and we need this kind of help."[23]

While the Church is an organization with its own traditions and patterns, the question of sabbatical leaves and refresher courses suggests comparison with other American institutional models. It is safe to say that the clergy who taught in the Catholic institutions of higher learning began to take regular sabbatical leaves only after the custom had been firmly established in other American colleges and universities. It may be helpful to note also that many large industrial firms pay for executive development courses for their men for varying periods of time, and do not expect employees to use vacation time for this. Smaller companies are much less likely to make this kind of personnel investment, mainly because they do not have enough management people on the payroll. The analogy for the Church is that the larger dioceses will provide such development courses for priests in specialized work and for junior administrators.

CLERGY CONFERENCES

In a much less formalized sense it seems logical to include, as a species of continuing education, the periodic clergy conferences held under the auspices of the diocese or the local deanery. The pattern of such clergy meetings differs from diocese to diocese and we have no information concerning the frequency with which they are held. The priests who helped construct this questionnaire, however, suggested that the purpose of these conferences was to inform and stimulate the clergy. The findings in Table 5.7 seem to support the dismal

Table 5.7 Distribution by type of employment of responses rating the diocesan clergy conferences

	Full-time curate	Part-time	Non-curate	All respondents
Both informative and stimulating	17%	15%	21%	18%
More informative than stimulating	25	24	23	24
More stimulating than informative	3	5	5	4
Neither informative nor stimulating	55	56	51	54
(Number of respondents)	(1,600)	(577)	(699)	(2,876)

comment of a Minnesota curate in his late twenties who reports that "we have had one deanery meeting during the past year, and it was about as pre-Vatican II as anything you could find this side of the Alps."

It is clear from the data in Table 5.7 that the diocesan priests are somewhat less than enthusiastic about their clergy conferences with more than half in each type of employment rating them as neither informative nor stimulating. If we combine the percentaged responses of those who were not quite so negatively critical, we find that more of them (42%) rated them as informative than rated them as stimulating (22%). This minority, then, tended to learn something from the experience of clergy conferences, but tended also to be bored by it. When we broke down the responses by age categories, we found that the youngest men were much more likely (59%) than the oldest (44%) to give the most negative rating to the clergy conferences.

With the development of clergy senates and voluntary associations of diocesan clergy, we may anticipate a revision of both the form and the content of diocesan conferences. In most large dioceses there has been an appointed "moderator" who planned the agenda for these meetings, selected the topics for discussion and invited priests to prepare papers. In many places the bishop himself is a regular attendant, using the opportunity to make known his mind to the priests. As a consequence of the Vatican Council, as implemented since this survey was taken, the procedures seem to be less rigid and the content more broadly defined, with the clergy evidencing a deeper interest in such conferences.

Table 5.8 Distribution in 1960 survey by curates and pastors of responses rating the deanery clergy meetings

	Curates	Pastors	All respondents
Stimulating	5%	11%	8%
Fairly interesting	22	24	22
Just average	27	31	29
Dull and drab	21	16	19
A waste of time	25	18	22
(Number of respondents)	(1,008)	(804)	(1,812)

In the 1960 survey of diocesan pastors and assistants we asked only about deanery meetings but did not consider their educational aspects. Here we found, as shown in Table 5.8, that all respondents were more likely to give a negative (41%) than a positive (30%) ap-

praisal, but that the curates were more negatively critical (46%) than
the pastors (34%). From the point of view of age we found in that
study also that the younger men were less satisfied than the older
men with the deanery meetings they attended.

SPIRITUAL RENEWAL

In preparing the areas of inquiry to be investigated in the current
survey we deliberately omitted questions about the personal spiritual practices and religious attitudes of the diocesan priests.[24] We
did ask them, however, about days of recollection and the yearly retreat. The Council Fathers said that the Bishop "should be concerned
about the spiritual, intellectual, and material condition of his priests,
so that they can live holy and pious lives and fulfill their ministry
faithfully and fruitfully. For this reason, he should encourage institutes and hold special meetings in which the priests can gather
from time to time for the performance of lengthier spiritual exercises
by way of renewing their lives and for the acquisition of deeper
knowledge of ecclesiastical subjects, especially sacred Scripture and
theology, the social questions of major importance, and the new
methods of pastoral activity."[25]

The continuing education of priests comprises more than the
acquisition of academic and practical knowledge. The constant effort
for renewal includes the several kinds of "spiritual exercises" that
are traditional to the priesthood.[26] Table 5.9 reveals the unexpected
finding that seven out of ten (71%) of all respondents did not
attend a day of recollection during the past year. It is not clear why
more of the men in specialized work (76%) than of those in the

Table 5.9 Distribution by type of employment of attendance at days of recollection during past year

	Full-time curate	Part-time	Non-curate	All re-spondents
Yes, on weekly day off	18%	15%	17%	17%
Yes, given day off for it	14	14	7	12
No, did not make one	68	71	76	71
(Number of respondents)	(1,636)	(590)	(740)	(2,966)

full-time parish ministry (68%) failed in this regard. We have seen in Table 5.6 that the opposite was true of attendance at summer institutes and courses. The fact is that the specialists report themselves busier than do the curates, and it is probably true that these more highly trained men have a certain dislike for traditional forms of spiritual exercises like days of recollection.

In general, it appears that this exercise in spiritual renewal is dwindling in importance and frequency. Unlike the question of summer institutes, where we found that younger men attend more frequently than older men, there is no age differential in the responses concerning days of recollection. In some places attendance is voluntary and in others it is mandatory for diocesan priests. The Table reveals that more men perform this exercise on their regular day off (17%) than on an extra day made free for them (12%). A California curate in his late thirties complains that the pastor controls this situation and thinks "there should be a diocesan policy that we be given an extra day for recollection instead of making it on our day off."

The traditional pattern of the annual clergy retreat has involved the establishment of fixed dates by diocesan officials, the appointment of a retreat master, and the mandate that all diocesan clergy must attend the retreat. Some of the comments of respondents indicate that a certain amount of experimentation has recently been introduced. Several curates want the opportunity to make a personal private retreat, a cursillo, or some arrangement separate from the regular diocesan retreat. "Does the clergy always have to do everything together?" queries one of the youngest part-time curates from Washington. In some dioceses, however, "our retreats are the discussion type, with our own priest leaders, and without the usual retreat master." In other dioceses, "this year we made the new seminar type retreat, and it was one of the best experiences I ever had."

Table 5.10 reveals a similar range of attitude toward the annual retreat among these men, regardless of whether they are in parishes or in specialized work. More of them (42%) indicate satisfaction than dissatisfaction (28%). More than half of them (54%) thought that the experience was "spiritually refreshing," but a somewhat larger proportion (60%) thought that it was well-conducted. Satisfaction with the quality of the annual retreat undoubtedly varies from year to year and from diocese to diocese. The fact that new "forms" are being introduced, as in the Oklahoma diocese, probably means that the norms against which these judgments are made are also changing.[27]

Table 5.10 Distribution by type of employment of responses rating the last annual diocesan priests' retreat

	Full-time curate	Part-time	Non-curate	All respondents
Well-conducted and spiritually refreshing	43%	39%	44%	42%
Well-conducted but not spiritually refreshing	18	18	17	18
Spiritually refreshing, but not well-conducted	12	13	10	12
Neither well-conducted nor spiritually refreshing	27	29	29	28
(Number of respondents)	(1,592)	(568)	(717)	(2,877)

The two most common complaints registered by the diocesan clergy about days of recollection and retreats are that the priest director in charge of the exercises is either a religious order priest or is too old and out-of-date for the work. A curate in a California diocese says that "priests should have something to say in choosing the retreat master." A young noncurate from Texas believes that "religious order priests are out of tune with the modern world, and especially with the life of the secular clergy." One of the youngest curates from a New York diocese reports that "our retreat was conducted by a religious priest who proceeded to undermine any desire a man might have for an original thought or for a decision of his own. He gave a magnificently untheological defense of priestly celibacy and in doing so undermined both the sacrament and the state of matrimony. I would be ashamed to give such talks to my parishioners."

The appointment of old men as retreat masters also evokes much criticism. "Because of their age," comments a Massachusetts curate in his late thirties, "most of our recent retreat masters have been stale rather than refreshing." A non-curate in his early thirties from

Illinois says that "our last retreat was a disaster. Our particular group was made up of all young priests and the director had no idea of our interests and problems." A young Michigan curate says that "the Bishop ought to look for a retreat master who knows what is going on in the Church and the world today." The fact is, of course, that the giving of spiritual retreats is highly specialized work for which special training is needed, and there is probably a shortage of such trained men in the Church.

Since educational requirements differ according to the type of employment a diocesan priest has, we have made most of our comparisons between parish priests and those in specialized work. Table 5.1, however, shows that levels of formal schooling differ also by age categories. The data reveal also that priests under thirty-five years of age are much more likely (43%) than those of fifty and over (18%) to have attended a summer institute or study week, although about the same proportion of both (32% to 30%) made a day of recollection during the year. The youngest priests are much more (90%) favorable than the oldest (69%) to the suggestion that the diocesan clergy should have sabbatical leaves for refresher courses. The difference of approval, however, is not large (89% to 84%) on the matter of encouraging priests to prepare for specialized work. On two other items the youngest priests are more critical than the oldest. They were much more ready (59% to 44%) to say that the clergy conferences they attended were "neither informative nor stimulating," and also (31% to 19%) to complain that their last annual retreat was "neither well-conducted nor spiritually refreshing."[28]

SUMMARY

We have seen in this chapter that the level of formal schooling, as attested by the earning of academic degrees, is rising among the diocesan clergy. Men who are in the specialized ministries are more likely than those in parish work to have, or to anticipate acquiring, graduate and professional degrees. They are also, on the average, somewhat older than parish assistants. Across these occupational lines there is remarkable and high agreement that curates who want to get specialized training should be encouraged to do so, and that the diocesan clergy should have time off to take refresher courses. Those in special assignments attend summer institutes more often, but attend days of recollection less often, than the full-time curates in the parishes. From the appraisals made by these two types of priests, who agree substantially on the matter, we may conclude that the general programs of clergy meetings at both the deanery and diocesan levels are in need of improvement before they can be termed a significant instrument for the continuing education of the clergy.

Most of these respondents seem to agree with the remark that "there is a growing need, especially in our day, for a continuing education and formation of the clergy after ordination. They have to keep up with new developments in theology as well as in pastoral methods."[29] As John McKenzie suggests, "unless the world suddenly stops moving, the education of the priest must continue as the priest grows in age; there will be an unceasing process of adaptation to fit new conditions and new needs."[30]

NOTES

1. See Regis Appel, "The Two-eyed Priest," *American Ecclesiastical Review*, Vol. 154, No. 4, October 1966, pp. 258–62.
2. *Priestly Formation*, Article 22.
3. See the references in Winthrop S. Hudson, *Religion in America* (New York: Scribner's, 1965), pp. 154 ff.; also William W. Sweet, "The Rise of Theological Schools in America," *Church History*, Vol. 6, September 1937, pp. 260–73.
4. As an example, see Kenneth K. Bailey, *Southern White Protestantism in the Twentieth Century* (New York: Harper & Row, 1964).
5. See, for example, Part Two in Daniel Callahan, *The Mind of the Catholic Layman* (New York: Scribner's, 1963).
6. For background information see John Tracy Ellis, "A Short History of Seminary Education," in Lee and Putz, *op. cit.*, pp. 1–81.
7. Walter W. Wagoner, *The Seminary—Protestant and Catholic* (New York: Sheed and Ward, 1966), pp. 196–98. See also Stafford Poole, *Seminary in Crisis* (New York: Herder and Herder, 1965), and John L. Murphy, "The Seminary College Course," *American Ecclesiastical Review*, Vol. 155, No. 4, October 1966, pp. 242–57.
8. *Priestly Formation*, Article 18.
9. As in every other profession there are, of course, anti-intellectuals in the priesthood. See the remarks by Stafford Poole, "The Diocesan Priest and the Intellectual Life," *Commonweal*, Vol. 82, No. 3, April 9, 1965, pp. 78–81.

10. As a generalization of motivation this opinion is highly questionable, but the data in the present survey show somewhat more dissatisfaction among the parish priests than among the specialists.

11. The category of "part-time curates" does not refer to a group of under-employed priests. They are in both parochial and nonparochial work and thus have "two jobs." They constitute one fifth of all respondents to this survey.

12. *The Church's Missionary Activity*, Article 39.

13. For a description of "priestly functions," see *Ministry and Life of Priests*, Articles 4–6. The variety of priestly activities at the parish level is described in Joseph H. Fichter, *Social Relations in the Urban Parish* (Chicago: University of Chicago Press, 1954), Chapter 10, "Social Roles of the Parish Priest," pp. 123–37. For the manner in which the laity view these activities, see *Priest and People*, Chapter 11, "The Image of the Parish Priest," pp. 183–203.

14. James Lee, "Overview of Educational Problems in Seminaries," in Lee and Putz, *op. cit.*, p. 84.

15. *Priestly Formation*, Article 12.

16. *Ministry and Life of Priests*, Article 19. James Keller and Richard Armstrong, eds., *Apostolic Renewal in the Seminary* (New York: Christophers, 1965), p. 27, remark that "since it is only after some years of pastoral experience that priests usually come to appreciate the fuller dimensions of their apostolic work, it is hoped that increasing numbers of priests with such experience be given the opportunity for further theological and pastoral studies."

17. For references to the main documents dealing with this training of newly ordained priests, see Abbott, *op. cit.*, p. 456, footnote 65.

18. See the discussion in Joseph H. Fichter, *Religion as an Occupation*, (Notre Dame, Ind.: University of Notre Dame Press, 1961), "The Apostolic Internship," pp. 106–09.

19. *Priestly Formation*, Article 12.

20. See the editorial by Aidan M. Carr on "Priests' Study Centers," *Homiletic and Pastoral Review*, Vol. 64, July 1966, p. 900. For a preliminary report on the survey sponsored by the Midwest Association of Theological Schools, see Cletus Wessels, "A Refresher Course in Theology," *America*, April 29, 1967, pp. 648–49.

21. The Council Fathers recommended vacations for priests, saying that their "recompense should be such as to allow priests a requisite and sufficient vacation each year. Bishops should see to it that priests can have a vacation of this sort." *Ministry and Life of Priests*, Article 20.

22. *Ibid.*, Article 19.

23. The Council Fathers seemed to be aware of the difficulties that hinder priests from continuing education because they say that the bishops should work out "some easier way for their priests to attend courses." *Ibid.*, Article 19.

24. Some of the respondents, however, suggested this as an area of future inquiry among diocesan priests. See below, Appendix C.

25. Bishops' Pastoral Office in the Church, Article 16.

26. See A. M. Charue, The Diocesan Clergy (New York: Desclee, 1963), Fourth Part, "Spirituality of the Diocesan Clergy," pp. 165–224.

27. The decree on the Ministry and Life of Priests, Article 18, recommended retreats, spiritual guidance, methods of mental prayer, but it was careful not to "canonize" any particular school of spirituality, as is pointed out by Abbott, op. cit., p. 570, footnote 218. The decree says also, "Above all, upon the bishop rests the heavy responsibility for the sanctity of his priests. Hence, he should exercise the greatest care on behalf of the continual formation of his priests," Article 7.

28. We have seen above, Chapter 2, that age is an important factor in the priests' attitude toward the rate of change in the diocese.

29. See Keller and Armstrong, eds., op. cit., p. 27.

30. John L. McKenzie, "Theology in the Seminary Curriculum," pp. 405–28 in Lee and Putz, op, cit., (p. 415).

LOCAL WORKING CONDITIONS

Because the Council said that the bishop "should regard priests as his brothers and friends," it is possible to idealize this relationship as one of intimate fraternity or familial love.[1] It must be remembered also that priests have a "hierarchial communion with the order of bishops" and that in large American dioceses the relationship resembles more closely that between a corporate president and the persons who are at various levels of subordination. The realistic version of this relationship, as it emerges from the facts of this survey, is that there exists a wide social distance between the bishop and the lower-echelon diocesan clergy. In the pragmatic day-by-day functioning of the priests, especially in the parishes—but also in almost any assignment outside the chancery office—the work gets done with hardly any reference to the bishop or contact with him.[2]

This is not the case in the relationship between the ordinary priest and his pastor or local superior. This is a face-to-face, day-by-day functional contact which is the stuff of human living. The parish curates are usually known as "assistants," although some of the more progressive pastors are now calling them "associates." The Council Fathers said that "as cooperators with the pastor, assistant pastors make an outstanding and active contribution to the pastoral ministry under the authority of the pastor. Therefore, there should always be fraternal association, mutual charity, and respect between the pastor and his assistants. They should assist one another with counsel, help and example, furthering the welfare of the parish with united purpose and energy."[3]

PASTOR–ASSISTANT RELATIONS

The pastor–curate relationship elicited more voluntary comments and suggestions from our respondents than any other area of inquiry in this survey.[4] This means that their immediate concerns and personal actions are bound up with the man who has working authority over them, and that their daily life and ministry are greatly affected by the manner in which their pastor treats them. It does not mean that they are largely dissatisfied with their present pastor. As a matter of fact, Table 6.1 shows that almost seven out of ten (68%) curates in our earlier survey reported happy or friendly relations in the parish rectories with which they are acquainted.

Table 6.1 Distribution of appraisal of rectory relations by pastors and curates in 1960 survey of diocesan priests

	Pastors	Curates	All re-spondents
Happy family relations	14%	8%	11%
Fairly friendly	65	60	62
Formal and correct	10	16	13
Fairly strained	10	14	12
Unhappy relations	1	2	2
(Number of respondents)	(929)	(1,226)	(2,155)

A Georgia curate in his late thirties thought that we should have centered this whole survey exclusively around pastor–curate relationships. "It seems to me that the basic reason for the major problems and scandals in the priesthood is rooted in the very atmosphere of the rectories where ordained men live in the same house but as strangers. A happy rectory is a wonderful place in all respects but a cold and strained one is the breeding ground of problems." A young California curate says that "a lot of assistants are tense because of personality conflicts. It is nerve-racking for a grown man, the assistant, to have to clear everything with the pastor; and it is difficult for the pastor to have to tell the assistant what to do. In many rectories neither is completely at ease in the other's presence."

Good working relations among the priests who live in the same house are undoubtedly the result of a complex of factors: personality traits, work expectations, mutual respect, shared responsibilities, and others.[5] There appears to be much ambiguity about the manner in which the pastor–curate role should be interpreted, whether it is a father–son relationship, employer–employee, master–apprentice, or an association of senior and junior professional colleagues. We had assumed that joint planning was an important factor, but we found that only one third of the pastors and one fifth (21%) of the curates said that there was much of this going on in the parish rectories they know. Table 6.2 looks at the parish priests working together, while Tale 6.1 viewed them living together. The comparison between the data indicates that friendly relations are more prevalent than work relations.[6]

Table 6.2 Distribution of appraisal of degree to which priests in rectories plan jointly, by pastors and curates in 1960 survey

	Pastors	Curates	All respondents
Very much so	9%	5%	7%
Quite a bit	24	16	19
More or less	44	42	43
Hardly at all	19	27	24
Not at all	4	10	7
(Number of respondents)	(919)	(1,229)	(2,148)

Table 6.1 shows that the majority, but pastors more than curates, gave a positive appraisal of personal relations in the rectory. When we asked them to what extent they thought these priests cooperate in planning parish projects, (Table 6.2) a much lower percentage gave a positive answer, but pastors were again more positive than assistants. Obviously, pastors and curates are looking at these questions from different perspectives, and although both are looking at the rectories "they know best" they are also both personally involved in such relationships. We found that curates who were most satisfied with

their current assignment in a parish gave as the chief reason for that satisfaction the fact that they had a "good boss." The pastor's satisfaction with his current assignment came from other reasons like large parish, few debts, good people.

COMMUNICATION

In the current survey we did not question pastors and superiors, and tried a different approach to the matter of personal relations. On the basis of research findings among American professionals, we hypothesized that professional colleagues who are working closely together tend to call each other by their first names. A California curate in his late thirties has a different view, and from his own experience, when he writes that "I was never on a first-name basis with any of my four pastors. I think that pastors are afraid their authority will suffer if they get too friendly with us or if they treated us as brother Christians." In Table 6.3 we find that four out of ten (39%) of our respondents are usually on a first-name basis with their pastor or local superior, but that this proportion is much lower (33%) for men who are in the parish than for those who are in specialized nonparochial assignments (55%). The latter, by their work and training, are likely to have the kind of professional orientation that is basic to our hypothesis.[7]

Table 6.3 Distribution of frequency with which respondent calls pastor or local superior by first name, by type of employment

	Full-time curate	Part-time	Non-curate	All re-spondents
Usually	34%	32%	55%	39%
Sometimes	11	9	6	9
Seldom	8	9	6	8
Never	47	50	33	44
(Number of respondents)	(1,669)	(598)	(692)	(2,959)

This criterion of good working relations must be looked at also from the point of view of youth's genuine respect for the aged. Only one third of the priests who are under thirty-five years of age, as compared to half of those who are over fifty, are on a first-name basis with their local superior.[8] A young curate from a Connecticut diocese remarks, "although I always call the pastor 'Father,' he is very open and friendly and we have an excellent working relationship. He has been ordained over thirty years but is definitely 'new breed' in his thinking and acting." A curate in his early thirties from Nebraska writes, "I don't think being on a first-name basis with my pastor is important, especially if he is quite a bit older than I. A very important source of difficulty for me is my pastor's notion that he is my employer, and that whatever I do, or do not do, is subject to his approval."

Let us take this query a step further. Granting that there can be good working relations between superior and subordinates whether or not they are on a first-name basis and even when there is a large difference between their ages, we may ask to what degree the priest has free and open two-way communication with his pastor or local superior. We have seen previously (Table 3.3) that only one fifth of these rank-and-file priests have such positive communication with their bishop, and that (Table 3.6) the same proportion report that such communication exists throughout the entire diocesan structure. Since we are here concerned with communication between men who are living in the same residence we should expect from them a much more positive appraisal.

The data in Table 6.4 show that about half (52%) of all these diocesan priests give a positive appraisal of the degree of communication that exists between them and their local superior, but that the

Table 6.4 Degree of free and open two-way communication with pastor or local superior, by type of occupation

	Full-time curate	Part-time	Non-curate	All respondents
Very much so	30%	27%	39%	31%
Quite a bit	20	21	22	21
More or less	21	24	21	22
Hardly at all	17	16	11	16
Not at all	12	12	7	10
(Number of respondents)	(1,658)	(594)	(672)	(2,924)

proportions are considerably higher among those in specialized non-parish work (61%) than among both the full-time (50%) and the part-time curates (48%). Many of the men in specialized work are listed as "in residence" at a parish rectory and are not directly under the authority of the local pastor as is the case with the parish assistants. This fact apparently gives them a more "comfortable" relationship with the man who is technically their local superior.

The curates are, by ecclesiastical legislation, subordinate co-operators with the pastor, a position that is difficult for them to maintain with equanimity as they grow older.[9] One assistant in his late forties from a Pennsylvania diocese says that "the pastor considers the rectory his private domain, whose wishes and comfort come before all other considerations. The curate is permitted to make no decisions whatever in the conduct of parish activities. The result is constant tensions between us." A Massachusetts curate in the same age bracket remarks that "in a well-established diocese like ours, a good portion of the assistants have become functionaries who obediently perform routine duties defined by the pastor. In my own case I find it hard to see the will of God in the will of my pastor who is well over eighty years of age and whose ideas and ways of acting belong to another age."

There is an interesting contrast between full-time curate and full-time specialist when they make an estimate of the quality of communication with their immediate superiors. The older curates do not report good communications with their pastor, while the older specialists do say that they communicate well with their superiors. When we look at curates alone, and compare the satisfied with the dissatisfied, we find that a much larger proportion (58%) of the former than of the latter (33%) give a positive estimate of free and open two-way communication with their pastors. This finding underlines one of the most important factors of job satisfaction among parish curates.

SEPARATE RESIDENCE AND OFFICE

What we have found so far is that about half of the curates are not on a first-name basis with their pastor and that about three out of ten give a negative appraisal of their manner of communicating with him. We felt that part of the problem may lie in the fact that these men live together in the same residence. Unlike some other countries, where each diocesan priest maintains his own apartment or home, the pattern in the United States has been a common rectory residence for each parish. The Council Fathers seem to approve this American arrangement. "To render the care of souls more efficacious, community life for priests is strongly recommended, especially for those attached to the same parish. While this way of living encourages apostolic action, it also affords an example of charity and unity to the faithful."[10]

We asked these diocesan priests whether "curates should have a choice of their own separate residence or of living in the parish rectory." This seemed to be a novel suggestion for some of the men. Table 6.5 shows that one fifth of all respondents could not make up their minds about it. Among the rest there is more disagreement (50%) than agreement (30%) with the idea of freedom of choice of a separate residence. Oddly enough, the older the men are the more they dislike this notion; a larger proportion of those in the oldest age group (58%) than in the youngest (46%) are against it. Those who are doing specialized work and who already have a degree of independence of the local superior are more likely to be against it (57%) than are the others.

Table 6.5 Distribution of responses concerning choice of separate residence, by type of employment

	Full-time curate	Part-time	Non-curate	All respondents
Agree	33%	32%	23%	30%
Disagree	48	47	57	50
Not sure	19	21	20	20
(Number of respondents)	(1,685)	(597)	(759)	(3,041)

Despite the difficulties that exist in some parish rectories because of the manner in which the pastor perceives his role, the curates for the most part are not ready to say that they want to break away from the community life of the rectory. Besides the problems of living together, however, there are also work complaints. An Illinois curate in his early thirties insists that "there must be room for more independence for assistants. It is very demeaning when assistants are expected to be receptionists, secretaries, part-time janitors, errand boys, and such. It can 'un-priest' a priest."

More significant perhaps, if not typical, is the remark of a Pennsylvania priest in his early forties. "Something should be written into Church legislation protecting the right of an assistant to fulfill his duties to the parishioners. From personal experience I can say that there are pastors who go to great lengths to keep their curates away from parishioners—no contact allowed in the office, by phone, even in parish organizations, prohibitions against visiting hospitals. Such men are sick, I know, but legislation is needed to prevent the Bishop from humoring such a man at the expense of a curate's priestly life."[11]

The notion that a clergyman could do a better professional job if his place of work, his office, were separated from his place of residence, was suggested by a number of priests in the preparatory stages of the inquiry schedule. In this case the assumption was that there would be less interference from the pastor, more direct contact with the parishioners, more efficiency in the performance of the parochial role.[12] We therefore asked them whether or not they agreed with the statement that "each priest should have his own office separate from his place of residence." The responses in Table 6.6 reveal an even greater uncertainty (26%) among them than had been the case in the question of a separate residence (20%).

This is another case in which there is much more disagreement (52%) than agreement (22%) among the total respondents, and in which again the largest proportion (57%) of men who are in spe-

Table 6.6 Distribution of responses concerning priest's office separate from place of residence, by type of employment

	Full-time curate	Part-time	Non-curate	All respondents
Agree	24%	24%	16%	22%
Disagree	51	48	57	52
Not sure	25	28	27	26
(Number of respondents)	(1,686)	(598)	(758)	(3,042)

cialized work and who in most cases have their own separate offices, disagreed with the suggestion. Yet a curate in his late thirties from a California diocese says "I definitely think each parish priest should have his own separate office. The whole question of the nonprofessional circumstances in which many priests are forced to work should be studied in detail. Even the matter of how poorly the phone is answered and messages transmitted in many rectories needs to be treated."[13] A Missouri priest in his early thirties who has good relations with his pastor, attributes this harmony mainly to the fact that he has his own office, adequate secretarial help, and a pastor who delegates authority and deals with him like a mature professional.

The survey findings indicate that the diocesan priests are more or less in accord with the prevailing arrangements whereby the parish clergy live and work together in the same rectory. There are some age differences of preference. The oldest men are more unwilling (58%) than the youngest men (46%) to choose separate living quarters, as well as to have their office separate from their residence (66% to 48%). Quite aside from the differences of age, however, we have here another key to the problem of job satisfaction among the parish assistants. Satisfied curates are twice as likely (61%) as dissatisfied (28%) to accept common residential pattern, and also much more likely (60% to 32%) to accept the current arrangement of locating the office in the rectory.

HORIZONTAL MOBILITY

Whether or not a parish assistant enjoys pleasant working and living conditions and gets along well with his local superior, he seldom has any control over the decision to continue or to change his present assignment. Among the oldest men in this survey there has been an average of 5.15 different full-time assignments per priests, but 9 percent of these oldest men report that they are still in the first assignment they received after ordination. We shall see later that the great majority of all respondents want to change the manner in which they get their job appointments.[14] Meanwhile we were curious to know what they thought about shifts from one parish to another, and asked them whether they agree with the statement that "curates should rotate parishes periodically to get a variety of experience."[15]

Table 6.7 demonstrates that eight out of ten (79%) of all respondents favor the concept of rotation of parishes, and that there is no significant difference according to the type of employment they currently have. There is also no significant difference of opinion according to differences in age. The younger professional man in America usually expects and experiences a certain amount of occupational mobility before he settles down to a permanent place, sometimes with tenure. This shifting of jobs has overtones of career improvement, a concept which is hardly involved in the shifting of a curate from one parish to another.

We were unable to discover a pattern of routine rotation of parish appointments among the parish curates although a Wisconsin curate who has been ordained for six years says that he is "beginning to

Table 6.7 Distribution of opinion, by type of employment, on statement that "curates should rotate parishes periodically to get a variety of experience"

	Full-time curate	Part-time	Non-curate	All respondents
Agree	77%	80%	80%	79%
Disagree	10	7	6	8
Not sure	13	13	14	13
(Number of respondents)	(1,687)	(596)	(760)	(3,043)

detect a trend in this diocese to indicate that after seven years in one place a transfer is probable." They are in favor of rotating but their comments on the matter raise the question of frequency of change. A California priest in his late thirties says that "an assignment should not be too short. A priest's most effective work is done between the second and the fifth year of his assignment. It takes time for parishioners to get to know a priest and to have confidence in him. In parishes where priests are frequently changed because of a difficult pastor, the people suffer spiritually."

There is an interesting variety of opinions in this matter. An Alabama curate in his early thirties thinks that assistants should not be in one place more than five years, and pastors not more than ten years. A Massachusetts priest in his early thirties makes the daring suggestion that "there should be a rotation of pastor and assistant, and not just of parishes. In other words, after a man has been a pastor for six years he should become an assistant for six years, and vice versa. Isn't this what keeps the Jesuits both effective and humble?" A curate in his early forties from a Michigan diocese thinks that "curates should rotate parishes until they reach forty years of age. After forty a man gets tired of moving; he has the range of experience; and he should 'stay put' till he becomes pastor of his own parish."

THE PROBLEM OF SALARIES

One aspect of the working conditions of these lower-echelon priests that has merited some attention is the question of financial income. The diocesan clergy are not bound by a vow of poverty, although many of them exhibit a spirit of detachment from this world's goods and in practice are quite poor. The Vatican Council pointed out that a just recompense is due to priests. "Where a fitting recompense is not otherwise provided, the faithful themselves are bound by a genuine obligation to see that the needed means can be procured for them to lead a respectable and worthy life. For it is in behalf of the faithful that priests labor." Furthermore, "depending on the nature of the office itself and the conditions of place and time, the recompense should be fundamentally the same for all those operating in the same circumstances."[16]

In our 1960 survey of diocesan parish priests we asked them about their financial situation, and in the companion survey of their lay friends we asked what impression these lay people had of the financial status of the parish priest they knew best.[17] Table 6.8 reveals that more priests are in debt (13%) than the laity realizes, (6%), but also that more of the clergy (55%) have savings than the laity (41%) think they have. The Table tells us that the youngest priests are more likely (19%) than the oldest (4%) to be in debt, a not surprising outcome. When compared to American white families headed by fathers under thirty-five years of age, the youngest priests show an unusually low percentage who are in debt.

Table 6.8 Financial status of diocesan parish clergy in 1960 survey, by age categories, and estimates by laity

	Under 35 years	35 to 49 years	50 years and over	All priests	Estimate of laity
Considerable money	6%	3%	6%	5%	7%
Some money	48	48	59	50	34
About solvent	20	26	23	23	47
Always broke	7	11	8	9	6
In debt	19	12	4	13	6
(Number of respondents)	(742)	(939)	(501)	(2,182)	(2,144)

In the current survey we did not ask any direct question about either financial status or salaries, but were advised to include the following statement: "Stipends and stole fees should be abolished in favor of a graduated annual salary." Both stipends and stole fees are voluntary contributions made by the laity, the stipend when they request the priest to celebrate a Mass for their intention, the stole fee when they receive some other special service from the clergy, as for baptisms, weddings or funerals. The youngest priests are much more in agreement (89%) than the oldest (68%) that this system of contributions should be abolished, but Table 6.9 shows relatively no difference of opinion by type of employment.

That the matter of salaries and income is of some concern to the

Table 6.9 Distribution of responses concerning replacement of stipends and stole fees with graduated yearly salary, by type of employment

	Full-time curate	Part-time	Non-curate	All respondents
Agree	84%	87%	86%	85%
Disagree	8	6	6	7
Not sure	8	7	8	8
(Number of respondents)	(1,687)	(598)	(759)	(3,044)

diocesan clergy is demonstrated by the variety of comment made by the respondents in relation to this survey question. A young curate from a New Jersey diocese wants the Mass stipends given directly to the parish church where the Mass is celebrated. A noncurate in his late thirties from a Kansas diocese is "in favor of abolishing stipends, but equally in favor of retaining stole fees because of the special service rendered." A young curate from Florida believes that "there is need for a complete revamping of clergy salaries. I don't want to get rich but I want to meet my expenses. It cost me twelve hundred dollars a year to furnish the parish with a car." Several of the priests are unsure about the manner in which an annual salary would be "graduated" and prefer "a flat salary, with no fringe benefits, for all —bishops, pastors and assistants alike."

The problem of priests' income has been among the first questions discussed in the newly formed clergy senates and diocesan councils. Monthly salaries as such, aside from so-called "fringe benefits" have been nominal and varied from diocese to diocese, being fixed at two levels for pastors and assistants. Costs of food and lodging are borne by the parish. In the spring following this survey, upon advice of a predominantly lay coordinating committee, Bishop Primeau, of Manchester, abolished the system of stipends and stole fees, and fixed pastors' salaries at $350, and assistants' at $225 per month.[18]

Some of the respondents think that the salary received should be somehow adjusted to the amount of work the priest does. A Pennsylvania curate in his late twenties thinks "it is reasonable that the priest working in a large busy city parish should receive more salary than the priest who has nothing to do in a 'dead' parish." An Illinois curate in his early thirties opines that "the Church that preaches justice and charity should also practice just, reasonable, and charitable remuneration for curates. How many pastors are there whose business acumen is limited to the counting of money they receive for the work their assistants performed?" A curate in his late forties from an Ohio diocese, who does not get along well with his pastor, says that "it seems a grave injustice that assistants have to take care of all baptisms, as well as the funerals and marriages the pastor doesn't want, and then hand over the stipends to the pastor." It is evident that this question is still open for much debate.[19]

ATTITUTES AND RELATIONS

At this point we decided to test the hypothesis that the attitude a curate has toward his working conditions is colored by the kind of relationship he has with his pastor. In order to test this hypothesis we selected only those who reported that they are full-time curates, and then compared those who have good working relationships with their pastor with those who complain about their pastor. The first group is made up of men who say that they are "usually" on a first-name basis with their pastor and who also report that there is "very much" free and open communication with the pastor. This group (266 men) we are here comparing with a smaller and contrasting group (138) men who say that they "never" call the pastor by his first name and also say that there is "not at all" free and open communication with him.

Before testing the hypothesis concerning attitudes toward working conditions in the parish, we were curious to know what the age spread was on these polar categories of curates. Table 6.10 demonstrates the interesting fact that the largest proportion (58%) of curates who have poor relations with their pastors are in the middle years, thirty-five to forty-nine years old. These men seem to feel the frustrations of their subordinate role. One of them in this age bracket from a large eastern diocese complained that "we now have to wait about thirty years after ordination before we become pastor and meanwhile we are still assistants doing the same kind of work we did one year after ordination."[20] The absence of significant career mobility seems related to estrangement from one's current pastor.

Table 6.10   Age distribution of full-time curates who have close and distant relations with their pastor

	Close to pastor	Distant	All full-time curates
Under 35 years of age	49%	38%	52%
35 to 49 years	45	58	42
50 years and over	6	4	6
(Number of respondents)	(266)	(138)	(1,688)

The assumption that the quality of curate–pastor relationship would differentially affect the opinions of full-time curates is established in the first two items of Table 6.11. The curates who are not getting along well with their pastor are much more likely than those with close curate–pastor relations (41% to 26%) to say that they want the choice of their own home separate from the rectory, as well as (33% to 20%) their own office separated from their place of residence. We have seen in Tables 6.5 and 6.6 that only a minority of all respondents are desirous of this expression of professional independence from their local superior. If the "conflict" between assistant and pastor is as serious as it is reputed to be, one would expect that more curates want this kind of change.[21] It is apparent, however, that most of the diocesan priests prefer some kind of community living and working arrangement.

The third and fourth items in Table 6.11 seem to have no causal connection with the particular pastor–curate relationship. The majority of full-time diocesan assistants are in favor of gaining more experience through the rotation of parish appointments, whether or not they get along well with their current superior. There is no significant difference of opinion on this matter by age categories. The abolition of stipends and stole fees is favored by a large majority of the full-time assistants, with relatively no difference of opinion between those who have close and those who have distant relations with their pastor.

Table 6.11 Proportions of full-time curates with close and distant relations with pastor who agree on these statements

	Close to pastor	Distant	All full-time curates
Curates should have own residence	26%	41%	33%
(Number of respondents)	(266)	(137)	(1,685)
Priest's office separate from home	20	33	24
(Number of respondents)	(265)	(138)	(1,686)
Curates should rotate parishes	78	75	77
(Number of respondents)	(265)	(138)	(1,687)
Abolish stipends for annual salary	84	89	84
(Number of respondents)	(266)	(138)	(1,687)

Let us see whether there are other ways in which attitudes of full-time curates differ according to the kind of relationship they have with their pastor. We find that the men who have poor working relations with the pastor are also more likely than the others to say that there should be a definite retirement age for pastors (95% to 87%), priests should be promoted to the pastorate on ability rather than seniority (81% to 73%), and that the Church should dispense with the title of monsignor (81% to 65%). Those who do not get along well with their pastor are also more likely than the others to answer "not at all" to the question whether their bishop has a personal and positive interest in them (64% to 37%), whether there is open and free communication with the bishop (61% to 25%), and whether such communication exists throughout the diocesan structure (48% to 20%). Since we have made no personality tests of the respondents we must be careful to avoid judgment whether the "fault" of these poor relationships lies in the pastor or the assistant.

WHO WORKS HARD?

In probing further into the conditions under which these diocesan priests carry on their tasks, we were curious to know whether the work demands, or job expectations, are heavier among parish assistants or among those who do specialized work in the diocese. In the 1960 survey of diocesan parish priests we asked the question: "In comparison with your fellow diocesan priests who are performing nonparochial functions, do you feel that your present work is harder or easier than theirs?" Table 6.12 shows that a little over one third

Table 6.12 Distribution of opinions whether parish work is harder or easier than nonparish work, by pastors and curates, in 1960 survey

	Pastors	Curates	All re-spondents
We work much harder	11%	8%	9%
Somewhat harder	25	27	26
About the same	42	46	44
Somewhat easier	17	16	17
Much easier	5	3	4
(Number of respondents)	(930)	(1,229)	(2,159)

of them (35%) thought they work harder than the men in specialized functions, but with practically no difference between the estimates of pastors and curates.

In the 1960 survey of diocesan parish priests we also asked them to compare their own work load with that of other professional persons like engineers, physicians, lawyers. "From what you know about the occupational demands made on other professional men, would you say your work is harder or easier than theirs?" Table 6.13 reveals an almost evenly distributed range of response with one third saying they work harder, one third "about the same," and one third "easier." In comparing the two Tables we find that there are fewer (21%) who think that parish work is easier than nonparish work than there are (32%) who think that their work is easier than that of professional men in the nonecclesiastical world.[23]

Table 6.13 Distribution of opinions whether parish priest's work is harder or easier than that of other professional men, by pastors and curates, in 1960 survey

	Pastors	Curates	All respondents
We work much harder	11%	10%	11%
Somewhat harder	21	27	24
About the same	33	33	33
Somewhat easier	24	20	22
Much easier	11	10	10
(Number of respondents)	(896)	(1,186)	(2,082)

In order to sharpen the whole question of the priests' work load we used a different approach in the current survey and asked them to measure their work expectations against their competence to do the work. "Considering your talents and training, do you feel that the work you are expected to do in your current assignment is more than you can handle, or calls for little of your abilities?" Here we found a remarkable contrast between those in the parish and those in specialized diocesan functions. By obtaining the self-estimates of both types of priests we are able to amplify and clarify the opinions given by parish priests in Table 6.12.

More than seven out of ten (72%) of those in nonparochial assignments, as compared to less than half (46%) of the full-time curates, say that they are working up to, and beyond, their capacity. The following complaint by a curate in his late thirties from a Connecticut diocese is paraphrased by others. "The daily work in the parish is piddling for the most part: writing Mass cards, unlocking the school door for the Boy Scout troop, copying baptismal records. The pastor always lays stress on being here to answer the door and the phone, and this is the main service to the parishioners. This is what he wants, but as a function for one's life career it is a maddening process. We cannot act on our own initiative because he controls us and the entire operation of the parish too closely."

The second column in Table 6.14 shows that the men who have two jobs work harder than full-time curates, but not so hard as those in nonparish work.[24] A young part-time curate from Colorado says "you should have asked about the amount of work one *voluntarily* takes upon himself, even at the displeasure of the pastor and the bishop." An Illinois priest in his twenties who is teaching "on the side" remarks that "it is difficult to sit in a rectory waiting for sick calls that never come. About all you can do is to think of some way of pushing yourself into special work. It's almost the only way to use your talents while you're still young. I don't think our bishops have any idea of the frustration felt by their young priests. We were told that we were to use our talents for Christ and yet we are forced to conform to unexplained directives and meaningless activities.[25] Some of the most talented men in our diocese have left the priesthood. I used to look at that with horror, but now I wonder."

Table 6.14 Distribution of responses concerning work expectations, by type of employment

	Full-time curate	Part-time	Non-curate	All respondents
More than I can handle	9%	13%	12%	11%
Extending me to capacity	37	44	60	44
Partly challenging my ability	39	35	21	34
Calling for little ability	15	8	7	11
(Numbers of respondents)	(1,680)	(595)	(750)	(3,025)

We have seen (Table 5.2) that the men who are in specialized nonparish work have considerably more formal education and graduate degrees than the full-time parish curates. They sometimes complained that they did not have sufficient professional training for their jobs. The curates, on the other hand, sometimes complained that they are doing work that any half-trained functionary could perform. As one young New York curate remarked, "It is not a question of how busy we are, or how much work we do, but the extent to which the work is utilizing our talents and training."[26]

One of the most revealing contrasts concerning the working conditions of priests in the parish is found in Table 6.15, indicating that the curates who get along well with their pastors work harder than those who do not. Putting this negatively, we note that more than half (54%) of all full-time curates report that they are not working up to their capacity, but this estimate jumps to eight out of ten (79%) where there are poor rectory relations, and declines to four out of ten (39%) where these relations are good. Our general supposition is that most priests are zealous and, at least in the beginning of their career, are willing to work hard.[27] It appears that the extent to which they employ their talents depends on the type of employment they have (Table 6.14) and also on the manner in which they are "managed" by the pastor (Table 6.15).

Table 6.15 Distribution of responses concerning work expectations of curates with close and distant relations with pastor

	Close to pastor	Distant	All full-time curates
More than I can handle	10%	5%	9%
Extending me to capacity	51	16	37
Partly challenging my ability	31	45	39
Calling for little ability	8	34	15
(Number of respondents)	(266)	(137)	(1,680)

One young full-time curate from New York who has a good working relation with his pastor sums up his thoughts as follows: "I think that if we are to be effective as priests we must work together as a team; therefore, I would like to see men with similar interests and outlooks on the apostolate assigned to the same rectory. This is the situation in my own rectory and I am very happy here."

SUMMARY

In summarizing these findings we must be careful not to conclude that the typical parish residence of diocesan priests is a place of conflict and turmoil.[28] The data show that the majority of parish clergy have a fairly high estimate of rectory relations, even though they do not see much joint planning of the work to be done. Nevertheless, a good personal relationship and frank communication are less likely to develop between the curate and his pastor than between the man in a specialized assignment and his local superior. Only a small proportion of the respondents want a choice of their own residence separate from the rectory, and a smaller minority want their office separate from their residence, but both of these are desired more by curates who have poor relationships than by those who get along well with their pastor.

Eight out of ten of all respondents think that curates should rotate parish assignments periodically to gain experience, and an even greater majority (85%) feel that stole fees and stipends should be abolished in favor of a graduated yearly salary. Parish priests have somewhat more savings than the parishioners think they have, but the youngest priests are not so well off financially as the oldest. Those who are in specialized diocesan assignments are busier and work harder than those who are in the parish, and parish clergy are more willing to admit this than they are to admit that professional men in general work harder than parish priests. Among the full-time assistants, the proper utilization of their talents depends largely on the kind of relationship they have with their pastor.

NOTES

1. *Ministry and Life of Priests*, Article 7.
2. Karl Rahner, *Bishops: Their Status and Function* (Baltimore: Helicon, 1964), pp. 48–50.
3. *Bishops' Pastoral Office in the Church*, Article 30.

4. More than the question of celibacy, which seemed to fascinate the journalists, and more than the clergy–bishop relationship, which seemed to bother the episcopal commentators on the press release.

5. See the two articles by S. Grabowski, "What Curates Expect from Pastors," and "What Pastors Expect from Curates," *Pastoral*, Vol. 12, May 1964, pp. 10–14, and June 1964, pp. 15–18.

6. For a description of a year's religious work by the priests of one parish, see Joseph H. Fichter, *Southern Parish* (Chicago: University of Chicago Press, 1951).

7. Probably because of confusion over the definition of "local superior," 9 percent of those in specialized work did not answer this question, and 13 per cent the question in Table 6.4.

8. It should be pointed out that the practice of using first names among professional colleagues is more customary in the United States than in most other countries.

9. See J. Smith, "New Frontier Problems: Old Curates," *Pastoral*, Vol. 11, March 1963, pp. 17–20; also Philip A. Hamilton, "A Sociologist Looks at the Pastor–Assistant Structure," *The Catholic Messenger*, Davenport, Iowa, August 4, 1966, p. 5f.

10. *Bishops' Pastoral Office in the Church*, Article 29.

11. It is a curious fact that the canon law of the Church largely neglects both the rights and the duties of the parish curate.

12. The problem of conflict between the familial and the professional roles in the Church is discussed in Joseph H. Fichter, *Religion as an Occupation*, (Notre Dame, Ind.: University of Notre Dame Press, 1961), Chapter 9, "Organized Social Relations."

13. In the 1960 survey of diocesan parish priests we found that more than three quarters (77%) reported that there was no full-time paid secretarial help in their parish rectory. See the general principles discussed and especially the bibliography by Leo V. Ryan, Chapter 13, "Management Responsibilities of the Pastor," in Eugene Weitzel, ed., *Pastoral Ministry in a Time of Change* (Milwaukee: Bruce, 1966), pp. 161–83.

14. See below, Chapter 7, "Facets of the Career."

15. In our 1960 survey of the lay friends of parish priests, only a little more than half (52%) agreed that "it would be a good idea if the diocesan parish priests were transferred once in a while."

16. *Ministry and Life of Priests*, Article 20.

17. In the 1960 survey of the laity we asked them to compare their own material standard of living with that of the diocesan parish priest they knew best. More than half (55%) said it was about the same; the others said it was higher (23%) or lower (22%) than that of their priest friend. These lay respondents rated their own yearly income as above average (27%), average (65%), below average (8%).

18. This action was commented upon in an editorial, "Salaries, Not Stipends," *America*, March 18, 1967, p. 365. C. Walter Weiss, "The Priest's Salary," *Homiletic and Pastoral Review*, Vol. 65, No. 1, October 1964, pp. 134–35,

offers a plan in which all Mass stipends and stole fees become part of parish income, and the priest's salary would be equal to that of a high school teacher, "a dignified but still common occupation."

19. The problem of clergy income looms large also among Protestants. See John C. Bramer, *Personal Finance for Clergymen* (Englewood Cliffs, N.J.: Prentice-Hall, 1964). "Most clergymen receive a grossly inadequate salary in comparison with that of others with comparable training," p. 21. See also James J. Kavanaugh, "A Priest's Income," *America*, April 23, 1966, pp. 585–87.

20. In the smallest dioceses the curate becomes a pastor much sooner. Joseph H. Fichter, *Priest and People* (New York: Sheed and Ward, 1965), pp. 173–77. This is why the current survey, which excludes pastors, contains so few curates from the smallest dioceses.

21. See J. R. Anderson, "Pastor Bonus: What a Curate Expects," *Priest*, Vol. 17, April 1961, pp. 314–16, and the editorial by Aidan Carr, "For Future Pastors Only; The Pastor and His Curate," *Homiletic and Pastoral Review*, Vol. 62, September 1962, p. 1104.

22. See the first column in Tables 6.5, 6.6, 6.7, and 6.9 above.

23. The lay friends of priests in the 1960 survey feel that the parish clergy works harder than the clergy think they do. In comparison with other professional men, according to the laity, the priests work harder (42%), about the same (37%), not so hard (21%).

24. In the 1960 survey we asked the parish priests, "Do you have other duties besides those ordinarily called parochial?" More of the curates (50%) than of the pastors (37%) answered affirmatively, mentioning with greatest frequency: high school teaching, hospital chaplains, Sisters' confessors, Newman Clubs, tribunal and chancery work.

25. For broader understanding see Sigmund Nosow and William Form, eds., *Man, Work and Society* (New York: Basic Books, 1962), Chapter 13, "Personal Adjustment in the World of Work," pp. 441–75.

26. This is a main theme of Charles W. Paris, "Clerical Manpower," *Homiletic and Pastoral Review*, Vol. 64, No. 3, December 1963, pp. 213–21. This article touches on most of the problems discussed in the present chapter.

27. From another point of view, more than four out of ten (43%) of the parish priests in the 1960 survey say they "can't quite finish their work" or are "always far behind," but a much smaller porportion (13%) of their lay friends say this about them.

28. For a Protestant study, see Kenneth Mitchell, *Psychological and Theological Relationships in the Multiple Staff Ministry* (Philadelphia: Westminster, 1966).

CHAPTER

7

FACETS OF THE CAREER

The man who prepares for and enters a professional career expects to advance through recognized stages of work, marked by achievement, promotion, age, income, and prestige. The diocesan priest prepares for the ecclesiastical career while in the seminary, enters it upon ordination and expects, ideally speaking, a "lifelong occupation that contains implications of direction, achievement, and progress."[1] The attempt to compare the life career of the priesthood with that of other American professions poses certain in-built paradoxes. The Council Fathers advised priests to practice docility, humility, abnegation, and other virtues that seem to preclude the motivations required for a successful careerist.

The priests who are appointed for parish work should have piety and knowledge of doctrine, but they also need "apostolic zeal and other gifts and qualities necessary for the proper exercise of the care of souls."[2] In the priestly career then, the paradox lies in the fact that "humility forbids ambition, but zeal encourages achievement. Yet zeal and ambition are characteristics of successful persons, and successful persons move forward in their careers."[3] Among the lower-echelon diocesan priests here under survey the principal recognition of career status is appointment to the pastorate. Yet we are told that in America, " a priest in a large diocese may get to be a pastor at an age when his lay contemporaries are ready for retirement. Meanwhile during his energetic and creative years, he has been deprived of power and

137

responsibility. Yet these are challenges that he needs to develop not only as a cleric, but as a man."[4]

HOW ASSIGNMENTS ARE MADE

Since the priest is in the holy service of the people and under the direction of his spiritual shepherd, the bishop, one may suggest that he is indifferent to the questions of assignment, promotion, and recognition. Yet a New York priest in his early thirties says that "of all the queries in this survey the one I feel most strongly about is the question of assignments. If something is not done about this soon, we shall see more 'de-humanizing' of the priesthood. To me, the proper appointment where a man can do his best work is more important than celibacy, relations with the bishop, etc." It appears that in most dioceses the practice has been simply to notify the curate, without interview or discussion, that he is to move to another parish by a certain date. A Michigan priest in his late thirties writes that "up until last year our own desires were simply not considered when the assignment was made, and we just felt that we had to stick it out in an undesirable assignment. But now our bishop has let us know that we are free to request a change in appointment."[5]

We must remember that we are speaking here, not of pastors, but of curates who may be full time or part time in the parish, and of men who are currently engaged in non-parochial work. It is to be expected that the longer a priest has been ordained, the greater the number of official appointments and transfers he is likely to have had. Table 7.1 shows that half of the youngest group are still on the first appointment they have had, while more than four out of ten (44%) of the oldest priests have had six or more assignments since ordination. The diocesan priest who is still not a pastor by the time he has reached fifty years of age can expect to have had an average of more than five different placements in his diocese.

Since we had already asked in the 1960 survey about the manner in which the priests obtained their current assignment, we did not repeat the question in this study. Table 7.2 shows that less than four out of ten pastors (36%) and hardly any assistants (3%) were asked ahead of time by the bishop or other diocesan official if they wanted

Table 7.1 Number of assignments, by age categories, that respondents have had since ordination

	Under 35 years	35 to 49 years	50 years and over
First	50%	15%	9%
Second or third	41	47	20
Fourth or fifth	8	27	27
Sixth or seventh	1	9	22
Eighth or more	*	2	22
(Number of respondents)	(1,521)	(1,322)	(205)
Average number of assignments	1.87	3.30	5.15

the assignment. The great majority of curates (84%) and half of the pastors were simply informed, with no prior consultation, that they were to report for duty at another parish. No other large-scale employment system, not even the military—except in time of national emergencies—transfers its professional personnel in this relatively abrupt manner.

Table 7.2 Manner in which pastors and curates in 1960 survey obtained their current assignment

	Pastors	Curates	All respondents
I was asked if I wanted it	36%	3%	17%
I asked for this position	5	1	3
I just asked for a change	5	7	6
Someone else interceded for me	4	5	5
Was simply told to report here	50	84	69
(Number of respondents)	(925)	(1,227)	(2,152)

Probably most of the diocesan clergy agree with the California curate in his late thirties who wrote that "the curate's personal preference should come second to the needs of the diocese, as seen by the Bishop,"[6] yet our research demonstrates that they do want to be consulted about their appointments and transfers. It is not that they are opposed to transfers and reassignments. We have seen, in fact, that the great majority (79%) of them agree to the suggestion that "curates should rotate parishes periodically to get a variety of experience" (Table 6.7), and there is no significant difference of opinion by age grades or by type of current employment. What bothers them is the manner in which these transfers occur. As one Illinois curate remarked, "You can't take a man almost fifty years old, as I am, change him around just any old time it seems convenient, and make him like it."

SATISFIED AND DISSATISFIED

In probing this matter further we asked three questions about the manner in which diocesan priests think they should receive appointments. More than four out of five respondents were in agreement with the following statements: "the diocese should have a personnel office to work out priests' assignments" (86% agree, 6% disagree); "curates should be interviewed before receiving their appointments" (83% agree, 8% disagree); "curates should have ample notice to prepare for new appointment" (90% agree, 6% disagree).[7] We did not ask whether and to what extent these three suggestions are currently followed in the diocese where these priests work. No repsondent volunteered the information in the affirmative, but several did so in the negative.

While large majorities of these priests favored these suggestions about the appointment system, we were aware of some differences of opinion when various categories of respondents were compared. We hypothesized that priests who could be termed "dissatisfied" would answer differently from the others. This category of dissatisfied is constituted by the minority (13%) of priests who said that if they "had the chance to do it over again" they would hesitate to enter the seminary to study for the priesthood. The contrasting and much larger group of satisfied priests are those who would not only enter the seminary again, but would do it at exactly the same age at which they did begin studying for the priesthood.[8]

We did not ask a direct question concerning satisfaction, nor try to elicit explanations why the priest is, or is not, satisfied with his life and work. The assumption that the youngest clergy, the men most recently out of the seminary, are more disgruntled than the others, is not demonstrated in Table 7.3, where we see that a larger proportion of the satisfied (48%) than of the dissatisfied (42%) are under thirty-five years of age. There is a suggestion in the Table that the youngest men have not yet "made up their minds" whether to be satisfied or dissatisfied.[9] They fall more heavily into the "all others" category, who may be called the "indifferent," while the opposite is the case with the men in the middle bracket.

Table 7.3   Age categories of respondents who are satisfied, dissatisfied, and "indifferent"

	Satisfied	Dis-satisfied	All others
Under 35 years of age	48%	42%	54%
35 to 49 years old	45	50	40
50 years and over	7	8	6
(Number of respondents)	(1,340)	(400)	(1,308)

On many items of this survey we have seen that the age differential accounts for significant differences of opinion, but even greater contrasts are found here between the satisfied and the dissatisfied priests. For example, when we asked them to what extent they are personally involved in attempting to interest boys in the priestly vocation (Table 4.6) more of the youngest men (45%) than of the oldest (32%) answered "very much" or "quite a bit," but the statistical difference is much greater between the satisfied (50%) and the dissatisfied (13%) who gave this same answer.

SUGGESTIONS FOR CURATE APPOINTMENTS

The great majority of all these diocesan priests, regardless of the type of employment they have, agreed to all three suggestions about the manner in which appointments should be made.[10] From the point of view of age, the youngest men are more in agreement than the oldest that the diocese should have a personnel office (88% to 74%), curates should be interviewed (85% to 78%), and should be given ample notice to prepare for a new appointment (91% to 86%). When we compare the opinions of the satisfied and the dissatisfied in the following Tables we find that in all three instances a higher proportion of the dissatisfied is in agreement with the suggestions. These comparative responses give us little more than a hint about the sources of dissatisfaction, which we shall have to probe further.

Table 7.4 Opinions of satisfied and dissatisfied priests concerning a personnel office to work out clergy assignments

	Satisfied	Dis-satisfied	All re-spondents
Agree	83%	89%	86%
Disagree	8	4	6
Not sure	9	7	8
(Number of respondents)	(1,333)	(400)	(3,038)

There was no suggestion in these three questions that every diocesan priest should have, or wants to have, only the assignment that would be most pleasing and satisfying to him. Indeed, in commenting about the "maldistribution" of the clergy some of them indicate that the needs of the diocese are not taken sufficiently into consideration. One New Jersey full-time assistant in his late thirties complains that "some pastors in traditional parishes demand three or more curates when they can get along with two, or even one. We lack chaplains for hospitals, mental institutions, schools and colleges, where part-time curates are appointed who are not competent for the job."

A Massachusetts curate in his fifties shows some sympathy for the diocesan officials who make the appointments. "The Chancery might

Table 7.5 Opinions of satisfied and dissatisfied priests concerning curate interviews before receiving appointments

	Satisfied	Dis-satisfied	All re-spondents
Agree	78%	91%	83%
Disagree	12	4	8
Not sure	10	5	9
(Number of respondents)	(1,335)	(400)	(3,041)

have a hard time filling undesirable posts (tough pastors, in the 'sticks,' no extras in remuneration, etc.) Only the meek boys would say 'I'll go anywhere.' On the other hand, some trouble might be avoided from the individual priest's point of view (discontent, friction, etc.)." A Wisconsin curate in his early thirties feels that the waste of talent could be avoided by more care in the whole assignment process. "Qualifications should determine your field of work; for example, men with higher degrees should be put into school or seminary work." On the other hand, said a priest in his late twenties from the same diocese, "men who are successful in specialized work can't resist the temptation to take a pastorate when their turn comes. They aren't prepared for the parish and they're really starting a second career."[11]

Table 7.6   Opinions of satisfied and dissatisfied priests concerning curates' ample notice to prepare for new appointment

	Satisfied	Dis-satisfied	All respondents
Agree	87%	93%	89%
Disagree	8	3	6
Not sure	5	4	5
(Number of respondents)	(1,337)	(400)	(3,040)

In every large diocese there is general consensus among the parish assistants concerning the "better jobs." A transfer to one of these desirable parishes—judged almost always on the quality of the pastor —may be considered a kind of horizontal promotion. In the strict career sense, however, the only formal promotion to a status higher than curate is that to the pastorate.[12] Probably in the interests of justice and fair play, and to avoid charges of favoritism and nepotism, the general practice in American dioceses has been to fill the vacant pastorate with the man who is next in line by number of years in the priesthood. In the American employment system seniority is of great importance for industrial and white-collar workers, but in the professions, and in the managerial occupations, seniority seems to be less important than ability and achievement as a criterion of promotion.

SENIORITY OR ABILITY

As we have seen in Table 7.2, there are rare instances (3%) of diocesan priests who "apply" for a particular parish position, but there appear to be no regular forms for the applicants to fill out, or any regular examinations that they have to pass. In the United States, "suitability of priests for offices is determined by the bishop, assisted in so far as necessary, by officials deputed for examination of the clergy (synodal examiners.)"[13] The general notion among the lower clergy seems to be that the priest who applies for a change of job is either a malcontent or selfishly ambitious, or both. "In this diocese," writes a young part-time curate from Texas, "you don't ask for anything. You get told where to go and what to do."

In the long run it is the bishop who makes the decision, or at least gives final approval, for the promotion of an assistant to the pastorate. Up to now in the Catholic system there is no election of pastors by the parishioners, or their representatives, as is the case in most Protestant congregations. In the 1960 survey of diocesan parish priests (Table 7.7) we found that curates are more than twice as likely

Table 7.7 Opinions of pastors and curates in 1960 survey on the basis of promotion to pastorate in their diocese

	Satisfied	Dis-satisfied	All re-spondents
Seniority alone	25%	53%	41%
Achievement and seniority	42	32	37
Preferment by Bishop	24	12	17
Merit and achievement	4	1	2
Holiness and seniority	3	2	2
Holiness and achievement	2	*	1
(Number of respondents)	(919)	(1,231)	(2,150)

(53%) as pastors (25%) to say that promotion was based on seniority alone in their diocese.[14] The pastors tend more than the curates to combine achievement and seniority as a criterion (42% to 32%) and also to admit that the preferment of the bishop (24% to 12% is an important basis for promotion to the pastorate. There is no doubt, however, that far-reaching adaptations of this appointment system are now under consideration in those dioceses where progressive bishops are attempting to implement the Second Vatican Council.

In some dioceses there appears to be also a "rewards system" in which a "deserving" pastor is appointed to a more prestigious parish. It is a recognition of past performance, but also a policy that tends to "give the more important urban parishes to older priests whose energies are already declining. Younger priests, capable of more action, are restricted to minor responsibilities. And so, those who are responsible cannot work, whereas the workers are not responsible."[15] A curate from a diocese in the Mountain States, where priests become pastors at a relatively young age, complains that the younger pastors get the smaller parishes, "and by the time we get our large parishes we are worn out and tired."

In the current survey we asked the priests whether they agree with the statement that "promotion to the pastorate should be made on a basis of ability rather than seniority," and we found that only about one out of ten (9%) of all respondents thinks that seniority is preferable to ability as a criterion of promotion. One of these dissenters, a Wisconsin curate in his early forties, poses the question: "Who will decide about our abilities? Right now seniority is about the only thing left in the priesthood that remains reasonably free of diocesan politics. If this is changed, a lot of us might just as well forget about becoming pastors and let the ecclesiastical politicians run everything."

There is no significant difference of opinion in Table 7.8 between the satisfied and the dissatisfied on the preference of ability over

Table 7.8 Opinions of satisfied and dissatisfied priests on suggestion that promotion to pastorate be on ability rather than seniority

	Satisfied	Dis-satisfied	All respondents
Agree	76%	78%	78%
Disagree	9	10	9
Not sure	15	12	13
(Number of respondents)	(3,326)	(399)	(3,023)

seniority as the basis for promotion. We found also that the type of employment the priests have does not seem to influence their opinion in this regard, but the oldest men, who are more nearly "in line" for promotion, are much less likely (61%) than the youngest men (84%) to agree with this suggestion. It should be pointed out that the Fathers of Vatican II did not mention seniority as a criterion for appointment to a pastorate. On the other hand, they suppressed the law of *concursus*, the competitive examination held to determine the qualifications of prospective appointees. "In making a judgment on the suitability of a priest for the administration of any parish, the bishop should take into consideration not only his knowledge of doctrine, but also his piety, apostolic zeal, and other gifts and qualities necessary for the proper exercise of the care of souls."[16]

The distribution of replies in Table 7.8 shows that the great majority of these diocesan priests do not like the present system of promotion by seniority.[17] A Massachusetts curate in his early thirties says that "there is something wrong with a system that permits men to reach their late fifties before they are put at the helm of a parish and are given the opportunity to exercise some pastoral initiative." One young New England curate makes the bold suggestion that there "should be some kind of rotation system whereby a priest goes from curate to pastor and back to curate. A man should be a pastor in his most energetic and productive years, say from thirty-five to fifty-five, and then go back to being a curate for the rest of his life. This would also solve the question of an age for retirement from the pastorate. There would then be a built-in system of retirement without waiting until a pastor is in his seventies or eighties."

ON BECOMING A MONSIGNOR

Another kind of promotion, one that is honorific rather than juridical, is that by which a priest becomes a monsignor. Titles like domestic prelate, papal chamberlain, and prothonotary apostolic are supposedly granted to priests who have made an outstanding contribution to the Church or are in certain higher-ranking positions in the diocese for which these titles are deemed "fitting." In the 1960 survey we asked the priests to indicate what characteristics best describe those who actually become monsignors in their diocese. No monsignors were questioned in this survey and therefore the data distributed in Table 7.9 comes only from "potential" monsignors.

Table 7.9 Opinions of pastors and curates in 1960 survey of the types of priests who are made monsignors in their diocese

	Pastors	Curates	All respondents
Those with the best "connections"	45%	38%	41%
The best organizers	17	20	19
The oldest men	16	16	16
The successful builders	11	15	13
Best money raisers	5	7	6
Most popular men	5	4	4
The holiest men	1	*	1
(Number of respondents)	(634)	(879)	(1,513)

The proportion of monsignors to nonmonsignors differs from diocese to diocese and seems to depend on the attitude of the bishop in the recommendation of priests for such honors.[18] Four out of ten (41%) respondents in Table 7.9—but pastors (45%) more than curates (38%)—think that the monsignor is one who had the best "connections" which apparently means an approved relationship with the bishop or one of his trusted advisers. A minority (16%) of these priests think of seniority, or advanced age, as a factor in their diocese, while others think that past achievement as organizers (19%) or as builders (13%) help to obtain this title. Not many of them (6%) feel that raising money is an avenue to this recognition, but a New Jersey curate in his early forties says that in his diocese "the average pastor thinks the purpose of the parish is to pay off the debt and thus receive the 'most valuable player award' (it's red!) from the chancery which shares his views."

We asked the diocesan pastors and curates: "What is the most common attitude toward the prospect of becoming a monsignor among your closest friends in the priesthood." The curates are younger men and the great majority of them (71%) say that their priest friends either do not discuss the prospect or are not interested in it. Table 7.10 shows, however, that among the priest friends of the pastors, who are older men, a large minority (44%) exhibit a certain amount of interest in the possibility of becoming a monsignor. None of these respondents was in specialized diocesan employment where the prospect of receiving this honor is often greater than it is among parish priests.

Table 7.10 Opinions of pastors and curates in 1960 survey of their fellow priests' attitudes toward becoming monsignor

	Pastors	Curates	All respondents
They hardly ever discuss it	31%	49%	41%
They are not interested in it	25	22	24
Would like it, but not aspiring	28	20	23
Would like it	14	7	10
Are working for it	2	2	2
(Number of respondents)	(940)	(1,237)	(2,177)

Among the respondents to this survey one of the oldest part-time assistants from Pennsylvania appears bitter about the fact that "the presence of many youngster monsignori, some of them ill-mannered, worldly, and unintelligent, has destroyed the seniority system of ordination date, and belittled the priesthood." A New York curate in his late thirties remarks that these titles are sometimes given to the undeserving and "this constitutes a rebuff to the hard-working priest who has been passed over, and brings dissatisfaction to those who are more deserving than some of the monsignors we now have." As long as monsignors are appointed and not elected the ordinary diocesan priest is not asked to judge who is worthy and who is not.

One of the questions that seemed to arouse the most interest in these lower-echelon diocesan priests (only one priest failed to answer it) was the suggestion that "it would be better if the Church dispensed with titles (like domestic prelate, papal chamberlain, prothonotary apostolic, etc.) for its priests." The data in Table 7.11 reveal that almost three quarters (73%) of all respondents are in favor of abolishing these honorific titles by which monsignors are known, and this high vote (72%) was given also by those who are in specialized nonparochial work, which sometimes leads to the monsignor's title. As may be expected, the oldest men were not quite so ready (63%) as the youngest (79%) to agree to this suggestion.

From a secular sociological point of view the absence of status symbols, as well as the long wait for the important promotion to a pastorate, appear to be potential sources of frustration among the ordinary diocesan clergy. Even if the title of monsignor were popular among them—and it demonstrably is not—they have little hope of attaining it. An Illinois part-time curate in his later thirties remarks that "while the present titles are out-dated and no longer relevant— some type of ranking—and consequently of titles—is customary in every large organization." A Pennsylvania curate in his early thirties thinks that the title of monsignor should be made even more rare, "given only to certain diocesan officials and to pastors on their retirement from office."

Table 7.11 Opinions of satisfied and dissatisfied priests on suggestion that ecclesiastical titles be abolished

	Satisfied	Dis-satisfied	All respondents
Agree	67%	80%	73%
Disagree	14	9	11
Am neutral	15	9	13
Don't know	4	2	3
(Number of respondents)	(1,340)	(399)	(3,047)

We note in Table 7.11 that a larger proportion of the dissatisfied priests (80%) than of the satisfied (67%) want to get rid of the monsignor title. A similiar dissatisfaction was expressed during the Council by Cardinal de Camara who asked, "Shall we take the initiative to suppress our own titles of Eminence, Beatitude, Excellency? Shall we lose our obsession to be of the nobility, and drop our coats of arms and mottoes? This seems like nothing, but how this creates distance between the clergy and the faithful. It separates us from our own century, which has already adopted another style of life."[19] The Cardinal was not opposed to rank, status, and recognition among Churchmen, but to the undemocratic, outmoded titles and trappings of ecclesiastical office.

CELIBACY AND PROMOTION

At this point we introduced another and speculative criterion for promotion in the Church. We wanted to know whether they agreed to the suggestion that "if there were a married priesthood, promotion to the pastorate and to the episcopacy should be allowed only for celibates." The next two Tables show that these diocesan clergy are much more willing to have married pastors (62%) than married bishops (38%). A curate in his late thirties from a Massachusetts diocese thinks that "our bishops should be celibate as they are in the Oriental Church, leading a higher life and showing forth a greater commitment. I don't think the laity in this diocese could every get used to the idea of a married bishop, and perhaps they never even thought about it."[20]

Table 7.12 Opinions of satisfied and dissatisfied priests on suggestion that in event of a married clergy only celibates be promoted to the pastorate

	Satisfied	Dis-satisfied	All re-spondents
Agree	22%	14%	18%
Disagree	57	74	62
Not sure	21	12	20
(Number of respondents)	(1,319)	(393)	(3,005)

In the several questions concerning a prospective married clergy in the Roman Catholic Church we shall see that the age of the priest respondent has an influence on his opinion.[21] The oldest priests are much more likely than the youngest to say that only celibates should be pastors (35% to 13%) and that only celibates should be bishops (53% to 35%). The difference of opinion between the satisfied and the dissatisfied in Tables 7.12 and 7.13 is also statistically significant and also suggests a partial explanation of the latter's dissatisfaction.

When we asked whether the diocesan priest should have the freedom of choice to marry, the satisfied priests were four times as likely (52%) as the dissatisfied (13%) to answer in the negative. When we asked them about the probable effectiveness of a married clergy in the parish ministry, the satisfied were much more likely (67%) than the dissatisfied (25%) to opine that they would be less effective.

A hypothetical suggestion of this kind is difficult to answer because a change from a celibate to a married clergy would necessarily involve other and complicated changes. One of the youngest curates from Massachusetts points out that "the present canonical legislation allows the pastor to be one of the last absolute monarchs and he would probably be even more intolerant if he remained celibate while his assistants married. As far as the bishop is concerned, he is fre-

Table 7.13   Opinions of satisfied and dissatisfied priests on suggestion that in event of a married clergy only celibates be promoted to the episcopacy

	Satisfied	Dis-satisfied	All respondents
Agree	44%	31%	39%
Disagree	34	44	38
Not sure	22	25	23
(Number of respondents)	(1,322)	(396)	(3,011)

quently unable to understand his priests even as the situation now exists. I fear it would become impossible if some of 'his' clergy were married and he were not." Several of the respondents feel that celibate superiors and married subordinates among the American priests of the Latin rite would simply widen the cleavage that already exists in the Church between administrators and lower-echelon clergy.[22]

RETIREMENT AND RESIGNATION

In the American employment system the end of the professional or occupational career comes with retirement, either voluntary or mandatory. The Fathers of the Second Vatican Council said that pastors who can no longer perform their duties "properly and fruitfully" because of age or some other reason "are urgently requested to tender their resignation voluntarily or upon invitation from the bishop."[23] In the same document they said also that bishops who have become less capable because of age or some other serious reason "are earnestly requested to offer their resignation from office either on their own initiative or upon invitation from the competent authority."[24] The responses of the priests in this survey, as seen in Tables 7.14 and 7.15, are clearly in agreement with the recommendations of the Council.

Table 7.14   Opinions of satisfied and dissatisfied priests on a definite retirement age for pastors

	Satisfied	Dis-satisfied	All re-spondents
Agree	88%	93%	91%
Disagree	7	4	5
Not sure	5	3	4
(Number of respondents)	(1,339)	(399)	(3,044)

The responses distributed in these two Tables demonstrate where the overwhelming majority of the lower-echelon clergy stand in answer to this question: "In general, and perhaps allowing for some exceptions, are you in favor of a definite retirement age for pastors and bishops?" As may be expected, the dissatisfied priests are in both cases in higher agreement with the suggestion than are the satisfied. This is not simply the reaction of the "restless" younger clergy. The priests who are fifty years of age and older also favor a definite retirement age for pastors (86%) and for bishops (84%). Relatively few other questions in this survey elicited such almost complete agreement of response.[25]

These diocesan priests made many comments about both promotion and retirement. They suggested that there should be a limited term in office for both pastors and bishops, and that the clergy should have a vote in the election or appointment of the bishop.[26] "No bishop should be in office more than ten years." "Pastors should rotate parishes every seven years." A young curate in a New Jersey diocese says, "It would be beneficial for the Church if pastors and bishops had a fixed term in office as happens with superiors in religious communities. I don't think that a retirement policy would solve the problems of either the diocese or the parish, but a term appointment would certainly help to alleviate these problems."[27]

Table 7.15   Opinions of satisfied and dissatisfied priests on a definite retirement age for bishops

	Satisfied	Dis-satisfied	All re-spondents
Agree	87%	93%	89%
Disagree	7	3	6
Not sure	6	4	5
(Number of respondents)	(1,339)	(398)	(3,039)

Pope Paul VI gave renewed impetus to the whole discussion about clerical retirement when he suggested that bishops should relinquish their office at the age of seventy-five. Even earlier, when Pope John was Nuncio in Paris he suggested that certain bishops might retire after the liberation of France, but few did. He gave reasons why the Holy See did not impose a retiring age on bishops. "He explained that the relationship was paternal rather than official, and that parents do not retire, though if they become in need of help their work may have to be done for them. The weakness of this argument of the paternal relationship is that it cuts across the habit of translating bishops to more important sees, which is like a man leaving his family for a larger or more promising one, something the Church has always set her face against."[28]

There is a problem of judgment common to both promotion and retirement. Some of the priests ask: If promotion is based on ability rather than seniority, who is to judge ability? Similarly, if retirement is based on lack of ability, who is to judge this lack of ability? It is a well-known fact of psychology that most men in executive positions who reach the mandatory age of retirement feel that they still "have a few good years in them." Most bishops and pastors are no exceptions to this generalization.[29] Decreasing competence occurs only gradually in most persons, and it is difficult for a man to admit to himself at some point of his career that he is now "less capable" than he used to be. Furthermore, as Barnard points out, "the resistance to loss of status is in general stronger than desire to achieve status," and this may help to explain why so few prelates and ecclesiastical administrators voluntarily resign. The day after they resign, they are "has-beens."

The bishop or pastor who relinquishes his office is still, of course, an ordained minister of God who can still perform important spiritual functions for the people of God. Even if he should go further and cease functioning as a clergyman he is still considered "a priest forever." Nevertheless, one southern curate in his late thirties suggested, "Why not have a temporary priesthood alongside the permanent priesthood? It seems to me that the irrevocability of ordination is a deterrent to many generous and zealous young men who would like to enter the seminary." Another southern priest in his early thirties and in nonparish work says, "I believe there should be some way for dissatisfied priests to get out similar to the way religious brothers and sisters can get dispensed from solemn vows."

The responses distributed in Table 7.16 were made to the suggestion that "as in other professions and occupations, it should be possible to have voluntary resignation, or an honorable discharge,

Table 7.16 Opinions of satisfied and dissatisfied priests on voluntary resignation from the priesthood

	Satisfied	Dis-satisfied	All re-spondents
Agree	55%	86%	64%
Disagree	26	8	20
Neutral	8	3	7
Don't know	11	3	9
(Number of respondents)	(1,333)	(397)	(3,027)

from the priesthood." In the light of the Catholic tradition of a permanent priesthood, it is noteworthy that only one out of five of all these diocesan priests flatly disagreed with the suggestion. As may be expected, the dissatisfied clergy are much more likely (86%) than the satisfied (55%) to agree to this proposition, yet it seems remarkable that so many of the latter are also in favor of some honorable way of leaving the priesthood. It may be expected too that only half (51%) of the oldest priests, as compared to two thirds of the youngest (65%) answered this question affirmatively.

Among the dissenting opinions to this proposition, several alluded to the permanancy of marriage. A Wisconsin curate in his early forties asked, "Since when is the priesthood a profession or occupation? I always considered it a vocation, like matrimony. If we priests are allowed an honorable discharge from the sacrament of holy orders, why are not laymen allowed an honorable discharge from the sacrament of matrimony?" An Ohio curate in his early thirties says, "If you permit voluntary resignation for priests then married men will want it also from their marriage—then what?"[30]

The possibility of giving up the priesthood is discussed nowhere in the Council documents except as a failing or defection. "With active mercy a bishop should attend upon priests who are in any sort of danger or who have failed in some respect."[31] Not only bishops but also priests "should realize that they have special obligations toward priests who labor under certain difficulties. They should give them timely help and also, if necessary, admonish them prudently. Moreover, they should always treat with fraternal charity and magnanimity those who have failed in some way, offering urgent prayers to God for them and continually showing themselves to be true brothers and friends."[32]

SUMMARY

The data of this chapter have dealt with the professional career of the lower-echelon diocesan priests. As in other occupations, the priests have an expected amount of job mobility, but it is horizontal and not vertical until the single promotion to the pastorate. The manner in which they receive their appointments from the bishop or the chancery office is not typical of American men in professional or occupational careers. As they grow older in the priesthood they accumulate increasing experience from the various assignments they have had, but these transfers can hardly be considered promotions in the "progressive stages" in an ecclesiastical career. For the most part, and without previous interview, the priests are simply ordered to move to another parish or to take up another diocesan task, and they definitely dislike this procedure.

What they want is nothing more than any mature American professional man expects from his superior or employer. They want some kind of personnel officer or manager in the diocese who knows their training, qualifications, talents, and interests, and can make intelligent decisions about their work assignments. They want a chance to be interviewed, and to discuss their prospects in a normal adult manner before they are shifted to a new assignment. They do not want sudden and immediate changes, in which they lack time to settle affairs in their previous post and to prepare for their next post.

In contrasting the satisfied with the dissatisfied among these priests we find a consistently higher proportion of the latter in favor of a mature procedure of clerical assignments. They agree with the others in overwhelmingly large proportions that promotion to the pastorate should be on the basis of ability rather than of seniority and that a retirement age should be fixed for both pastors and bishops. Many comments were made, however, similar to those of the Second Vatican Council, that competence or incompetence to perform the tasks of office should be a more important criterion than age for the mandatory retirement of pastors and bishops.

Recognition comes to diocesan priests when they are "elevated" to the honorific status of a monsignor. The diocesan priests take a realistic view of the criteria for this promotion, are relatively uninterested in it for themselves, and are greatly in favor of abolishing such ecclesiastical titles. Significant statistical differences occur between the satisfied and the dissatisfied on whether only celibate clergy should be promoted to the pastorate and the episcopacy. The dissatisfied are much more likely than the others to answer negatively. In general, however, less than one in five (18%) of all respondents agrees that in the event of a married clergy in the Roman rite only celibates be promoted to the pastorate; but more than twice as many (39%) think that bishops should follow the rule of celibacy. The dissatisfied priests are much more concerned about celibacy than are the satisfied, and they are much more in agreement than the others that there should be some voluntary and honorable way of resigning from the priesthood.

NOTES

1. See Robert Dubin, *The World of Work* (Englewood Cliffs, N.J.: Prentice-Hall, 1958), p. 278, who points out that "not all who work are following careers" because not all occupations involve successive and progressive stages in related functions.

2. *Bishops' Pastoral Office in the Church*, Article 31.

3. Joseph H. Fichter, *Religion as an Occupation* (Notre Dame, Ind.: University of Notre Dame Press, 1961), p. 171.

4. Francis Canavan, "Reforms That Priests Want," *America*, Vol. 114, April 23, 1966, pp. 582–89, says that "a 35-year-old priest in the United States today is regarded by his superiors as a boy and is treated as such. This is a basic defect in the ecclesiastical system that cries out to be remedied."

5. This is one of the practical consequences of the Council. The pre-Conciliar research finding (Table 7.2) was that less than one out of ten (9%) actually requested a change of assignment.

6. "If the Bishop is wrong," he continues, "the National Conference of Bishops should deal with him." Given the autonomy of diocesan jurisdiction there is little likelihood that the Bishops' Conference will establish a grievance committee to sit in judgment on any member Bishop's relationship with his clergy. The suggestion itself bespeaks the clergy's sense of dependence on higher authority. The "needs of the diocese" are better known by the local priests than by a national group of bishops.

7. The missing percentages represent those who are "not sure."

8. For a more detailed view about preferable age at entrance see above, Chapter 4, "Seminary Training," and Joseph H. Fichter, *Religion as an Occupation*, Chapter 1, "Vocation as an Occupational Choice."

9. See the relevant discussion in Edward Gross, *Work and Society* (New York: Thomas Y. Crowell, 1958), Chapter 5, "The Career," pp. 143–221.

10. See the suggestions of Joseph Mastrangelo, "Needed: A Vicar for Priests," *The Priest*, Vol. 22, No. 9, September 1966, pp. 717–20. This liaison man between bishop and priests "could be used as a consultant in making changes and appointments."

11. This willingness to shift careers may mean that the man did not have a genuine professional attitude toward the work in which he previously specialized. Professionals are generally less willing to seek a "second career" than are business executives. Yet there has been a significant shift of Protestant clergymen into other careers. See James Gustafson, "The Clergy in the United States," in Kenneth Lynn, ed., *The Professionals in America* (Boston: Houghton Mifflin, 1965), pp. 70–90.

12. Joseph H. Fichter, *Religion as an Occupation*, "Criteria for Promotion," pp. 168–71.

13. Abbott, *op. cit.*, p. 419, footnote 61.

14. Arthur X. Deegan, "Significant Factors in the Choice of Pastors," *The American Ecclesiastical Review*, August 1964, pp. 97–111, reports on a re-

search study which shows that "there is a tendency to choose parish administrators (pastors) on a basis of seniority." Most significant was the fact that only 9 per cent said that their own promotion was based mainly on seniority, but two thirds said that the promotion of other pastors was on seniority.

15. Ronald Creagh "Parish Probe," *Perspectives*, Vol. 10, No. 1, January–February, 1965, pp. 20–22.

16. *Bishops' Pastoral Office in the Church*, Article 31. *Concursus* is described in the Code of Canon Law, #459, also by Abbott, *op. cit.*, p. 419.

17. Some pastors also have negative views of the "seniority over merit procedure," according to Thomas R. O'Donovan, "Some Career Determinants of Church Executives," *Sociology and Social Research*, Vol. 48, October 1963, pp. 58–68, who analyzed the same research materials discussed by Arthur X. Deegan (see above, footnote 14).

18. Statistics derived from the 1966 edition of Kenedy's *Catholic Directory* show that monsignors accounted for 4.6 per cent of all nonpastor diocesan clergy in the United States. Among the large dioceses, New York, Washington, and Chicago had the highest proportions of these nonparochial monsignors, while Brooklyn, Detroit, and Philadelphia had the lowest.

19. Helder Cardinal Camara, "The Church—On Bishops," *Perspectives*, Vol. 8, No. 5, September–October, 1963, pp. 152–54. During the final session of the Council twenty bishops concelebrated a Mass in the Roman catacombs and made a pledge that included the following: "In meeting with people I will shun any title that implies grandeur or power." "I will shun both the semblance and the reality of wealth, especially in my dress and insignia." The text of this pledge was revealed by Bishop Alberto Devoto, of Goya, Argentina, in his pastoral letter of Easter, 1966, reprinted in *U.S. Catholic*, December 1966, p. 55.

20. Nor apparently did the Council Fathers when they said that in the Eastern Churches, "in addition to all bishops and those others who by a gift of grace choose to observe celibacy, there also exist married priests of outstanding merit." *Ministry and Life of Priests*, Article 16.

21. See below, Chapter 8, "Married Clergy."

22. This was certainly the case in the Russian Church before the Revolution, where the married parish priests were of very low status and subordinate to the unmarried prelates and administrators.

23. *Bishops' Pastoral Office in the Church*, Article 31.

24. *Ibid.*, Article 21. Xavier Rynne, *The Second Session* (New York: Farrar, Straus & Giroux, 1964), pp. 195–98, describes the debate on the proposition that bishops should retire at sixty-five. Cardinal Suenens favored forced retirement because bishops would not agree to resign voluntarily. Archbishop Mingo, of Sicily, said it was a "harsh but necessary law"; Bishop DeVito, of Lucknow, India, opposed it, saying "it would be just as outrageous as attempting to change the course of the moon."

25. Other instances of high approval concerned the clergy senate, personnel committee, and grievance committee (see above, Tables 3.8 to 3.10).

26. "Archbishop Young of Hobart, Australia, recently spoke in favor of priests working in a diocese having a voice in the appointment of their new bishop. He also thought that the day would come when the laity would have the same right." Quotation from *The London Tablet*, "Electing Bishops," in *The Priest*, Vol. 22, No. 10, October 1966, p. 810; see also John Tracy Ellis, "On Selecting American Bishops," *Commonweal*, March 10, 1967, pp. 643–49.

27. The question has also been asked about the Pope. "Would the collegiate nature of the Church be best served by electing the Pope for a single non-repeatable term of ten years? . . . And what would prevent the Church from now returning to the faithful their ancient privilege of electing the Bishop?" Joseph O. Donogue, "Elections in the Church," *The Commonweal*, Vol. 82, No. 9, May 21, 1965, p. 284. Canon 454 says that pastors should have "stability" in their parishes, but it seems likely that this canon will be revised to find ways of "making the pastoral clergy more mobile." See the discussion of "Stability of Parish Priests," *The Clergy Review*, Vol. 49, 1964, pp. 105–08.

28. See the quotation from *The London Tablet*, "Would Pope John Have Approved?" in *The Priest*, Vol. 22, No. 10, October 1966, p. 794.

29. See John R. McCarthy, "Clerical Retirement," *Homiletic and Pastoral Review*, Vol. 67, No. 3, December 1966, pp. 197–206. Pope Innocent III in 1206 gave six causes sufficient to warrant a bishop to ask permission to renounce his office, only one of which was "weakness of body." See Gerald V. McDevitt, *The Renunciation of an Ecclesiastical Office* (Washington: Catholic University Press, 1946), pp. 21–22. Here we read also that "an incumbent may revoke his resignation provided that he notify the superior of this intention before he has received notification of the superior's acceptance of his resignation" (p. 156).

30. When commenting about a possible married clergy, a young Oregon curate made another comparison. "If the priests get married, what's going to happen to the Sisters' communities? The Sisters will want to get married too; then what will happen to our hospitals and schools?"

31. *Bishops' Pastoral Office in the Church*, Article 16.

32. Decree on *Priestly Formation*, Article 8. Here Editor Walter Abbott adds a footnote reference to ex-priests, "the Church's heart and mind go out to the shepherds wandering in the mist," a term reminiscent of E. Boyd-Barrett, *Shepherds in the Mist* (New York: McMullen, 1945), and *A Shepherd Without Sheep* (Milwaukee: Bruce, 1956).

MARRIED CLERGY

The Fathers of the Second Vatican Council leave no doubt in anyone's mind concerning their preference for a continuation of the celibate priesthood in the Latin rite. They say that "total continence embraced on behalf of the kingdom of heaven has always been held in particular honor by the Church as being a sign of charity and stimulus towards it, as well as a unique fountain of spiritual fertility in the world."[1] When speaking of the training of seminarians they say that "students who, according to the holy and fixed laws of their own rite, follow the revered tradition of priestly celibacy should be very carefully trained for this state."[2]

In discussing the ministry and life of priests the Council spelled out the advantages of celibacy and the many ways it accords with the priesthood. This was prefaced by the remark that celibacy "is not, indeed, demanded by the nature of the priesthood, as is evident from the practice of the primitive Church, and from the tradition of the Eastern Churches. In these Churches, in addition to all bishops and those others who by a gift of grace choose to observe celibacy, there also exist married priests of outstanding merit. While this most sacred Synod recommends ecclesiastical celibacy, it in no way intends to change that different discipline which lawfully prevails in Eastern Churches."[3]

THE FEARFUL TOPIC

Some accounts by observers at the Council give the impression that the delegates were afraid to discuss the topic of a married clergy in the Western Church.[4] As a matter of fact, when the debate began on the restoration of the diaconate, Cardinal Bacci of the Curia said it was "dangerous" because it would lead to the proposal that deacons be allowed to marry. Bishop Franič, of Yugoslavia, thought that a married diaconate would endanger the status of the celibate priesthood and pointed out that the Orthodox Churches have difficulties with priests who are married. European journalists began to speculate about the married priesthood so that the French bishops felt impelled to issue a statement of denial that the Latin Church intended to change in this regard. "They noted also that no Father had suggested any such change in the existing legislation on the floor of the Council."[5]

There has been much uncertainty concerning the extent to which the American clergy have taken an interest in this formerly "closed" question and have discussed it among themselves. One of our respondents questioned the propriety of even asking about this matter and felt that it would be a "grievous sin" on the part of any celibate priest to speculate about whether he would marry if the Church law were changed. Bunnick remarks that "it is sometimes said that discussions of celibacy will only arouse doubts and uncertainties, which will impede the quiet living out of a priest's vocation. This cannot be denied, and we must regret the probability of such unrest. Nevertheless, we should also recognize that an artificial peace is no real peace, and that the subject would never have come up if there had been no difficulties with it."[6]

On the advice of our preliminary consultants, and perhaps at the risk of offending some consciences, we included the following statement in the survey questionnaire: "There has been much written lately on the question of married clergy in the Roman rite. During the past year have you discussed this question with your fellow diocesan priests?" The distribution of responses in Table 8.1 shows how the age groups differ in this regard.

Table 8.1 Frequency of discussion with fellow diocesan priests during past year about married clergy, by age categories

	Under 35 years	35 to 49 years	50 years and over	All respondents
Frequently	37%	30%	11%	33%
Occasionally	51	54	62	53
Seldom	11	13	19	12
Never	1	3	8	2
(Number of respondents)	(1,515)	(1,318)	(204)	(3,037)

The question of a married priesthood was a frequent topic of conversation among one third of all respondents, and only a small minority (14%) report that they had seldom or never talked about it with their fellow priests during the past year. Those who are under thirty-five, men who are normally still in the "marriagable age" bracket, were more than three times as likely (37%) as the oldest group (11%) to say that they had frequently discussed the matter. These statistics demonstrate unquestionably that the subject of a married Catholic priesthood is not a topic avoided or excluded from the conversation of these diocesan priests. The number of books and articles written about it in the past few years shows that the subject is now discussed much more than in the past, by the laity as well as by priests.

There were relatively few comments added to this statement about the frequency with which the priests do talk about it. One of the youngest curates, however, from a Connecticut diocese, is dissatisfied with the quality of the conversation. He believes that "the question of clerical marriage and celibacy should be aired, but much of the discussion, both pro and con, seems very immature. The one side is too juridical and abstract. The other side does not seem to recognize the deep value of a freely consecrated virginity." A non-curate in his late thirties from a Wisconsin diocese would "like to see the topic discussed more openly and frankly. At the present time there is something less than intellectual honesty in the debates and arguments."[7]

It does not necessarily follow that priests who talk about a married clergy are also in favor of a change in the law. We saw in Table 8.1

that the great majority (86%) of all respondents talked about it frequently or occasionally during the past year, but in Table 8.2 we find a smaller proportion (62%) who approve a change in Church legislation on the matter of clerical celibacy. We asked the question: "In general, would you be in favor of the *diocesan* priest's freedom of choice to marry?" and allowed for alternative answers. The resultant finding, that six out of ten are in favor of this freedom of choice, received more publicity by the news media in the original press release than any other item in the survey.[8]

Table 8.2 Opinions concerning diocesan priest's freedom of choice to marry, by age categories

	Under 35 years	35 to 49 years	50 years and over	All respondents
Only before ordination	12%	7%	6%	9%
Only after ordination	6	6	4	6
Both before and after	54	41	24	47
Not at all	28	46	66	38
(Number of respondents)	(1,478)	(1,291)	(199)	(2,968)

Almost two out of five (38%) of all respondents said that they are "not at all" in favor of this freedom of choice. Table 8.2, however, reveals the dramatic difference by age groups, with this negative answer being given by less than three out of ten (28%) of the youngest category, as compared with two thirds of the oldest. It will be noted that we asked whether there should be any limitation to this freedom of choice to marry, and that among the minority the youngest men are twice as ready (12%) as the oldest men (6%) to impose the qualification that only candidates for the priesthood may get married. In other words, they are saying that men who are now ordained priests should not be allowed to marry. Nevertheless, the largest single category (47%) of all respondents give approval without any qualification or limitation.

The difference of opinion by age groups becomes significant if we realize that any adaptation in Church legislation on clerical celibacy depends upon the approval of the bishops, most of whom fall into the oldest age category. Thus, if our oldest respondents, fifty years of age and over, reflect the mind of the hierarchy we may expect that two thirds of the bishops would vote against a priest's freedom of choice to marry. The agendum of the National Conference of Catholic Bishops, meeting in Chicago in April 1967, was said to be too crowded to allow discussion of the matter, but the proposal was made to include this question in a broad survey of the American priesthood.

A Michigan curate in his early forties felt that "this question should never have been asked because all priests of the Roman rite were plainly told before ordination to major orders that they were freely choosing a life of celibacy." An Illinois priest in his late thirties who is a part-time curate reflects on this same notion. "Much of the problem with celibacy today comes from the fact that before they were ordained many of the priests simply accepted it as one of the conditions of the priesthood rather than a good in itself. I think the special vocation to celibacy should be positively fostered for its own good in the Church, both before and after ordination." This positive approach to celibacy is recognized in the sensitive treatment O'Neill gives the subject: "It is only when seen as a total dedication of love and service centering in the inner core of the person that the celibacy of the priest takes on its proper meaning."[9]

If the large majority (86%) talk about a married priesthood and a smaller majority (62%) think that priests should be allowed to marry, how many of them would opt for the state of matrimony if Church regulations were changed? In the opinion of one young assistant from Florida, the crucial personal question about marriage was put "rather bluntly" in this survey. We simply asked: "If a married priesthood were permitted in the Roman rite, do you think that you would marry?" In Table 8.3 we find that only one out of twenty (5%) is sure that this is what he wants for himself; at the other end of the scale almost four times as many (18%) are just as definite that they do not want marriage.

It is in the definitely negative answers where the sharpest difference of response is found between the youngest (11%) and the oldest (47%) priests. Age makes a difference, according to a California curate who commented, "Perhaps if I had to do it over again I might want to marry, but I am now thirty-six years old. My life is happy and settled. It probably would be difficult at this late date to try to adjust to married life and to the new problems this would bring." The younger priests are aware that their attitudes and behavior have been patterned to the single life and that a change in this regard would require a major adjustment for them. A New England curate in his early thirties writes, "I have been a bachelor too long and have become very independent, and would consequently make married life very difficult for the woman." One of the youngest curates, from Minnesota, says, "I don't think I could do justice to a wife and family—not enough time."[10]

Table 8.3   Responses, by age categories, to question whether respondent himself would marry

	Under 35 years	35 to 49 years	50 years and over	All respondents
Yes, unquestionably	6%	5%	2%	5%
Very likely would	11	7	2	9
Probably would	21	14	10	17
Probably would not	31	28	15	28
Very likely not	20	25	24	23
Definitely would not	11	21	47	18
(Number of respondents)	(1,490)	(1,304)	(202)	(2,996)

Speculation about whether one would marry if given the chance becomes even more hypothetical when it turns to the problems of adaptation to the married life. Even among Protestants, writes Douglas, "it is striking how seldom books on the Protestant ministry take account of the fact that most ministers are married, with responsibilities as husbands and fathers. The guiding image, after the Protestant Reformation as well as before it, appears to be a celibate priesthood, in which the clergyman gives his undivided loyalty and time to the Church. Few authors meet realistically and constructively the conflicts faced by a minister who seeks to balance the competing demands and responsibilities of his family and his congregation."[11]

Some of the priests feel that there is "a problem behind the problem." A New York curate in his late twenties believes that men "who want to marry are seeking a union, a personal relationship, a community. This points up the problem behind the problem—the diocesan priesthood is not really such a community. There is something in our training that tends to develop a group of rugged (and not so rugged) individualists, not a true brotherhood." A young New England curate is concerned about the "system." He says that "the success or failure of a married clergy is contingent on our ability to reassess the parish structure and to redirect it to Christian ends." Others point to practical problems like living accommodations in parish rectories and an adequate family wage for the married priest.

SOME HAVE MARRIED

The penalty of excommunication from the Church is visited upon the priest who enters matrimony. In the recent past there has been much publicity given to some of the clergy who left the Church and married, as well as to their explanations of why they took this step. Up to now, however, we have had no reliable statistics of the frequency of this occurrence in the United States, nor of the proportions of ex-priests who are later reconciled with the Church. Table 8.4 demonstrates an apparently genuine sympathy for these men.[12] The overwhelming majority (87%) of these diocesan respondents, and the youngest (91%) more than the oldest (69%) are in favor of receiving such ex-priests back into the fold and allowing them to receive the sacraments and to remain married, whether or not they have children. Previously, since the Latin rite has ruled against a married priesthood, such a marriage was canonically invalid and the priest had to leave his wife before he could be reinstated as a practicing Catholic layman. Less than one out of ten (8%) of our

Table 8.4   Opinions, by age categories, on whether the married ex-priest should be allowed to return to the sacraments and remain married

	Under 35 years	35 to 49 years	50 years and over	All respondents
Should leave wives first	5%	9%	25%	8%
Only if they have children	4	5	6	5
Yes, with or without children	91	86	69	87
(Number of respondents)	(1,481)	(1,287)	(197)	(2,965)

respondents thinks that this should still be the case, with the oldest five times as likely (25%) as the youngest (5%) to hold this opinion.

The question of the permanency of the priesthood as a functional role has already been raised in this survey. Almost two thirds (64%) agreed, and again more of the youngest (65%) than of the oldest (51%), that it should be possible to have voluntary resignation, or an "honorable discharge," from the priesthood. What seems most significant is that only one fifth of these ordained men disagreed with the suggestion.[13] Table 8.4 shows that sympathy is expressed by these men for their fellow priests who have resigned, but in some quarters there is also alarm expressed about what appears to be a "trend."

Nobody really knows how many ex-priests there are in the United States, or whether there has been an increasing rate of defections over the years. O'Neill says that he was informed by "senior priests and diocesan officials" that those who gave up the priesthood amount to about 10 per cent of the number of priests in good standing in America.[14] This would mean that almost six thousand ordained American priests are no longer functioning in the priesthood.[15] Others suggest that there are about two thousand "shepherds in the mist" scattered around the country. There is also the conjecture that the rate of exit has remained fairly steady from year to year, but that men who had in former times quietly shifted from clerical to lay status are now being replaced by men whose departure from the priesthood is accomplished in the glare of publicity.[16] The editors of the Christian Century suggest that the frequent reports of Catholic priests who marry are no longer news stories and should be taken off the front page and put on the society page of the paper.

The attempt to obtain factual information on this matter presents a particularly vexing statistical problem.[17] No one has devised a simple and reliable way of gathering accurate data, although several approaches have been suggested. It is probable that every diocesan chancery office and every provincial headquarters of religious orders has a fairly reliable record of the priests who have defected and, less probably, some knowledge of their present whereabouts. Many of these officials are understandably reluctant to release such information, often in protection of the reputation of the individual involved. It may well be that some Vatican bureau maintains records of priestly resignations for every country in the world, but as far as we know, this information—if it does exist—has not been divulged.

In the present survey we asked for data that would help us to make some basic generalizations along these lines. We asked three related questions: first, how many priests were in your ordination class; second, how many of these priests have left the priesthood; and third, how many of those who left have married. Given the importance of the subject and the fact of communication among the clergy we assumed that a diocesan priest would have such information about his former seminary classmates. The fact that practically all of them provided specific statistical answers to these questions indicates that this was a valid assumption and lends credence to the information displayed in the following Table.

Table 8.5 Distribution of diocesan priests, by year of ordination, who left the priesthood, and who married

Years of ordination	Left the ministry	Left and married
1964–1966	0.50%	0.27%
1961–1963	1.50	0.81
1958–1960	2.89	1.56
1955–1957	2.81	1.72
1952–1954	2.51	1.49
1949–1951	3.47	2.71
1946–1948	3.48	2.16
1943–1945	3.29	2.13
1942 and earlier	3.73	2.42

The data that form the basis for Table 8.5 are provided by diocesan priests from all regions of the country, of whom 23 per cent became priests in the three most recent ordination classes, while 5 per cent were ordained twenty-five years or longer. The numerically superior younger priests represented more dioceses and more ordination classes than did the older. The size of the ordination class varies from year to year and particularly from diocese to diocese. Some of the priests are from places that do not have their own major seminary and were ordained in dioceses other than their own, but made numerical distinctions between those who belonged to their diocese and those who did not. This is admittedly a circuitous way of calculating the data, and the conclusions are as reliable as the estimates made by our respondents. They are certainly more reliable than the offhand guesswork of the "senior priests and diocesan officials" from whom O'Neill got his information.

Obviously the year of ordination is an important datum since the numbers who leave the priesthood are likely to grow, and the proportion increase, with the length of years in the priesthood. The longitudinal statistics in Table 8.5 fulfill the expectation that those who were ordained twenty-five years or longer show a larger loss than those ordained in recent years. These are not yearly rates of loss, but the cumulative percentage of loss over the years of the original ordination class. The progressive increase in both columns of Table 8.5 shows some fluctuations and we have no data that would explain, for example, why those ordained in the classes of 1952 to 1954 show a lower proportion of loss than those who were ordained from 1958 to 1960.

In the present survey we did not ask about motivation or for any explanation of the reasons why some of their classmates decided to leave the priesthood. In the 1960 survey of diocesan parish clergy we asked this open-end question without satisfactory results: "You probably know a few priests who have quit the priesthood. What principal reason, in your opinion, is the most significant one why they left the priesthood?" The answers were so varied, and often in combination, that they were difficult to categorize. Most frequently mentioned were spiritual faults like pride, selfishness and disobedience; the problem of celibacy was mentioned in second place, and in third place various facets of the relationship between superiors and subordinates. In the present study the comparison between the two columns of Table 8.5 shows that about one third of those who left the priesthood did not do so in order to marry.

WHAT WILL PEOPLE SAY?

Some of the advocates of a married Catholic clergy feel that the married priests would best be employed in nonparochial assignments.

The underlying notion here seems to be that the American lay people are not ready to accept a married pastor or curate. We asked these respondents about parishioner approval: "In your own parish at the present time, do you think that the introduction of a married clergy would be approved by the parishioners?" Almost one hundred priests did not answer this question, most of whom are in non-parochial specialized work. We may assume, therefore, that the great majority who did answer it have sufficient knowledge of the lay persons' attitudes on which to base their own estimates.

We found that the type of employment a priest currently has is apparently not a factor in this opinion, both those in and those out of parish work giving about the same proportionate answers. Table 8.6, however, reveals that the oldest priests are much more likely (62%) than the youngest (35%) to say that "hardly any" of the parishioners would accept a married clergy. This may reflect also age differences of opinion among the laity. A part-time curate from Kansas in his later forties thinks that the age level of the parishioners would make a difference. He is convinced that in the newer suburban parishes made up of young families most of the lay people under forty years of age are ready to accept a married clergy in the Catholic parish. If this is the case one would expect that more of the men under thirty-five years of age in Table 8.6 would have indicated it.

Table 8.6 Estimate by priests of extent of parishioner approval of married Catholic clergy, by age categories

	Under 35 years	35 to 49 years	All respondents	50 years and over
Most would approve	9%	8%	8%	9%
More than half of them would	8	6	3	7
About half	16	15	12	15
Less than half	32	26	15	28
Hardly any	35	45	62	41
(Number of respondents)	(1,493)	(1,267)	(193)	(2,953)

The Newsweek Poll, taken by Louis Harris and Associates several months after the present survey, reports that nearly half (48%) of the adult Catholic laity approve the priest's freedom to marry.[18] The answers distributed in Table 8.6 refer to the immediate parish situation and not to the general question of freedom to marry. They show that only a minority (16%) of the priests think that more than half of the parishioners would accept a married clergy. On the other hand, seven out of ten (69%) believe that less than half of the people would accept the change. One may speculate that the priests do not really know the mind of their parishioners, or perhaps that their divergence from the Harris Poll may mean that the attitudes of the laity have changed as a consequence of the wide publicity attending the preliminary release of the findings of the present survey.

There is evidence in their comments that these priests are concerned about the attitudes of parishioners on this subject. A non-curate in his early thirties from a Kansas diocese says that "all the questions about marriage in this survey are presuming that an ideal situation existed, namely that the Catholics would accept married priests. While I favor it now, maybe it will be fifty years before the people accept it." A curate in his late twenties from Pennsylvania remarks cautiously that before he would ask permission to marry he "would first want to observe the reaction of the laity to such a revolutionary change. I don't expect this challenge to occur in twentieth-century America. And after that—who cares?"

There was also the atypical remark of a Kentucky curate in his late thirties who thinks that "the question is none of the parishioners' business. This touches intimately on the personal life of the priest and not his parishioners. It should be his and only his decision. I believe that a married priest could serve his parish as well as a celibate and that the parishioners should not be involved in the decision." Yet there can be no doubt that the effectiveness of the parish priest depends heavily on the kind of relationship he has with the parishioners and that the attitudes of the laity are an important element in that relationship. We therefore asked this question in the survey: "Do you think that in America the married clergy would be more, or less, effective than the celibate clergy in the parish ministry?" We were not asking then whether marriage would benefit the individual priest, but whether it would benefit his work in the parish. The following Table distributes the answers to this question.

Table 8.7   Estimate by priests on whether married clergy would be more effective than celibate clergy in parish ministry, by age categories

	Under 35 years	35 to 49 years	50 years and over	All respondents
Married clergy less effective	48%	58%	74%	54%
More effective	16	13	8	14
Makes no difference	36	29	18	32
(Number of respondents)	(1,478)	(1,293)	(201)	(2,972)

The largest difference of opinion, as we note in Table 8.7 is a difference of age, with the oldest priests much more likely (74%) than the youngest (48%) to say that married clergy would be less effective. We have seen that the younger men discuss the question more and are more in favor of a married clergy; they are also less negative about laity reaction and about the parochial effectiveness of the change. Nevertheless, there remains the opinion that the effectiveness of the married priest depends also on the kind of assignment he has in the diocese. A young curate from Rhode Island refines this concept even further in relation to the parish: "It would be bettter to have two types of parish priests: a full-time celibate clergy who would always be available to the people; and a part-time married clergy who would serve as auxiliaries to the parish on week-ends but would have lay occupations during the week." A Virginia curate in his late twenties believes that the real question is not whether the priests should be allowed to marry, but whether married men should be ordained to the priesthood.[19] It is, of course, a well-known fact that the Church has accepted and ordained some married men who were former Protestant ministers.

One of the most frequently repeated arguments in support of the celibate clergy is the belief that marriage and family would tend to distract the priest from his main function and thus make him less effective in his work. An Alabama curate in his late thirties says simply that "a married clergy has less time for the apostolate and is, therefore, generally less effective. But I also believe that this should be a matter of free choice." On the other hand, a Michigan curate in the same age bracket says, "I think that I could be a better, holier, more effective priest if I had the right companion." Probably any married man in any occupation is affected in his work performance by the kind of wife he has, but there is hardly any research on this question among the married clergy of the Protestant churches.[20]

If we leave the matter of parochial effectiveness for a moment and note that a substantial minority (25%) of these lower-echelon priests are in nonparish assignments, we may consider the comment of a New York curate in his early thirties. He says that "the parish clergy should remain celibate. Members of the diocesan curia, catechetical directors, teachers and others in nonparochial work, should be allowed to marry. Celibates serving in the parish should retain the option, but if they marry they should go into nonparochial jobs." The work demands on the parish priest are not heavier than those on the priest specialist, but they are of a different kind involving the clergy differently with the people they serve. We have seen in Table 8.7 that the respondents generally (54%) think married clergy would be less effective than celibate clergy in the parish ministry. When we look at the answers by type of employment we find that somewhat more of the specialists (58%) than of the full-time curates (53%) hold this negative opinion.

In the comparison between the married and the celibate life we are able to provide another research finding that seems relevant. We asked both the clergy and the laity in the 1960 survey whether they thought the "worries" of the parish priest are heavier, or lighter, than those of the average married man. We have already seen (Tables 6.12, 6.13) that the lay friends of priests believe that the work demands on the parish clergy are greater than the priests themselves think they are. Here, in Table 8.8, we find that a large number of

Table 8.8 Estimates of clergy and laity in 1960 survey on whether parish priests' "worries" are greater than those of married men

	Clergy	Laity
Priests' are much heavier	6%	25%
Somewhat heavier	13	20
About the same	19	28
Somewhat lighter	34	19
Much lighter	28	8
(Number of respondents)	(2,161)	(2,197)

the laity (45%) think that the parish priest has heavier burdens than the married man, but only one out of five (19%) priests would agree with them.

It appears, then, that diocesan parish priests have a sympathetic appreciation of the married man's worries and burdens. More than three out of five of them (62%), as compared to less than three out of ten (27%) lay people, think that the worries of the parish priest are "much" or "somewhat" lighter than those of married men. It is an interesting fact that the opinions of married and single people differ in this regard. As we found in the earlier survey, "it is fairly clear that the married parishioners are not quite so sympathetic to the hardships of the priest's job as are the unmarried. Perhaps it is true that the work, worry, and responsibility of the married men are greater—or seem greater to themselves—than those of either the single layman or the parish priest."[21] Comparative opinions of this kind indicate that the image that one group of people has of another is colored by the personal experiences of the people making the judgment.

FOR AND AGAINST MARRIAGE

As far as we can estimate from the data in Table 8.5, approximately one third of the men who left the priesthood did not enter marriage, yet there can be little doubt that the demands of celibacy on the one hand and the attractions of marriage on the other have an influence on most men who give up the priesthood. It is clear from the data in this chapter that some look with favor on a married clergy and some do not. We were curious to test the hypothesis that the attitude of the priest toward this question would be a factor also in some of his other responses. We, therefore, selected two opposite categories from the respondents in Table 8.2 and Table 8.3, those who most favor a married clergy (338 men) and those who most favor a celibate clergy (777 men) among the diocesan priests. One group favors freedom of choice to marry both before and after ordination and also says that they "unquestionably" or "very likely" would marry if the Church permitted it. The contrasting group is made up of those who are against freedom of choice to marry and who also say that they "definitely" or "very likely" would not marry if given the choice. Let us see how they differ in their answers in Table 8.9.

Table 8.9 Responses of priests who are pro-marriage and pro-celibacy to selected questions on priestly career

	Approve married clergy	Approve celibate clergy	All respondents
Would hesitate now to enter seminary	42%	4%	13%
(Number of respondents)	(333)	(763)	(2,977)
Does not attempt to interest boys in priestly vocation	40	17	23
(Number of respondents)	(337)	(776)	(3,032)
Unwillingness to lead single life is very serious hindrance to seminary	72	24	39
(Number of respondents)	(332)	(740)	(2,948)
Voluntary resignation from priesthood should be allowed	82	44	64
(Number of respondents)	(336)	(769)	(3,027)

We may say then that these two polar categories take the strongest stand on either side of the controversy over a married clergy. The most convinced proponents of celibacy are more than twice as numerous (25%) as the most convinced proponents of a married clergy (11%) in proportion to the total number of respondents to this survey. We would expect then that these two opposing groups express very different opinions about other relevant issues in this survey. Table 8.9 shows that those who approve a married clergy are about ten times (42%) as likely as the others (4%) to say that if they could choose again they would hesitate to enter the seminary. They are much more ready than the others (40% to 17%) to admit that they are "not at all" or "hardly at all" personally involved in attempting to interest boys in the priestly vocation. They are three times more convinced (72% to 24%) that the unwillingness to lead a single life is a "very serious" reason why young men do not enter the seminary.

They are also much more ready to say (82% to 44%) that it should be possible to have voluntary resignation or an honorable discharge from the priesthood. Table 8.9 shows that these two sets of men differ enormously in their views on the priestly career. Let us see, in Table 8.10, how they differ on questions more relevant to celibacy.

Table 8.10   Responses of priests who are pro-marriage and pro-celibacy to selected questions about the married clergy

	Approve married clergy	Approve celibate clergy	All respondents
Talk frequently with fellow-priests about question of married clergy	65%	18%	33%
(Number of respondents)	(337)	(775)	(3,037)
Married clergy more effective than celibate in parish ministry	52	1	14
(Number of respondents)	(336)	(775)	(2,972)
More than half the parishioners would accept married priests	47	1	16
(Number of respondents)	(333)	(755)	(2,953)
Only celibates should be promoted to pastorate	8	33	18
(Number of respondents)	(334)	(754)	(3,005)
Only celibates should be promoted to episcopate	25	55	39
(Number of respondents)	(337)	(757)	(3,011)
Married ex-priests should leave their wives before reacceptance to the sacraments	1	20	8
(Number of respondents)	(336)	(746)	(2,965)

The contrasting responses reported in Table 8.10 are simply a confirmation of the fact that these two groups of priests disagree very widely on all the items that are in any way relevant to the question of a married priesthood in the Latin rite. Except for the first item, about the frequency of discussing the subject, the other responses are judgments and opinions. Those who want a married clergy tend to think that they would be effective in the parish ministry and that the parishioners would accept them as married priests.[22] Since these are hypothetical questions there are no research data to verify or deny either of these opinions. The three remaining items in the Table deal with what "should" be done. No one knows what will happen about promotions to the pastorate and episcopacy in the event of a married clergy in the Latin rite. On the final question it appears that Rome is currently much more lenient than it was in readmitting to the sacraments ex-priests who have married, a change applauded by more than nine out of ten respondents to this survey.

If we look at the last column in Table 8.9 and Table 8.10 we find that the priests who oppose each other on the question of married clergy are far to either side of the opinions expressed by the total universe of respondents. In this sense neither group is truly representative of the general thinking of the lower-echelon diocesan clergy, nor are they expected to be. They represent extremes of attitudes and opinions. Certain other characteristics may be noted about these two sets of diocesan priests. Most of those who favor a married clergy are under thirty-five years of age, and they are more likely than the advocates of clerical celibacy to have made their high school in a minor seminary. What seems of more pertinence, however, is the fact that those who want a married clergy do not communicate so well with their pastor or immediate superior, they feel themselves more remote from their bishop, and they do not feel that their talents are being well used.

SUMMARY

The survey data discussed in this chapter show that the possibility of a married priesthood in the Latin rite is widely discussed among the priests themselves. Three out of five of these diocesan clergy think that Catholic priests should have freedom of choice to marry, but they are not so sure about either the effectiveness of married priests in the parish ministry or the willingness of parishioners to accept them. In all of these questions the youngest clergy are more affirmative than the oldest, and this includes the small minority who think that they themselves would marry if the Church changes its regulations.

The overwhelming majority of these respondents believe that ex-priests who have married should be reinstated as practicing Catholics without having to break up their marriage. They report that only a very small proportion of their ordination class has abandoned the priesthood and an even smaller proportion has married. In comparing the responses of those who hold extreme views of pro-marriage and pro-celibacy, we find that they have contrasting attitudes about the seminary and about resignation from the priesthood. It appears that neither the strongest advocates of celibacy nor the strongest advocates of a married clergy are representative of the average diocesan priest.

NOTES

1. *On the Church*, Article 42, where we read also that celibacy, or virginity, is a "precious gift of divine grace which the Father gives to some men" so that by it "they can more easily devote their entire selves to God along with undivided heart."

2. *Priestly Formation*, Article 10, where celibacy is shown to be "a kind of freedom at the service of charity," a point made by David P. O'Neill, *Priestly Celibacy and Maturity* (New York: Sheed and Ward, 1965), p. 159, where he says that "In this spending of himself in the service of Lord and people, the priest is witnessing to love through the total commitment of his celibacy."

3. *Ministry and Life of Priests*, Article 16. Xavier Rynne, *Letters from Vatican City* (New York: Farrar, Straus & Giroux, 1963), pp. 168–69, tells of a Dominican theologian who was first barred from Rome for publishing a pamphlet discussing changes in clerical celibacy, and then was brought back by Pope John.

4. Michael Novak, *The Open Church* (New York: Macmillan, 1964), p. 123, observes that "there seemed to be an almost absolute block in the minds of some of the bishops against uniting marriage to holy orders in any form. It seemed to outsiders that the celibacy of these bishops had been so precarious, at least unconsciously, that if they had had the choice, they would never have accepted it. How else explain the claim that if deacons could marry fewer would wish to be priests?"

5. Xavier Rynne, *The Second Session* (New York: Farrar, Straus, 1964), p. 104. Nevertheless, Pope Paul's encyclical on celibacy pointed out that Vatican II "foresaw the possibility of conferring holy diaconate on men of mature age who are already married."

6. R. J. Bunnik, "The Question of Married Priests," *Cross Currents*, Vol. 15, 1965, pp. 407–31, and continued in Vol. 16, pp. 81–112. One may select out of the growing literature on this subject two books with opposing views, Ida Gorres, *Is Celibacy Outdated?* (Westminster: Newman Press, 1965) and Pierre Hermand, *The Priest, Celibate or Married?* (Baltimore: Helicon Press, 1966).

7. The National Association for Pastoral Renewal has encouraged wider surveys of clerical opinion. In June, 1967, Pope Paul noted that ecclesiastical celibacy has today been examined more penetratingly than every before, but suggests that a further study may be allowed of married Protestant clergymen and of the "possibility of admitting to priestly functions" those who would join the Catholic Church. This break with the traditional pattern has already been made in a number of cases of former Protestant ministers who remained married when they became Catholic priests.

8. See Joseph H. Fichter, "That 'Celibacy' Survey," *America*, January 21, 1967, pp. 92–94.

9. O'Neill, *op. cit.*, p. 33. See also Jean Rosenbaum, "A Psychoanalyst's Case for Celibacy," *The Catholic World*, May 1967, pp. 107–110. For some historical perspectives on the subject see the entire issue of *Resonance*, Fall 1966, "The Law on Celibacy: Soundings from Its History," which includes a useful selected bibliography.

10. See the amusing piece by John Cope Stanton, "A Hen-Pecked Clergy?" *The Priest*, Vol. 22, No. 10, October 1966, pp. 795–96, who concludes that the law on celibacy "is in no danger, immediate or even remote." Also in the lighter vein is P. J. Laux, "Fly Now, Pay Later," *America*, September 24, 1966, pp. 340–41.

11. William Douglas, *Ministers' Wives* (New York: Harper & Row, 1965), p. 260. For a rather somber historical account see Roland Bainton, "The Office of the Minister's Wife in New England," *Harvard Divinity School Bulletin*, Vol. 21, November 5, 1956, pp. 37–59.

12. A California curate in his late thirties says that "we go out of our way to help non-Catholics who have been married three or four times to become Catholic and get married in the Church. But the married priest who had served the Church faithfully for years is often treated as though he had commited the unforgivable sin."

13. See above, Chapter 7, "Facets of the Career," Table 7.16.

14. O'Neill, *op. cit.*, p. 43.

15. In May 1967, the Chancellor of the Archdiocese of Cincinnati, Henry Vogelpohl, announced that during the years from 1946 to 1966, only seven out of 619 diocesan priests left the priesthood, a little more than 1 per cent (*Cincinnati Enquirer*, May 21, 1967). See J. Abbo, "The Problem of Lapsed Priests," *Jurist*, Vol. 23, April 1963, pp. 153–79; also *The Priest*, Vol. 19, October 1963, pp. 839–42. Bunnik, *op. cit.*, p. 103, cites *Paris Match*, September 11, 1963, pp. 60–63, for "unofficial estimates" that 10 per cent of the priests in the Western Church "are in open conflict with the law of celibacy."

16. See *Religion as an Occupation*, Chapter 8, "Giving Up the Vocation," pp.

185–209. According to the Pope's encyclical on celibacy, defections from the priesthood are due to either the priest's moral failure or to an error of judgment by those who approved the fitness of the candidate. "The responsibility falls not on consecrated celibacy in itself."

17. This problem is recognized also in studies of Protestant clergymen. See Edgar W. Mills, *Career Change Among Ministers* (Harvard University, Center for Research in Careers, 1966), pp. 1–3, 21–28.

18. "How U.S. Catholics View Their Church," *Newsweek*, March 20, 1967, pp. 68–75. The *Tablet* of London reported in October, 1966, that 68 per cent of Dutch Catholics prefer married clergy.

19. This is advocated also in an editorial, "Married Priests?" in the *Commonweal*, May 15, 1964, pp. 223–24. "There are many married men who would make excellent priests, but who do not feel called to celibacy." See also Aiden M. Carr, "Celibacy and Convert Clergymen," *Homiletic and Pastoral Review*, November 1962, pp. 167–69. The notion that celibacy is "part of a package deal" if a man wants to be a priest is discussed by John L. McKenzie in his column Q.E.D., *The Critic*, June–July, 1967, pp. 6–8, 91–92, and in other words by Leo J. Trese, *A Man Approved* (New York: Sheed and Ward), pp. 54–56.

20. See, however, John Scanzoni, "Resolution of Occupational-Conjugal Role Conflict in Clergy Marriages," *Journal of Marriage and Family*, Vol. 27, August 1965, pp. 396–402. There is ample evidence that the Protestant parish minister is sometimes forced to put his wife and family in second place to Church work. See the study of the wives of Baptist ministers by John Koehler, "The Minister as a Family Man," *Pastoral Psychology*, September 1960, pp. 12–15.

21. See *Priest and People*, p. 76.

22. Although there are exceptions, Protestant congregations expect and prefer their pastor to be a married man, exactly the opposite of the Catholic expectation. Among other reasons is the notion that a married man is more competent than a bachelor in counseling others. For an excellent discussion see J. C. Wynn, *Pastoral Ministry to Families* (Philadelphia: Westminster, 1957), Chapter 8, "The Pastor as a Family Man," pp. 181–201.

CHAPTER

9

MATTERS OF CONSCIENCE

Western culture, with the strong influence of Christianity, has gradually evolved a social system in which the freedom of the individual conscience is of paramount importance. The Fathers of the Second Vatican Council underscored this concept with the words: "Conscience is the most secret core and sanctuary of a man. There he is alone with God, whose voice echoes in his depths. In a wonderful manner conscience reveals that law which is fulfilled by love of God and neighbor. In fidelity to conscience, Christians are joined with the rest of men in the search for truth, and for the genuine solution to the numerous problems that arise in the life of individuals and from social relationships. Hence, the more that a correct conscience holds sway, the more persons and groups turn aside from blind choice and strive to be guided by objective norms of morality."[1]

The traditional teaching that a man must have the liberty to exercise his conscience according to objective norms of morality is easily and widely accepted. In the concrete situation, however, problems of human relations arise when there is disagreement about the "objective" norms of morality. Inner conflicts of conscience arise when this disagreement appears in a social system like the Church between a subordinate who has voluntarily promised obedience and a superior who possesses legitimately constituted authority. The explanation that "I was only following orders—like a good soldier," has not been acceptable in our day in obvious instances of cruelty and atrocity. Indeed, the main moral thrust of the Nürnberg trials of war criminals was precisely this point: a person is guilty if he obediently performs an action that "everybody knows" is evil.

Conversely, a priest can no longer be expected to accept conscientiously a statement like this from his Bishop: "You have made a vow of obedience. Just do what you are told, and it will be on my conscience, not yours." In the priest–bishop relationship, the moral problem becomes acute when the morality of an action is not clear-cut, or when it is obvious to either the bishop or the priest, but not to both. Nevertheless, the Council Fathers solemnly declared that "in all his activity a man is bound to follow his conscience, in order that he may come to God, for whom he was created. It follows that he is not to be forced to act in a manner contrary to his conscience."[2]

PRIESTS' RIGHTS IN CONSCIENCE

In a religious organization like the diocese or the parish, in which both the superior and the subordinate are presumed to have "good will," that is, the desire to follow a "right conscience," the problem involves the correct interpretation of obedience and authority. MacNutt uses the following simple example: "Suppose a superior (or pastor) objects to carrying out the changes in the liturgy. Should the subjects (or assistants in a parish) calmly accept his decision, knowing that the mind of the Church demands an implementation of the liturgical renewal? Should the assistants say nothing to a man who does not himself comply with the mind of the Church? And the laity, too: should they suffer in silence?"[3]

In many instances of disagreement of this kind, it seems fairly easy to decide who is right and who is wrong. In other cases, especially in areas where moral latitude is allowable, much confusion exists. For this reason some of the clergy advisors in the preparatory stage to this survey strongly urged that the question of the priests' rights in conscience be included. Their feeling was similar to that of a California curate in his early thirties who wrote on the questionnaire: "Maybe it is sad ignorance on my part but I am terribly confused about the question of freedom of conscience versus authority. I wish this matter were more fully discussed by the experts and clear directives given for us to follow. It seems that years ago the person in authority was always right and that strict obedience was the order of the day. Nowadays things are certainly different, and I think all for the better, but also very confusing."

In this day, when clergy and religious sometimes become involved in protest movements that oppose higher policy, both political and ecclesiastical, the problem of their rights in conscience becomes of some practical importance. We therefore asked the following question of these lower-echelon diocesan priests: "Some priests are impelled by conscience to speak out, and act, on controversial issues (race, Vietnam, strikes, etc.). Would you agree that they have this right in conscience?" Table 9.1 distributes their responses according to age groupings.

Table 9.1 Response, by age categories, on priest's right in conscience to speak out and act on controversial issues

	Under 35 years	35 to 49 years	50 years and over	All respondents
Agree	80%	70%	53%	74%
Disagree	9	17	29	14
Neutral	7	8	12	8
Don't know	4	5	6	4
(Number of respondents)	(1,514)	(1,312)	(201)	(3,027)

Since freedom of conscience is a deep-rooted traditional principle of Christian morality, it is to be expected that the great majority (74%) of these priests agree that a man has the right in conscience to speak out and to act on controversial issues.[4] If this is a traditional teaching of the Church, one wonders why the oldest men are more than three times as likely (29%) as the youngest (9%) to be in disagreement. The general attitude of the young clergy seems to be expressed by an Ohio curate in his late twenties who says that he "has not only the right, but also the duty, to protest." One of the older noncurates from Massachusetts shows a degree of hesitation in his comments. He defends the right of conscience but adds that "a priest is viewed by the public as speaking for the Church.

If he is to speak out he should make it clear that he does so as an individual; that he does not speak for all priests or for the Church."

It seems then a curious finding, as demonstrated in Table 9.1, that the attitude about the expression of one's right of conscience is largely a function of age. Among these respondents it does not depend on the position, or the kind of employment, the priest has. The answers are distributed in approximately the same proportions for full-time curates, part-time curates, and those in specialized diocesan work. Regardless of age or function, however, they probably all agree to the importance of prudence, if that virtue is correctly defined. One of the oldest curates from a western diocese uses an almost frivolous example to demonstrate that "the right conscience does not justify imprudence or self-righteousness. Impelled by conscience, I once booed the officials at a football game. My priest companions took me home at the half, and I later thanked them because the importance of the game had taken precedence over the dignity of my collar."

In order to concretize this abstract principle we added the following question: "Would you stand up for a priest's right in conscience to speak, write, march, demonstrate, picket, etc., when this conflicts with the bishop's wishes?" The responses given in Table 9.2 indicate that it is one thing to proclaim an abstract principle but quite another to support the person who acts on the principle.[5] The fact that this question evoked many comments from the respondents who felt it necessary to make distinctions and explanations seems to indicate that this is a matter of much concern to the diocesan

Table 9.2 Response, by age groups, on type of support for the priest's right in conscience to act when this conflicts with the Bishop's wishes

	Under 35 years	35 to 49 years	50 years and over	All respondents
Publicly	24%	17%	11%	20%
Privately	43	36	25	39
Silently	9	9	12	9
Not at all	24	38	52	32
(Number of respondents)	(1,446)	(1,279)	(201)	(2,926)

clergy. Some of them wanted an example spelled out showing whether the priest or the bishop was "right." One Ohio priest in his early forties said, "I presume here that the Bishop's wishes are rational and for the good of the public order." A part-time curate in the same age bracket from Wisconsin wanted to list some qualifications "because in our diocese the matter of rights in conscience has so often been clouded by the matter of civil disobedience."

One third (32%) of all respondents say that they would not in any way support a priest who follows his conscience against the wishes of the Bishop, and here again the age difference in attitude is considerable, with the oldest priests more than twice as likely (52%) as the youngest (24%) to answer in the negative. A California curate in his late thirties says frankly, "I would really like to support him publicly, but I hate to admit that I am afraid of the disapproval of the chancery." One of the youngest curates from New York explained, "If I did not agree the priest has the right to speak out, I obviously would not support him against the bishop. If I did agree with the priest, I hope I would not refuse to support him out of cowardice. But should I support him publicly? In some cases a public revolt might not be justified. In other cases, it might be justified but not beneficial. In still others, it might be demanded."

It is typical of the casuistry taught both in seminaries and in law schools that clergymen, like lawyers, tend to qualify their answers in a particular moral judgment. There would be no point in asking the question if we had stated clearly that the bishop was right, or that the priest was right. In any particular case it may be easy to judge by norms of objective morality that the expressed wishes of the bishop are right and the external action of the priest is wrong, or vice versa. We did not ask the respondents whether the bishop or the priest is morally justified when they are in conflict. We found that only a small minority (14%) disagreed with an abstract principle in Table 9.1, but that more than twice as many (32%) disagreed with the specific exercise of the principle. What made the difference between these two questions is the obedience-authority relationship as it operates concretely in the diocese. Put very simply, it means that eight out of ten of these respondents are so accustomed to accepting the wishes of their bishop that they are not willing to give public support to a felow priest's right in conscience to act against those wishes.

It appears then that freedom of conscience has its risks, and that clergymen who have patterned their lives on obedience to authority find it difficult to stand in public support of a fellow priest who is acting on his conscience. "Only in freedom can man direct himself toward goodness," say the Council Fathers. "Our contemporaries make much of this freedom and pursue it eagerly; and rightly so, to be sure."[6] They say further that "the gospel has a sacred reverence for the dignity of conscience and its freedom of choice," and further that "in the divine arrangement itself the rightful autonomy of the creature, and particularly of man, is not withdrawn. Rather it is re-established in its own dignity and strengthened in it."[7]

DUE PROCESS FOR PRIESTS

The lowly status of most of the diocesan priests who answered this survey makes particularly pertinent the whole question of the rights of the clergy. When a priest gets in trouble with the chancery or does something to which the Bishop takes offense he becomes subject to disciplinary action. We have no way of knowing how many diocesan priests are annually suspended or otherwise penalized without due process. Among the propositions that received the highest consensus on this survey is the almost universal agreement (95%) to the statement that "a priest should have a chance to defend his case

Table 9.3   Response, by age categories, concering opportunity of accused priest to defend his case and face his accusers

	Under 35 years	35 to 49 years	50 years and over	All respondents
Agree	95%	94%	95%	95%
Disagree	1	2	*	1
Neutral	2	3	2	2
Don't know	2	1	3	2
(Number of respondents)	(1,517)	(1,315)	(204)	(3,036)

and to face his accusers before being suspended or otherwise penalized." A proposition of this kind seems so obviously in accord with American standards of fairness and justice that one may say it should not have been asked in the first place in a survey of this kind.

In writing about the case of Father DuBay, the editors of *America* said that "canonical procedure is so different from what citizens take for granted as a matter of natural justice that, in their eyes, the proceedings of ecclesiastical courts are suspect *ab initio*. American lawyers are invariably shocked when they learn that, as an ordinary matter, canon law makes no use of confrontation, cross-examination, or oral argument." They write also that "for the diocesan clergy, what the bishop says has been the end of the line—at least in practice. This is so not only because of the spiritually motivated reluctance of the vast majority of the clergy to engage in open conflict with their bishops, but also because the law itself gives the bishops an almost insuperable advantage."[8]

One of the oldest curates from a Pennsylvania diocese brings the matter down to a very practical level when he says that "assistants are sometimes moved from one parish to another because of an accusation made by their pastor to the bishop. I think the curate should know what the charge is and have a chance to defend or explain himself. If he is falsely accused he should be fully exonerated; if he is correctly accused he will have the chance to avoid a similar downfall. Even without a grievance committee in the diocese, decisions about his behavior should not be left to the one-sided judgment of the pastor or the bishop."[9]

At the Second Session of the Vatican Council Cardinal Frings of Cologne remarked that "no one should be judged and condemned without having been heard, without knowing what he is accused of, and without having the opportunity to amend what he can reasonably be reproached with." He was not making this reference to any diocesan bishop, chancery, or curia, but to the Holy Office in Rome, "whose methods and behavior do not conform at all to the modern era, and are a cause of scandal to the world."[10] A modernization and reform of these methods both in Rome and in the local diocese may be expected, not only as a consequence of such high-level criticism but also because exposure of the methods is increasing in the communications media and among the clergy who are unwilling to accept the "seal of secrecy" so often imposed on them.[11]

CIVIL RIGHTS AND VIETNAM

We move now from these questions about the priest and his rights as a member of the Church into the area of broader social questions. We wanted to know how the respondents express their social conscience about several of the large public issues about which the American people are concerned. Individual clergymen, as well as Church organizations and councils, have become increasingly involved in some of these national questions. When the Vatican Council urged social responsibility and participation, it did not exclude the clergy from this admonition. No longer can anyone "content himself with a merely individualistic morality. It grows increasingly true that the obligations of justice and love are fulfilled only if each person, contributing to the common good, according to his own abilities and the needs of others, also promotes and assists the public and private institutions dedicated to bettering the conditions of human life."[12]

It would be presumptuous to suggest that Vatican II lends approval to every large social movement in every country, or to the four specific American social programs about which we questioned the clergy in this survey. For example, the Council said that "the Church rejects, as foreign to the mind of Christ," any discrimination against men or harassment of them, because of their race, but this does not imply an endorsement of the current Negro civil rights movement in the United States.[13] Table 9.4 reveals that more than three quarters (77%) of the lower-echelon diocesan priests approve this movement.

It is probably to be expected that clergymen who support their fellow priests in their right of conscience would also be strongly in support of the Negro civil rights movement. We have seen in Table 9.3 that the age of the respondent was not a factor of differential attitudes on the right of a priest to defend his case and face his accusers.[14] Age does make a difference, however, in the matter of the civil rights movement, with the youngest much more likely (80%) than the oldest (65%) to express approval. The problem of legalism, of obedience and authority, was raised in this connection. A curate from Florida, in his early thirties, wrote "I approve

Table 9.4 Distribution of attitudes, by age categories, on the Negro civil rights movement

	Under 35 years	35 to 49 years	50 years and over	All respondents
Approve	80%	75%	65%	77%
Disapprove	10	13	14	12
Neutral	10	12	21	11
(Number of respondents)	(1,510)	(1,311)	(201)	(3,022)

the civil rights movement in principle, but believe at this stage that it is going too far and actually hurting itself by turning the neutrals and lukewarm against it. Now is the time to stop and solidify the progress already made. Later on a new thrust can be made if necessary."[15]

Some of these priests made the usual distinctions concerning civil disobedience in commenting about civil rights.[16] An Ohio curate in his early thirties writes, "I am all for civil rights if this means the attainment of racial equality, but I do not approve the rabble-rousing speeches and marches, in which people try to glorify themselves." A New York curate in his late forties says, "I do not approve a movement which preaches and encourages civil disobedience in the implementation of its program. I favor the movement in so far as it obeys the laws of the land and uses restraint in attaining its rightful objectives."

Although racial disturbances have not subsided in the United States, the majority of Americans seem to have accepted the principle of civil rights for all. The Vietnam war seems to have replaced the civil rights movement as the most controversial issue among the American people. We asked in this survey whether the priests approve or disapprove "the Administration conduct of Viet War." A national Gallup Poll taken at the same time as this survey asked: "Do you approve or disapprove of the way President Johnson is handling the situation in Vietnam?" The resultant comparative findings showed that 54 per cent of Catholics gave approval, as compared with 39 per cent Protestant and 41 per cent Jewish.[17]

The statistics in Table 9.5 show that approximately the same proportion (56%) of priest respondents as of American Catholics (54%) in the Gallup Poll also expressed approval. One of the differences, however, is that a higher percentage of the Catholic laity (31%) than of these diocesan priests (22%) showed disapproval. The remaining proportions in both instances were neutral or of no opinion. The internal age comparison in Table 9.5 reveals that

Table 9.5   Distribution of attitudes, by age categories, on Administration conduct of the Vietnam war

	Under 35 years	35 to 49 years	50 years and over	All respondents
Approve	50%	61%	69%	56%
Disapprove	26	18	11	22
Neutral	24	21	20	22
(Number of respondents)	(1,494)	(1,304)	(204)	(3,002)

the oldest group of priests was much more ready (69%) than the youngest (50%) to approve the way in which the Administration is conducting the war.

Opinions about the Vietnam war are more sharply divided than are those on the three other public issues discussed in this survey. These differences are discussed in the Catholic press where the generally favorable attitude of Cardinal Spellman, for example, has been both praised and deplored. Some of the Catholic clergy, Sisters, and lay people have participated in protest marches, demonstrations, and proclamations against the war in Vietnam. Other Catholics, including some members of the hierarchy, some representatives of the Knights of Columbus and of the Catholic War Veterans, have been highly critical of these peace protesters. This discrepancy of behavior and attitudes on both sides bespeaks a conflict of values as well as a confusion over the objective morality of the way the war is conducted.

POVERTY AND MEDICARE

In attempting to probe further the social awareness of these diocesan priests we asked also for their opinion about the domestic war on poverty. Three quarters of all respondents give their approval to this program, but here again, in Table 9.6, we see a dramatic contrast between the youngest (78%) and the oldest (65%) who express approval of the war on poverty. It should be noted, however, that the oldest group are more neutral (20%) than disapproving (15%).

Table 9.6 Distribution of attitudes, by age categories, on the domestic war on poverty

	Under 35 years	35 to 49 years	50 years and over	All respondents
Approve	78%	74%	65%	75%
Disapprove	12	14	15	13
Neutral	10	12	20	12
(Number of respondents)	(1,507)	(1,310)	(202)	(3,019)

Most of the priests seem to appreciate the need for this public program of assistance to the poor and take it for granted. Only a few made comments about the manner in which the program is being put into practice, complaining about inefficiency and "political bungling." One Pennsylvania curate in his late thirties, however, took this occasion to reflect about what he called the "poverty program" in his own diocese, saying that "the poor do not have the Gospel preached to them. The Catholic Church has given them no significant assistance here. A multi-million dollar minor seminary was built overlooking the city where there are numerous pockets of poverty wherein thousands languish."

Whatever the practical involvement of churchmen in any particular diocese there can be no doubt about the Church's official stand on the poverty of the masses. The so-called "social" encyclicals have dealt in some detail with the questions of poverty and the maldistribution of wealth.[18] The Second Vatican Council made even more explicit the function of the Christian and of the organized Church as a servant to those who are in need. "A man can scarcely arrive at the needed sense of responsibility unless his living conditions allow him to become conscious of his dignity, and to rise to his destiny by spending himself for God and for others. But human freedom is often crippled when a man falls into extreme poverty, just as it withers when he indulges in too many of life's comforts and imprisons himself in a kind of splendid isolation."[19]

Criticisms of the manner in which the poverty program operates locally are much more numerous than those made against the Medicare Program. Among the four public issues discussed in this survey the highest approval was given to the Medicare Program, and Table 9.7 shows that it is the only one of the four on which liberal approval is expressed by a higher proportion of the oldest priests (84%) than of the youngest (80%). Since medicare is aimed mainly at the medical assistance of senior citizens, it appears that advancing age turns the attention even of priests to this question.

Table 9.7 Distribution of attitudes, by age categories, on the Medicare Program

	Under 35 years	35 to 49 years	50 years and over	All respondents
Approve	80%	86%	84%	83%
Disapprove	6	6	6	6
Neutral	14	8	10	11
(Number of respondents)	(1,513)	(1,318)	(203)	(3,034)

The Council Fathers took the trouble to affirm that the Church itself should take care of infirm and aged priests. "In some nations," they said, "social security is not yet properly organized toward the support of the clergy. In such places Episcopal Conferences should see to it that under the vigilance of the hierarchy sufficient provision is made for an appropriate program of preventive medicine and so-called health benefits, and for the necessary support of priests burdened by infirmity, ill-health, or old age. To this end there can be set up diocesan programs—and these can be amalgamated—or programs simultaneously instituted for various dioceses, or associations initiated for a whole territory."[20]

STATUS AND SOCIAL VALUES

The four social issues we are discussing here, and about which we questioned the respondents, are instruments for the testing of one's general adherence to the American value system. These values constitute in a sense the norms of social morality, as widely accepted by the American people. When we ask the priests to make a judgment about these issues we are asking them to make a personal judgment about the morality of national programs and issues, to decide whether their own conscience conforms to the social conscience of the nation.

One has the right to expect that dedicated and educated churchmen will not only exhibit social awareness and concern about these matters but that they will also take a moral position regarding them.[21] This is a problem of conscience: to discern the difference between right and wrong, and even to attempt to choose the better over the merely good. In a rough and general way, the attitudes and judgments one expresses on these issues tend to place him either in the liberal or the conservative camp. Since there is not complete agreement among these respondents it is obvious that the adherence of the diocesan priest to one camp or the other depends on factors outside his status as a professional clergyman.

The research results here show that age is clearly one of these factors. On each of the four public issues discussed, the youngest priests are consistently closer to the liberal position than are the oldest priests. The comparative statistics on the Medicare Program in Table 9.7 show that the age of the respondent acts as a factor that transcends the liberal–conservative dichotomy. On the civil rights movement and on the poverty war the oldest men are more likely than the youngest to declare themselves neutral. The proportion of "neutrals" is higher on the complicated question of the Vietnam war, but in this case the disapproval by the youngest men (26%) is much higher than that of the oldest (11%).

It seems reasonable to assume that a man's occupation influences his position on the continuum from social liberalism to social conservatism. Professionals have attitudes different from those of blue-collar workers; and if other characteristics were held constant the clergyman would tend to reflect the attitudes of the professional class. All our respondents are professionals, but we have already seen that their opinions differ according to their age levels. Let us see whether they differ also according to the type of employment they have within the priesthood.

Table 9.8 shows that, while the statistical differences are not large, the men in specialized assignments are proportionately higher

Table 9.8 Distribution of approval, by type of employment, on selected controversial issues

	Full-time curates	Part-time	Non-curate
Negro civil rights movement	75%	79%	81%
(Number of respondents)	(1,673)	(596)	(753)
Domestic war on poverty	73	77	78
(Number of respondents)	(1,667)	(598)	(754)
The Medicare Program	82	80	86
(Number of respondents)	(1,679)	(599)	(756)
Administration conduct of Vietnam war	55	53	60
(Number of respondents)	(1,662)	(591)	(749)

in approval of the civil rights movement, the war on poverty and the medicare program. This finding gains added significance from the fact that the nonparochial priests are somewhat older than the parochial curates so that the conservative influence of age seems to be more than counterbalanced by their education and position.[22] If the nonparish priests have liberal attitudes on the three social issues already mentioned, they indicate more conservative attitudes on the question of the Administration's conduct of the Vietnam war. In this case they show a higher proportion of approval (60%) than do the men in full-time parish work (55%).

SUPPORTERS OF CLERGY RIGHTS

In order to probe more deeply the matters of conscience with which this chapter is concerned we decided to test the hypothesis that the strongest supporters of clergy rights also have the most liberal social attitudes on the several public issues we have discussed. For comparative purposes the data we have already seen in Tables 9.1 and 9.2 allow us to select and discuss two contrasting types of re-spondents. On the one side are the strongest supporters of clergy rights (573 men) who agree that the priest has a right in conscience to speak out and act on controversial issues and who say also that they would publicly support him in the exercise of that right. On the other side are those who seem to be opposed to clergy rights, a smaller number (364 men) who disagree that this right in conscience exists and who also say that they would in no way support the priest who attempts to exercise it against the wishes of the bishop.

As is already evident from Tables 9.1 and 9.2, the supporters of clergy rights are younger than the nonsupporters. When we look at them in this new comparison we find that six out of ten of them, as compared to one third (34%) of the latter, are below thirty-five years of age. Their opinions differ widely on many of the important questions of this survey. They show much more approval of a clergy senate, a personnel office and a grievance committee for priests. They are much more liberal in their attitudes toward a married clergy and toward ex-priests. They are more critical of their seminary ex-periences and of the diocesan communication system between superiors and subordinates. When we compare their answers in Table 9.9 we find that their social attitudes place them in two op-posing camps.

Table 9.9 demonstrates dramatically how widely divergent the social attitudes of these diocesan priests can be. It shows also that there is a relationship between personal convictions about matters of conscience and social convictions about matters of public concern. If the third column of the Table represents the "norm" or the average thinking of the lower-echelon diocesan priests, the other columns show how far these opposite groups of priests depart from

Table 9.9   Distribution of approval by supporters and nonsupporters of clergy rights, on selected controversial social issues

	Support clergy rights	Against clergy rights	All respondents
Negro civil rights movement	92%	48%	77%
(Number of respondents)	(570)	(375)	(3,022)
Domestic war on poverty	85	56	75
(Number of respondents)	(568)	(358)	(3,019)
The Medicare Program	88	75	83
(Number of respondents)	(570)	(364)	(3,034)
Administration conduct of Vietnam war	38	72	56
(Number of respondents)	(563)	(361)	(3,002)

that norm. They are farthest apart on the controversial issues of the Vietnam war and the civil rights movement, which have been prominent yardsticks for the measurement of liberal and conservative positions among Americans. It appears then that a priest's attitude toward change in the larger society is correlated with his attitude toward change within the Church.

We have seen time and again that various types of priests are contained within this totality of respondents. Besides the groups differing by age and type of employment, there are the alienated and the accepted, the satisfied and dissatisfied, those who are pro-marriage and those who are pro-celibacy. Here we seem to have discovered a factor of social style that tends to condition a man's organizational and personal relationships. The strongest supporters of clergy rights tend to be radicals who are not yet alienated but who have adopted an anti-status-quo style which may in time lead them to frustration and eventually perhaps to bitterness or defection.

SUMMARY

In this chapter we have found that the majority of respondents agree that priests must not be excluded from the traditional Christian teaching on the right of conscience, but that one third of them would in no way support the expression of this right of conscience against the wishes of the bishop. On both of these matters, the youngest priests hold views markedly different from the oldest, but regardless of age, there is almost unanimous opinion that a priest should have the right of self-defense against his accusers.[23]

Large majorities, but young priests more than the old, are favorable to the Negro civil rights movement and the domestic war on poverty. The oldest men are much more ready than the youngest to approve the administration conduct of the Vietnam war, and they are somewhat more in approval of the Medicare Program. Comparing them by type of employment we found that the men in specialized work were more likely than the full-time parish assistants to take a more liberal stance on public issues—the exception being the question of the war in Vietnam. More significant than age or type of employment was the attitude the priests had on the rights of the clergy. Those who were strongest in upholding the priest's private right of conscience were also strongly liberal on social issues of importance.

NOTES

1. *Church in the Modern World*, Article 16.
2. *On Religious Freedom*, Article 3. Perhaps more applicable in the context of the priest's right to social action is the next sentence of the document: "Nor, on the other hand, is he to be restrained from acting in accordance with his conscience, especially in matters religious."
3. Sylvester S. MacNutt, "The Problem of Obedience," *America*, Vol. 112, No. 1, January 2, 1965, pp. 14–18.
4. Paul Blanchard, the perennial critic of Catholicism, points out that in the Council discussions the rights of Church members themselves "were somehow maneuvered into the background out of the range of religious liberty." *Paul Blanchard on Vatican II* (Boston: Beacon Press, 1966), pp. 74–122.
5. The *Declaration on Religious Freedom*, Article 7, says that "the usages of society are to be the usages of freedom in their full range," to which Abbott, *op. cit.*, p. 687, footnote 21, adds: "Secular experts may well consider this the most significant sentence in the Declaration. It is a statement of the basic principle of the free society." John XXIII added the term freedom to those of truth, justice, and charity, previously asserted by his predecessors.
6. *Church in the Modern World*, Article 17.
7. *Ibid.*, Article 41.
8. Editorial in *America*, August 27, 1966, pp. 200–01.
9. See similar statements in William H. DuBay, *The Human Church* (New York: Doubleday, 1966), Chapter 7, "The Democratic Church." On the

other hand, according to a news release in May 1967, a group of pastors and senior priests in Detroit complained that "we are aware that the Archbishop has seldom spoken out in defense of the older priests; that he has seldom, if ever, rebuked those younger men who have made unkind and unjust blanket accusations against all pastors. We fear also that he considers all pastors as unfair in their treatment of assistants." *Star-Herald,* Camden, June 2, 1967.

10. Xavier Rynne, *The Second Session* (New York, Farrar, Straus & Giroux, 1964), p. 182.
11. See for example, John O'Connor, "The Bishops and the Press," *America,* February 4, 1967, pp. 180–82.
12. *Church in the Modern World,* Article 30.
13. *Relationship of the Church to Non-Christian Religions,* Article 5. The Latin term for "reject" is *reprobat,* which is practically as strong as *condemnat.* Abbott, *op. cit.,* p. 668, footnote 31, says that "the Council finds racial and religious discrimination too disturbing not to condemn," although otherwise the Council Fathers refrained from condemnations.
14. Clerical or lay status also makes a difference in the opinions of survey respondents. In a study of subscribers to the *National Catholic Reporter* a higher percentage of lay people (72%) than of clergy (67%) feel that the Church in America is moving "too slowly" in protecting the rights of priests.
15. Such cautionary remarks are made at every step in every movement to procure justice and the rights of people. Progressive social actionists insist, however, that "justice delayed is justice denied."
16. Civil disobedience is certainly a matter of conscience when "public authority oversteps its competence and oppresses the people." Limits are imposed by natural law and the gospel, but it is lawful for people "to defend their own rights and those of their fellow citizens against any abuse of this authority" (*The Church in the Modern World,* Article 74). The conscience problem becomes more immediate and delicate for the clergyman in a situation like that of March 1965, when the Catholic, Episcopal, and Methodist Bishops of Alabama opposed the civil rights demonstrations in Selma.
17. Religious News Service release report in the *Star-Herald,* Camden, September 30, 1966.
18. Pope Paul's 1967 encyclical on the *Progress of Peoples* is considered by many to be the "most advanced" social philosophy that has come from a papal document. See also Jean Calvez and Jacques Perrin, *The Church and Social Justice: Papal Social Teachings from Leo XIII to Pius XII* (Chicago: Regnery, 1961), and the subsequent volume by Jean Calvez, *The Social Thought of John XXIII* (Chicago: Regnery, 1964).
19. *Church in the Modern World,* Article 31.
20. *Ministry and Life of Priests,* Article 21.
21. There has been a growing recognition of the moral aspects of social values. For examples, see Robbin Williams, *American Society* (New York: Knopf, 1959), Chapter 11, "Value Orientation in American Society," pp. 372–442,

and Edward Tiryakian, ed., *Sociological Theory, Values, and Sociocultural Change* (New York: The Free Press, 1963).

22. Implicit here is the intriguing question of "reference group" influence. Since the full-time curates are "closer to the people," are they more likely to reflect the thinking of their parishioners? By their relative removal from such contacts can the specialized noncurates be freer of such influence?

23. See the discussion about "Silenced Priests," *Ave Maria*, Vol. 103, No. 2, January 8, 1966.

IMPLICATIONS AND INTERPRETATIONS

From the point of view of social reform and organizational renewal it is probably safe to say that a great deal of social science research is "wasted." This may be partly due to the fact that the researcher often considers his task completed after he has presented the findings to his sponsors in the form of a report or to the public in the form of a book. A more important factor in this "wastage" seems to lie in the inability, or perhaps sometimes unwillingness, on the part of responsible managers in an organization to accept, understand, interpret, and apply the research findings.

This failure to utilize the fruits of research—or even to sponsor research in the first place—is more apparent in voluntary service organizations, like Churches, than it is in profit-making productive organizations, like business corporations. The utilitarian value of social science research has been more readily recognized by big industry than by big religion, and this recognition has been steadily increasing. This is the reason why greater emphasis has been placed recently on the combination of research and development. In other words, planning is more and more based on solid information. From this point of view research data do not have their greatest value because they represent interesting information or "pure" knowledge but because they offer a springboard for change, improvement and development.

The results of the present survey offer insights into why things are as they are among the lower diocesan clergy. They also, more importantly, give us leads about what should be done. In other words, we have in this study strong evidence of the social sources of satisfaction and dissatisfaction among these priests. We have also strong hints about the changes that are needed and about the direction in which the adaptations should move. Obviously we cannot offer a handbook of ready-made and easily applicable solutions. American dioceses are much too varied and complicated as social systems to allow both universal and specific recommendations. Yet the generalizations that emerge from the study are open to local interpretation and application.

What follows is a series of propositions focusing on these research findings that seem of most practical importance. The acceptance of these propositions implies that the judgment of peers in subordinate positions—as distinct from the judgment of ecclesiastical superiors—is to be taken ever more seriously if the *aggiornamento* of the Church is to succeed. An improvement in the status and performance of the lower-echelon diocesan priests requires attention to these generalizations. The sequence with which they are presented here reflects the sequence of chapters in this book rather than a rank order of importance.

CHANGE IS HERE TO STAY

1. The universality and rapidity of social change in contemporary society were noted by the Fathers of the Second Vatican Council, stressed by social scientists, and also recognized by the priests who answered this survey. What is more significant, and not so often perceived, is that social change is a permanent phenomenon of our technological and industrial society. The Church as a human institution is caught up in this phenomenon, and the *Ecclesia semper reformanda* means that the updating process is a continuing renewal and not something that is ever fully and finally accomplished.

There is a need in the Church, at the diocesan and parochial levels, as well as at Rome, to accept a "mentality of continuing change." Some of the priests who answered this survey seem to expect that the Church will someday "get back to normal," that what is going on now is simply a transition from the old Church to the new Church, that somehow out of it all will come the fixed and final version of a system in which they can get back to work without anxiety or uneasiness. They forget that the Council itself recognized the People of God as a Pilgrim Church constantly and even restlessly on the move.

Change in the Church, as in the secular society, is not an uncontrollable blind force. It can be accelerated or slowed down, but never stopped. What is more important is that its direction and quality can be planned and promoted. Our research data demonstrate this possibility of controlled change. Liturgical adaptations have been promoted by the hierarchy and clergy and largely accepted by the laity. Participation of the laity in parish planning has not been planned and promoted in a similar fashion and consequently little change has occurred. The racial apostolate, a prime area of inexpert decisions at the diocesan level, has also been moving at a slow pace.

Two significant conclusions can be drawn for the practical utility of the American Church. (a) The first is that the areas in which faster and qualitative change is desired can be recognized and selected. Experts must be consulted, development must be planned, and practical methods employed. Norms and values guiding change have already been supplied by the Vatican Council. (b) The second is that the younger diocesan priests are much more aware than the older priests of the expectations of the Vatican Council and of the extent to which they have been, or have not been, implemented on the local scene. They are much more ready for change and willing to promote it than are the older men. The relative resistance to change on the part of men over fifty years of age becomes crucially signicant when we realize that most bishops, chancellors, and big-city pastors are in this age bracket.

POLICY-MAKING AND IMPLEMENTATION

2. The conceptual framework against which we measured the findings of this survey was provided by the documents of the Second Vatican Council. This implies an almost unique relationship between

the policy makers of the Church and those who are mainly responsible for implementing the policy decisions. They are the same
people. This is not usually the case in the military, in industrial,
educational, political, and other large-scale organizations. When
Pentagon officials make decisions, another set of people, the field
commanders, carry them out. When the board of directors in a business corporation makes policy, another group of men, the managers,
put the policy into operation. This kind of arrangement is common
in all large-scale modern organizations: the legislators are distinct
from the administrators.

The bishops who assembled at Rome to vote at the Council are
also the men who went back to their own dioceses, either as
Ordinaries or as auxiliaries, to administer the agreed-upon renewal
of the Church. This does not mean that they can, or intend to, do
it alone. Indeed, they had determined at Rome to find ways of involving all the People of God, the clergy and laity at all levels, in the
reformation of the Church. There is the added fact that the spotlight of public information which was turned on the Council continues to focus on the regional and diocesan Church. As a
consequence there is a legitimate and widely publicized contrast between what the bishops at Rome said they were going to do and
what they are actually doing at home.

The priests who answered this survey are rank-and-file workers
in the local diocese that is supposed to be renewed and reformed as
a consequence of Second Vatican. It appears that most of them have
read the documents emerging from the Council, or are at least aware
of the major recommendations made in them. They seem to be particularly aware that the bishops are now supposed to emphasize
their pastoral and apostolic role over their administrative and juridical role, and they are waiting for this change to occur.

The basic expectation here is not that bishops must cease to be
administrators but that they must learn to "manage" their clergy in
a manner quite different from the traditional system. This modern
manner still requires responsible authority and direction at the top
of the diocesan system—as in all effective social organizations—but
it requires also wide consultation, free and open two-way communication between superiors and subordinates, a willingness to listen

to the lower-echelon priests and to credit them with maturity, an honest admission that neither the decisions nor their implementation can be the work of one man alone, the bishop ordinary of the diocese. It is quite probable that some of the bishops are too old to change their ways, and that all of them find it difficult to discard ways that have been deeply and traditionally imbedded in the Church.

ALIGNMENT OF TRAINING AND OCCUPATION

3. Like every other occupational or professional system of employment, the Catholic Church has to recruit and train men, and to utilize properly their services. The Council underscored the significance of this fact by producing two separate documents on the priesthood and by commenting on the priestly role at appropriate points in all the other documents. Every other employment system —with the exception of the military—recruits its professionals after they have been trained elsewhere, as in colleges and universities. No outside educational agency prepares men for the priesthood. The seminaries hold the only franchise to educate men for this vocation so that their training is under the control of the organization that accepts them and employs them.

Something seems to have gone wrong with this system. The priests themselves do not exhibit a great enthusiasm in attempting to enroll candidates for the seminary. The attractiveness of the priesthood, as a lifetime commitment, seems to have diminshed in comparison with the increasing number of alternative careers open to American Catholic youth. These facts obviously call for a double reform: one that will modernize and renew the status and role of the diocesan clergy so that this vocation achieves a new image in the minds of prospective recruits, and secondly a reformation of the seminary training system which produces these priests.

The central finding here is that these respondents report inadequate career preparation for the very functions that absorb most of their time and energy. They are constantly dealing with people, counselling them, serving them as other Christs, and yet they complain that they had practically no training in social relations. The parishioners whom they serve constitute a social organization, the parish, and are involved in various subgroupings, yet the priests report that they were not trained to handle practical parochial problems.

The relationship between the training program and the occupational field itself requires adaptation of one to the other. Some of the older clergy say they were not properly prepared to meet the demands of the priest's work in the modern Church; some of the younger clergy say that the parish and diocese are not yet ready for the "new" ideas they learned in the seminary. In both cases these priests think of themselves as "misfits." In some dioceses the seminary faculty is "behind the times," and their priestly products are not able to cope with the modernizing Church. In other dioceses the seminary faculty is "ahead of the times," sending newly ordained priests into a work system that has not yet adjusted to the fruitful utilization of their zeal and knowledge. The obvious need is an intelligent coordination of both segments of the ecclesiastical employment system.

UPDATING PROFESSIONAL COMPETENCE

4. The so-called "knowledge explosion" in Western society has not left the Church and its clergy unaffected. Like other professional men, the clergyman needs not only a better preparatory training for his life career, but also a continual updating of his knowledge. This has been an ideal recommendation written earlier into the Canon Law of the Church and reemphasized by the Fathers of the Second Vatican Council. The notion has had to be abandoned that the priest was "finally ready" for his priestly work on the day of ordination, as well as the notion that he was "finally ready" to assume the responsibility of a pastorate after a period of apprenticeship as parish assistant.

Just as there is no end in sight for the changes occurring in the Church, so also there is no end or completion to the priest's education. It may be asserted that the individual priest should recognize this and go about the process of keeping himself informed by study and reading. The Council went beyond this attitude and said that it is the duty of the bishops to provide opportunities for the continuing education of their clergy. In the American employment system this means not only establishing "intra-company" institutes, but also providing time off with pay so that men may take refresher courses and enjoy sabbatical leaves of absence. The present survey reveals that the lower clergy are overwhelmingly in favor of this arrangement but that very few of them have had these opportunities during the past year.

Most of the diocesan priests seem to have been educated for the role of "general practitioner" in the parochial apostolate. Those who are specialists on nonparochial assignments have had more years of formal schooling and higher academic degrees. Whether or not the role of the priest specialist is expanded in the new Church, there seems to be a need of supplementing the general education of every parish priest with some kind of specialization. This means that every priest will have a subsidiary area of knowledge in which he exhibits a certain degree of expertise. The Council strongly urged that the Church through her priests be of service to the total society and not only to members of the parish. This impact of service can be made best by men who develop a specialized interest and ability that go beyond their parochial and sacramental role.

For full-time specialists in nonparochial work there is a need to expand the educational process beyond training in canon law and the sacred sciences under Catholic auspices. The priest specialists who teach in high schools, colleges, and seminaries, who are in the Newman apostolate, Catholic charities, and other supra-parochial activities, need a professional background and continuing education from whatever sources these are available. For certain purposes, these sources may well be graduate and professional schools in "secular" universities, or even in Protestant theological seminaries.

THE PASTOR AND WASTE OF TALENT

5. The importance of the pastor's role was spelled out in the documents of the Vatican Council; and data from empirical research show that the pastor is the "key person" in the operation of the parish as well as in the lives of the parish assistants. He is the immediate representative of the bishop and is able in many ways to ac-

celerate or impede the renewal of the Church at the level where the people are. Where the bishop is serious about promoting the aggiornamento, and where the pastor is intelligently and zealously "on the bishop's side," there is almost certain to be an acceptance of Christian renewal on the part of the faithful.

The day-by-day working conditions of the parish curate do not depend upon the chancery or the bishop but upon the manner in which the pastor manages the parish enterprise. If his relationship with the curate is that of a professional associate, rather than that of a father to his son, or of a master to his apprentice, the working conditions are likely to be satisfactory. The curates in every large diocese develop an informal system of ranking the desirability of curates' assignments, and the principal criterion of judgment is the pastor. A good parish for the curate is one where the pastor treats him with respect, encourages his talents, allows him responsibility, and involves him in parochial decisions.

The measure of an unsatisfactory parish appointment for the curate is most often the pastor who restrains the curate's zeal and talents by confining him to a limited and monotonous routine of repetitive tasks. If we realize that both self-respect and social status are closely related to the quality of role performance we may appreciate the fact that the curate is sometimes resentfully frustrated in his lowly position. If he is not permitted to use his talents and his capacity for work, he is likely to be both bored and dissatisfied. It is difficult to believe that the "boredom of the rectory" emerges from the nature of the priestly occupation rather than from the manner in which the pastor interprets that occupation for himself and particularly for the curate who has been assigned as his co-worker.

One of the most important conclusions from the present study is the widespread waste of talent among the full-time parish assistants, and the consequent restlessness and dissatisfaction among the lower-echelon diocesan clergy. The data show that the men in specialized nonparish assignments work much harder than the full-time curates. Furthermore, the curates who have good relations with their pastor work harder than those who do not get along well with their pastor. In both types of employment the hard workers exhibit a more satisfied, healthy, and positive attitude toward the Church and the priest-hood. Where priestly zeal is curtailed and where priestly talent is allowed to lie dormant, the progress of the parish, the diocese, and the Church suffers.

LACK OF CAREER MOBILITY

6. Regardless of ancient traditions of priestly work, the modern American priest is living in a social system where professional careers are important. The diocesan priest is not a monk living in the mass anonymity of a rural monastery where thoughts of personal career progress are a sign of sinful pride. The Council's emphasis on service to the world implies that the parish priest has not, and can-not, withdraw from the world. If he is to perform adequately and use the talents that are now wasted, the concept of his employment must be changed from that of a job-holder to that of a professional careerist.

Almost all of the recognized elements which constitute the normal professional career are absent from the life of the parish assistant. In most cases he receives an appointment instead of being offered a position and thus has no choice of his place of work or control over the conditions under which he will function. He is not allowed the typical professional opportunity to employ and develop his talents up to their capacity. There are no authentic criteria for the recogni-tion of merit and achievement. He may be moved from a "poor" parish to a "better" parish, but he seldom has any way of knowing whether this is meant as a promotion in recognition of his past services. The single significant promotion of his life is that to the pastorate, and this is based on seniority rather than on professional competence. One of the more startling findings of this survey is the large proportion of men who favor some form of honorable exit from the priesthood, a negative attitude that is necessarily bound up with the unsatisfactory career pattern of the priesthood.

The obvious implication of these findings is the need for a com-plete reformation of the current system of appointments, transfers, and promotions for diocesan priests. More important than the re-form of the mechanism of employment is a new conceptualization of the clerical vocation, one that genuinely defines the diocesan priest as a professional career man. When we talked about the relationship between pastor and assistant, we were talking about personal qualities which may conform to or override the institutional system. In the present case we are talking about behavior patterns that have been built into the institution and that require revision.

The large minority of nonparochial specialists who responded to this survey exemplify a kind of imperfect and tentative professionalization of the diocesan priesthood. They are doing the kind of work, like teaching, writing, counseling, social work, that has already been professionalized in the secular society outside the ecclesiastical structure. This is, in a sense, their subsidiary role in which they can measure their performance and progress according to nonecclesiastical work standards. The parish ministry in the Catholic Church does not have clear professional criteria of this kind. It is almost imperative that such criteria soon be developed.

CELIBATE AND MARRIED PRIESTS

7. The contentious question of a married diocesan clergy in the Latin rite will not be solved by ignoring it, nor is it likely to be discarded as a result of the 1967 papal encyclical on clerical celibacy. Pope Paul prohibited official discussion of the subject on the floor of the Second Vatican Council, and many bishops seem to have taken their cue from him in their reluctance to place it on the agenda of the National Conference of Bishops. As far as we can judge, it is only in the relatively recent past that serious attention has been given to the prospect of a married Catholic priesthood in the United States. There is little evidence that it was widely discussed by American clergy and laity before the Council, but our research data show clearly that the rank and file diocesan priests were interested in it after the Council.

The most publicized finding of this survey was the fact that 62 per cent of the respondents favor the diocesan priest's freedom of choice to marry. This means not only that they accept the statement of the Council that celibacy is not demanded by the very nature of the priesthood, but also that they want to remove celibacy as a condition for ordination to the priesthood. This position is perfectly orthodox and unassailable on doctrinal grounds. One may debate for or against its implementation with personal, practical, and moral arguments. The main resistance to change, however, seems to come from the fact that the celibate Catholic priesthood has been strongly institutionalized in Western society.

Like every strongly established behavior pattern, the custom of a celibate diocesan clergy cannot be treated in isolation from the total institutional structure in which it exists. The shift to a voluntary married clergy would entail other changes: revision of residence for the multi-staff rectory, a new salary scale to assure an adequate family wage, a new design for recruitment and training of seminarians, and many other changes that are probably unforeseen. The present systems, both diocesan and parochial, are "geared" to the continuance of the celibate clergy. The acceptance of a married clergy would require a substantial redesign of that system.

Aside from its effect upon the ecclesiastical institution, one cannot ignore the personal consequences of such a change. The large majority of these priests do not want marriage for themselves, which means that celibate and married priests must develop good working relations. For a while, at least, the oldest priests, and probably most of the pastors and diocesan administrators, would constitute an authoritative celibate age grouping distinct from the younger married clergy. Since the priest is in a profession of service to people his relationship with the laity may be significantly affected by a change in marital status. Basic also to the personal aspects of this change is the effect it may have upon him as a man of God and a Church professional.

FREEDOM AND OBEDIENCE

8. The Second Vatican Council decided that the Church should take a stance of openness to the whole world and particularly to the technological, industrial, secular, and progressive society of the West. If the Church is to adapt itself institutionally to this kind of social system, it must face the modern conceptions of freedom and author-

ity which most westerners accept as part of the culture. This poses a problem of substantial change away from the traditional patterns of relatively rigid authority and obedience. It means that the consciences of subordinates must be respected in a practical, and not merely theoretical, fashion.

The contrast between theoretical and practical attitudes toward freedom of conscience is sharply delineated in the responses to this survey. The approval of a priest's right in conscience is something quite different from the willingness to support that right when he attempts to exercise it. When one proposes a concrete situation in which the interests of various parties are in conflict, one must expect a "situational" answer. In the diocesan situation that now prevails —partly through habits of thought-training, but perhaps more because of actual experience in the priesthood—priests are reluctant to stand up for a fellow priest who follows his own conscience rather than that of the bishop.

The question of a "right" conscience and what to do about it seems to be one of the most troublesome personal problems bothering these priests. They have studied the blueprint for the renewed Church and they are not sure that they must wait for it to be mediated through their bishops, pastors, and other superiors before they can start to work on its fulfillment. Yet they are caught in a web of institutionalized patterns of obedience through which there runs a strand of fear that reprisals may be visited on nonconformists. They are not treated like mature professionals who have confidence in their own judgments and who are encouraged by Church superiors to follow their conscience.

The practical implication of these research findings is that the updating of the Church in America will develop a clerical obedience that is less subservient and fearful, and a hierarchial authority that is more permissive and humane. The social awareness exhibited by these priests indicates that they know that improvements in the American social system have often forced a clarification of the social conscience. The problem of civil disobedience will probably never be completely solved in any dynamic progressive society. If the dynamic institutionalized Church is to deal with the problem of personal conscience (of both clergy and laity), it must learn to accept the fact that conscience cannot be controlled completely from above in this kind of Church in this kind of society. It may also well accept with humility the fact that there is a fallibility of judgments of conscience in both superiors and subordinates.

THE QUESTIONNAIRE

Reverend and dear Father:

1. Vatican II strongly recommended that suitable means," especially social research," be employed and that "religious and social surveys" be made so that the apostolate of the Church can become more effective and fruitful. As a diocesan priest you are cordially invited to participiate in this nation-wide survey of *non-pastors* and *non-monsignors*. More than six thousand diocesan priests are being asked these questions in what is probably the largest research project of its kind ever undertaken in this country.

2. This survey is being financed by your fellow priests in many dioceses. Its contents emerge from the queries raised by diocesan priests since before Vatican II. The present form of the questionnaire is the result of long consultation and wide pre-testing among the priests of several dioceses. Some of it is pretty personal, but please be as frank and outspoken as you wish.

3. The questionnaire is designed to guarantee anonymity. Almost all the questions can be answered by placing a check mark in the appropriate ( ) parenthesis. Responses will be machine-punched and machine-tabulated; only statistical information will be released. Please read each item carefully and unhurriedly before answering it.

4. A major study of this type can be an effective instrument for the renewal of the Church only with divine blessing. We cannot serve

God well without His constant grace and protection. In His name, may we ask your prayers, and thank you for your cooperation.

5. How long have you been ordained?

1. ( ) 3 years or less	4. ( ) 10–12 years	7. ( ) 19–21 years
2. ( ) 4–6 years	5. ( ) 13–15	8. ( ) 22–24
3. ( ) 7–9	6. ( ) 16–18	9. ( ) 25 and over

6. How old were you on your last birthday?

		5. ( ) 45–49 years
1. ( ) Under 30 years	3. ( ) 35–39 years	6. ( ) 50–54
2. ( ) 30–34	4. ( ) 40–44	7. ( ) 55 and over

7. How old were you when you entered the seminary (i.e., first started to study for the priesthood)?

1. ( ) 13–14 years old	4. ( ) 17 years old	7. ( ) 20 years old
2. ( ) 15	5. ( ) 18	8. ( ) 21 or over
3. ( ) 16	6. ( ) 19	

8. If you had the chance to do it over again, at what age would you enter the seminary to start study for the priesthood?
Or would you enter at all? At age _____ years, or would hesitate to enter at all ( )

9. To what extent are you personally involved in attempting to interest boys in the priestly vocation?

1. ( ) Very much so	3. ( ) More or less	4. ( ) Hardly at all
2. ( ) Quite a bit		5. ( ) Not at all

10–14. Here is a list of reasons sometimes given why boys hesitate to enter the seminary. To what extent do you see these as serious reasons among the boys you know? (Please check each line)

	Very Serious	Moderately Serious	Hardly Serious
10. Attraction of other occupations	1. ( )	2. ( )	3. ( )
11. Lack of contact with priests	1. ( )	2. ( )	3. ( )
12. Feelings of unworthiness	1. ( )	2. ( )	3. ( )
13. Lack of encouragement from parents	1. ( )	2. ( )	3. ( )
14. Unwillingness to lead single life	1. ( )	2. ( )	3. ( )

15–18. To what extent do you feel that your own training in the major seminary helped you in your priestly life to do the following things?

	Very much so	Quite a bit	More or less	Hardly at all	Not at all
15. Lead a holy life	1. ( )	2. ( )	3. ( )	4. ( )	5. ( )
16. Lead an intellectual life	1. ( )	2. ( )	3. ( )	4. ( )	5. ( )
17. Deal with lay people	1. ( )	2. ( )	3. ( )	4. ( )	5. ( )
18. Handle practical parish problems	1. ( )	2. ( )	3. ( )	4. ( )	5. ( )

19. How many official "transfers" have you had since (and including) your first assignment after your ordination?————

20. Please check your current status:

1. ( ) Fulltime parish assist- ant
2. ( ) Assistant, but with some non-parish assignments
3. ( ) Am living here, but my main work is non-parochial

21. Are you on a "first-name" basis with your pastor (or the superior of the residence where you live?)

1. ( ) Usually
2. ( ) Sometimes
3. ( ) Seldom
4. ( ) Never

22. In general during the past year, has it been your experience that the Bishop Ordinary of the diocese takes a positive and personal interest in you?

1. ( ) Very much so
2. ( ) Quite a bit
3. ( ) More or less
4. ( ) Hardly at all
5. ( ) Not at all

23. Every priest deals with the Chancery Office of the diocese, and looks for both efficiency and "humaneness" in this dealing. How do you rate your Chancery Office?

1. ( ) High in both efficiency and humaneness
2. ( ) More efficient than humane
3. ( ) More humane than efficient
4. ( ) Poor in both efficiency and humaneness

24. Would you agree that a priest should have a chance to defend his case and to face his accusers before being suspended or otherwise penalized?

    1. (   ) Agree   3. (   ) Neutral
    2. (   ) Disagree   4. (   ) Don't know

25. Some priests are impelled by conscience to speak out, and act, on controversial issues (race, Vietnam, strikes, etc.) Would you agree that they have this "right in conscience?"

    1. (   ) Agree   3. (   ) Neutral
    2. (   ) Disagree   4. (   ) Don't know

26. Would you stand up for a priest's right in conscience to speak, write, march, demonstrate, picket, etc., when this conflicts with the Bishop's wishes? I would support him:

    1. (   ) Publicly   3. (   ) Silently
    2. (   ) Privately   4. (   ) Not at all

27–30. Vatican II suggests that there be free and open "two-way" communication between superiors and subordinates in the Church. To what extent does this now exist in your diocese, major seminary, with your bishop and pastor?

	Very much so	Quite a bit	More or less	Hardly at all	Not at all
27. Diocesan structure as a whole	1. ( )	2. ( )	3. ( )	4. ( )	5. ( )
28. Major seminary (if there is one)	1. ( )	2. ( )	3. ( )	4. ( )	5. ( )
29. With Ordinary of diocese	1. ( )	2. ( )	3. ( )	4. ( )	5. ( )
30. Your pastor (or local superior)	1. ( )	2. ( )	3. ( )	4. ( )	5. ( )

31. Some suggest that a full-time personnel committee made up of experienced and qualified priests should work with priests who have problems. Does your diocese have such a committee, and what do you think of it?

    1. (   ) We don't have one, but I approve the idea
    2. (   ) We do have one and I approve of it

3. ( ) We do have one, but I disapprove of it
4. ( ) We don't have one and I disapprove the idea

32. Some think there should also be an intermediary "grievance committee," elected by the priests themselves, to which priests can bring their complaints. Does your diocese have such a committee, and what do you think of it?

1. ( ) We don't have one, but I approve the idea
2. ( ) We do have one and I approve of it
3. ( ) We do have one, but I disapprove of it
4. ( ) We don't have one and I disapprove the idea

33. There has been talk of a "senate of clergy," elective representatives of the presbytery to assist the Bishop in governing the diocese. Does your diocese have such a senate, and what do you think of it?

1. ( ) We don't have one, but I approve the idea
2. ( ) We do have one and I approve of it
3. ( ) We do have one, but I disapprove of it
4. ( ) We don't have one and I disapprove the idea

34. There has been much written lately on the question of married clergy in the Roman rite. During the past year have you discussed this question with your fellow diocesan priests?

1. ( ) Frequently   3. ( ) Seldom
2. ( ) Occasionally   4. ( ) Never

35. In general, would you be in favor of the diocesan priest's freedom of choice to marry?

1. ( ) Yes, but only before   3. ( ) Both before and after
   ordination
2. ( ) Yes, but only after   4. ( ) No, not at all
   ordination

36. What about those priests who have left the ministry and married? Should they be allowed to return to the sacraments and remain married?

1. ( ) No, they should leave their wives first
2. ( ) Yes, but only if they have children
3. ( ) Yes, whether or not they have children

37. Do you think that in America the married clergy would be more, or less, effective than the celibate clergy in the parish ministry?

    1. (   ) Less effective　　　3. (   ) Makes no difference
    2. (   ) More effective

38. In your own parish at the present time, do you think that the introduction of a married clergy would be approved by:

    1. (   ) Most parishioners　　4. (   ) Less than half
    2. (   ) More than half of them　5. (   ) Hardly any
    3. (   ) About half

39–40. If there were a married priesthood, promotion to the pastorate and to the episcopacy should be allowed *only for celibates*. What do you think?

    To the pastorate:　1. (   ) Yes　2. (   ) No　3. (   ) Am not sure
    To the episcopacy: 1. (   ) Yes　2. (   ) No　3. (   ) Am not sure

41. If a married priesthood were permitted in the Roman rite, do you think that you would marry?

    1. (   ) Yes, unquestionably　4. (   ) Probably would not
    2. (   ) Very likely would　　5. (   ) Very likely not
    3. (   ) Probably would　　　6. (   ) Definitely would not

42–43. Including yourself, how many priests were there in your ordination class?

    ——— priests in my ordination class

44–45. As far as you know, how many of these have left the priesthood? How many of those who left have married?

    ——— in my class have left the priesthood
    ——— in my class have left and married

46. As in other professions and occupations, it should be possible to have voluntary resignation, or an "honorable discharge," from the priesthood. What do you think?

    1. (   ) Agree　　　3. (   ) Neutral
    2. (   ) Disagree　　4. (   ) Don't know

47–48. In general, and perhaps allowing for some exceptions, are you in favor of a definite retirement age for pastors and bishops?

For the pastors: 1. ( ) Yes 2. ( ) No 3. ( ) Am not sure
For the bishops: 1. ( ) Yes 2. ( ) No 3. ( ) Am not sure

49–57. Here are some statements that we hear priests making. Do you agree or disagree with them? (Please check each one)

	Agree	Disagree	Not sure
49. The diocese should have a personnel office to work out priests' assignments	1. ( )	2. ( )	3. ( )
50. Curates should be interviewed before receiving their appointments	1. ( )	2. ( )	3. ( )
51. Curates should have ample notice to prepare for new appointment	1. ( )	2. ( )	3. ( )
52. Curates who want to prepare for specialized work should be encouraged to do so	1. ( )	2. ( )	3. ( )
53. Curates should rotate parishes periodically to get a variety of experience	1. ( )	2. ( )	3. ( )
54. Curates should have choice of own separate residence or of living in parish rectory	1. ( )	2. ( )	3. ( )
55. Each priest should have his own office separate from his place of residence	1. ( )	2. ( )	3. ( )
56. Stipends and stole fees should be abolished in favor of graduated annual salary	1. ( )	2. ( )	3. ( )
57. Promotion to pastorate should be made on a basis of ability rather than seniority	1. ( )	2. ( )	3. ( )

58. It would be better if the Church dispensed with titles (like domestic prelate, papal chamberlain, prothonotary apostolic, etc.) for its priests.

1. ( ) Agree   3. ( ) Neutral
2. ( ) Disagree   4. ( ) Don't know

59. It would be better if the Catholic clergy in America wore regular "civilian" suits on the street, instead of the black suit and Roman collar.

    1. ( ) Agree   3. ( ) Neutral
    2. ( ) Disagree   4. ( ) Don't know

60. Diocesan priests should have periodical sabbatical leaves to take "refresher courses" in the work and problems of the ministry.

    1. ( ) Agree   3. ( ) Neutral
    2. ( ) Disagree   4. ( ) Don't know

61. It would be better if priests restrict their close friendships to fellow priests and deal with the laity only on a professional, impersonal level.

    1. ( ) Agree   3. ( ) Neutral
    2. ( ) Disagree   4. ( ) Don't know

62–67. Some people think that the Catholic Church has been moving too fast and others think it moves too slowly on the following issues. How do you feel about the rate of change in your own diocese? (Please make a check on each line)

	Too Fast	Too Slow	About Right
62. Liturgical adaptations	1. ( )	2. ( )	3. ( )
63. Inter-faith dialogue	1. ( )	2. ( )	3. ( )
64. Change of seminary routine	1. ( )	2. ( )	3. ( )
65. Racial apostolate	1. ( )	2. ( )	3. ( )
66. Laity in parish planning	1. ( )	2. ( )	3. ( )
67. Rules for mixed marriage	1. ( )	2. ( )	3. ( )

68–71. Here are several public programs which some people approve while others disapprove. How do you feel about them? (Please make a check on each line)

	Approve	Dis-approve	Am Neutral
68. The medicare program	1. ( )	2. ( )	3. ( )
69. Administration conduct of Viet War	1. ( )	2. ( )	3. ( )
70. Negro Civil Rights Movement	1. ( )	2. ( )	3. ( )
71. Domestic War on Poverty	1. ( )	2. ( )	3. ( )

72. Considering your talents and training, do you feel that the work you are expected to do in your current assignment is:

    1. ( ) More than you can handle
    2. ( ) Extending you just about to your capacity
    3. ( ) Only partly challenging your abilities
    4. ( ) Calling for little of your abilities

73. How would you rate, as informative and stimulating, the clergy conferences you attended in your diocese during the past twelve months?

    1. ( ) They were both informative and stimulating
    2. ( ) More informative than stimulating
    3. ( ) More stimulating than informative
    4. ( ) Neither informative nor stimulating

74. In general, would you say that the last annual diocesan priests' retreat you made was:

    1. ( ) Well-conducted and spiritually refreshing
    2. ( ) Well-conducted, but not spiritually refreshing
    3. ( ) Spiritually refreshing, but not well-conducted
    4. ( ) Neither well-conducted nor spiritually refreshing

75. How about "Days of Recollection?" Did you make at least one during the past twelve months, and how did you arrange it?

    1. ( ) Yes, made it on my weekly "day off"
    2. ( ) Yes, and was given an extra day off to make it
    3. ( ) No, did not make one during last twelve months

76. During the past summer did you attend any "Institute" or "Study Week" or similar program? If so, did you do it on your vacation time?

    1. ( ) Yes, did it on my vacation
    2. ( ) Yes, but was given time besides vacation
    3. ( ) No, did not attend any such program

77. What is the highest academic degree you have earned, and do you intend to study for a further degree?

    1. ( ) Have no academic degree and will not get one
    2. ( ) Have no academic degree but intend to get one

3. (   ) Bachelor's but will not go for Master's
4. (   ) Bachelor's and intend to get Master's
5. (   ) Master's but will not go for doctorate
6. (   ) Master's and intend to get doctorate
7. (   ) Have the doctoral degree

78–80. We guarantee that your answers to this questionnaire will be held in the strictest confidence. Yet for purposes of analysis and comparison we need to know the name of the diocese or archdiocese in which you are carrying on your ministry.

(Name of diocese or archdiocese) _____

Reverend and dear Father:

We have tried to make the return of the questionnaire as convenient as possible. Simply seal it in the accompanying post-paid envelope and drop it in the mail without your name or address appearing anywhere on it.

If you wish a copy of the statistical report of this survey send us a separate postcard requesting it. Processing the data will take at least three months.

May God reward you for your patience, care and cooperation in providing the information for this study. We again ask your prayers that this research project may prove a useful instrument for His greater glory and for the renewal of the Church in America.

If you have any comments or suggestions that seem important to you and were not included in these questions, please feel free to add them here.

Cordially in Christ

September, 1966

(signed)
JOSEPH H. FICHTER, S.J.

MARGINAL TABLES
ON 3,048 RESPONDENTS

SURVEY QUESTION

5. How long have you been ordained?

	%
3 years or less	23.1
4–6	18.9
7–9	17.0
10–12	14.5
13–15	7.9
16–18	6.2
19–21	4.2
22–24	2.9
25 and over	5.3

(Total of replies   3,048)

6. How old were you on your last birthday?

	%
Under 30 years	22.4
30–34	27.5
35–39	24.9
40–44	11.8
45–49	6.6
50–54	3.6
55 and over	3.1

(Total of replies   3,048)

223

7. How old were you when you entered the seminary

	%
13–14 years	27.5
15	5.0
16	4.5
17	12.5
18	19.8
19	7.8
20	6.1
21 and over	16.9

(Total of replies   3,048)

8. At what age would you now enter (or would you hesitate to enter)?

	%
13–14 years	12.1
15	1.6
16	1.4
17	7.1
18	24.2
19	5.2
20	8.6
21 and over	26.3
Hesitate to enter at all	13.4

(Total of replies   3,048)

9. Personal involvement attempting to interest boys in vocation

	%
Very much so	15.4
Quite a bit	25.4
More or less	36.6
Hardly at all	17.7
Not at all	4.9

(Total of replies   3,032)

10. Attraction of other occupations as hindrance to vocation

	%
Very serious	52.5
Moderately serious	36.2
Hardly serious	11.3

(Total of replies   2,963)

11. Lack of contact with priests as hindrance to vocation

	%
Very serious	27.8
Moderately serious	45.7
Hardly serious	26.5
(Total of replies 2,903)	

12. Feelings of unworthiness as hindrance to vocation

	%
Very serious	5.3
Moderately serious	24.8
Hardly serious	69.8
(Total of replies 2,874)	

13. Lack of encouragement from parents as hindrance to vocation

	%
Very serious	37.0
Moderately serious	46.4
Hardly serious	16.6
(Total of replies 2,941)	

14. Unwillingness to lead single life as hindrance to vocation

	%
Very serious	38.9
Moderately serious	40.9
Hardly serious	20.2
(Total of replies 2,948)	

15. Extent to which major seminary prepared for holy life

	%
Very much so	21.3
Quite a bit	32.8
More or less	31.4
Hardly at all	12.0
Not at all	2.5
(Total of replies 3,032)	

16. Extent to which major seminary prepared for intellectual life

	%
Very much so	14.8
Quite a bit	30.2
More or less	34.2
Hardly at all	16.5
Not at all	4.3
(Total of replies 3,019)	

17. Extent to which major seminary prepared to deal with lay people

	%
Very much so	4.3
Quite a bit	8.7
More or less	21.8
Hardly at all	40.9
Not at all	24.2

(Total of replies   3,020)

18. Extent to which major seminary prepared for parish problems

	%
Very much so	3.1
Quite a bit	7.3
More or less	19.7
Hardly at all	42.2
Not at all	27.7

(Total of replies   3,017)

19. How many official assignments since ordination (including current)?

	%
One	32.2
Two	21.2
Three	20.9
Four	11.1
Five	6.6
Six	3.6
Seven	1.9
Eight	0.9
Nine or more	1.7

(Total of replies   3,048)

20. Current assignment status

	%
Full-time parish assistant	55.4
Assistant, but with nonparish assignments	19.7
Full-time nonparochial assignment	24.9

(Total of replies   3,048)

21. On a first-name basis with pastor or local superior

	%
Usually	38.7
Sometimes	9.4
Seldom	7.8
Never	44.1

(Total of replies   2,959)

22. Bishop's personal interest in you during the past year

	%
Very much so	8.2
Quite a bit	10.6
More or less	20.7
Hardly at all	23.8
Not at all	36.7

(Total of replies   3,038)

23. Efficiency and humaneness of the Chancery Office

	%
High in both efficiency and humaneness	36.9
More efficient than humane	44.9
More humane than efficient	5.5
Poor in both efficiency and humaness	12.6

(Total of replies   2,988)

24. Priest should have chance to defend case and face accusers

	%
Agree	94.5
Disagree	1.5
Neutral	2.4
Don't know	1.6

(Total of replies   3,036)

25. Priest has right in conscience to act on controversial issues

	%
Agree	73.6
Disagree	14.0
Neutral	7.8
Don't know	4.5

(Total of replies   3,027)

26. Would you support the priest's right in conscience to act when it conflicts with the bishop's wishes?

	%
Publicly	20.0
Privately	38.7
Silently	8.9
Not at all	32.4

(Total of replies   2,926)

27. Extent of free and open communication in whole diocesan structure

	%
Very much so	5.1
Quite a bit	13.9
More or less	28.2
Hardly at all	35.5
Not at all	17.4

(Total of replies   3,003)

28. Extent of free and open communication in major seminary

	%
Very much so	11.3
Quite a bit	22.3
More or less	27.7
Hardly at all	22.8
Not at all	15.9

(Total of replies   1,801)

29. Extent of free and open communication with bishop or diocese

	%
Very much so	6.8
Quite a bit	12.9
More or less	25.4
Hardly at all	30.7
Not at all	24.2

(Total of replies   3,017)

30. Extent of free and open communication with pastor or superior

	%
Very much so	31.2
Quite a bit	20.7
More or less	21.8
Hardly at all	15.7
Not at all	10.6

(Total of replies   2,924)

31. Experience and attitude on full-time personnel committee for priests

	%
We don't have one, but I approve the idea	88.7
We do have one, and I approve of it	6.6
We do have one, but I disapprove of it	0.6
We don't have one, and I disapprove the idea	4.1

(Total of replies   3,011)

32. Experience and attitude on intermediary grievance committee

	%
We don't have one, but I approve the idea	80.2
We do have one, and I approve of it	10.1
We do have one, but I disapprove of it	0.6
We don't have one, and I disapprove the idea	9.1
(Total of replies 3,005)	

33. Experience and attitude on diocesan clergy senate

	%
We don't have one, but I approve the idea	67.3
We do have one, and I approve of it	27.1
We do have one, but I disapprove of it	1.4
We don't have one, and I disapprove the idea	4.2
(Total of replies 3,001)	

34. Discussed question of married clergy with fellow priest during the past year

	%
Frequently	32.5
Occasionally	53.3
Seldom	12.1
Never	2.1
(Total of replies 3,037)	

35. Should diocesan priests have freedom of choice to marry?

	%
Yes, but only before ordination	9.4
Yes, but only after ordination	5.5
Both before and after	46.7
No, not at all	38.4
(Total of replies 2,968)	

36. Priests who left and married be allowed to return to sacraments

	%
No, they should leave their wives first	8.0
Yes, but only if they have children	4.6
Yes, whether or not they have children	87.4
(Total of replies 2,965)	

37. Would married clergy be less or more effective than celibate clergy in parish ministry?

	%
Less effective	54.2
More effective	13.9
Makes no difference	31.9
(Total of replies 2,972)	

38. Would parishioners accept a married parish clergy?

		%
Most parishioners would		8.5
More than half of them		7.0
About half		15.4
Less than half		28.1
Hardly any		40.9
(Total of replies	2,953)	

39. Should only celibate priests be promoted to pastorate?

		%
Yes		17.6
No		62.4
Am not sure		20.0
(Total of replies	3,005)	

40. Should only celibate priests be promoted to episcopacy?

		%
Yes		39.0
No		37.6
Am not sure		23.4
(Total of replies	3,011)	

41. If a married priesthood permitted in Latin rite, would you marry?

		%
Yes, unquestionably		5.0
Very likely would		8.9
Probably would		17.1
Probably would not		28.1
Very likely would not		22.7
Definitely would not		18.2
(Total of replies	2,996)	

42. Number of priests in ordination class

		%
Less than 10		11.3
10–19		20.8
20–29		22.8
30–39		19.0
40–49		10.8
50–59		6.4
60–69		3.9
70–79		2.6
80 or more		2.4
(Total of replies	3,040)	

44. Number in ordination class who since left the priesthood

		%
None		61.4
One		23.9
Two		7.5
Three		4.1
Four		1.6
Five		0.5
Six		0.7
Seven or more		0.3
	(Total of replies 3,040)	

45. Number in ordination class who left priesthood and married

		%
None left priesthood		61.4
Left but did not marry		12.3
One married		18.2
Two		4.4
Three		2.7
Four		0.5
Five		0.4
Six or more		0.1
	(Total of replies 3,040)	

46. Church should allow voluntary resignation, or honorable discharge, from the priesthood

		%
Agree		63.8
Disagree		19.7
Neutral		7.1
Don't know		9.4
	(Total of replies 3,027)	

47. Should be definite retirement age for pastors

		%
Yes		90.6
No		5.5
Am not sure		3.9
	(Total of replies 3,044)	

48. Should be definite retirement age for bishops

		%
Yes		89.5
No		5.5
Am not sure		5.0
	(Total of replies 3,039)	

49. Diocese should have personnel office to work out assignments

	%
Agree	85.6
Disagree	6.0
Not sure	8.4

(Total of replies   3,038)

50. Curates should be interviewed before receiving appointments

	%
Agree	83.0
Disagree	8.4
Not sure	8.6

(Total of replies   3,041)

51. Curates should have ample notice to prepare for new appointments

	%
Agree	88.9
Disagree	6.2
Not sure	4.9

(Total of replies   3,040)

52. Curates who want to prepare for specialization should be encouraged to do so

	%
Agree	86.5
Disagree	3.4
Not sure	10.1

(Total of replies   3,039)

53. Curates should rotate parishes periodically for experience

	%
Agree	78.4
Disagree	8.2
Not sure	13.4

(Total of replies   3,043)

54. Curates should have choice of own residence or of living in parish rectory

	%
Agree	30.5
Disagree	49.6
Not sure	19.9

(Total of replies   3,041)

55. Each priest should have his office separate from residence

		%
Agree		22.2
Disagree		51.7
Not sure		26.1
	Total of replies 3,042)	

56. Abolish stipends and stole fees for graduated annual salary

		%
Agree		85.0
Disagree		7.2
Not sure		7.8
	(Total of replies 3,044)	

57. Promotion to pastorate on ability rather than seniority

		%
Agree		78.2
Disagree		8.5
Not sure		13.3
	(Total of replies 3,023)	

58. Dispense with monsignor's titles

		%
Agree		73.5
Disagree		10.9
Neutral		12.7
Don't know		2.9
	(Total of replies 3,047)	

59. Priests should wear "civilian" suits instead of black suits and clerical collar

		%
Agree		19.5
Disagree		57.6
Neutral		14.7
Don't know		8.2
	(Total of replies 3,041)	

60. Priests should have sabbatical leaves for refresher courses

		%
Agree		86.2
Disagree		4.0
Neutral		7.4
Don't know		2.4
	(Total of replies 3,041)	

61. Priests should restrict close friendship to fellow priests and deal with laity in professional, impersonal manner

	%
Agree	13.9
Disagree	75.2
Neutral	8.0
Don't know	2.9
(Total of replies 3,025)	

62. Rate of change of liturgical adaptations in own diocese

	%
Too fast	5.3
Too slow	29.8
About right	64.9
(Total of replies 3,037)	

63. Rate of change of inter-faith dialogue in own diocese

	%
Too fast	4.9
Too slow	41.9
About right	53.2
(Total of replies 3,014)	

64. Rate of change of seminary routine in own diocese

	%
Too fast	9.0
Too slow	41.7
About right	49.3
(Total of replies 2,640)	

65. Rate of change in racial apostolate in own diocese

	%
Too fast	3.1
Too slow	53.6
About right	43.3
(Total of replies 2,940)	

66. Rate of change of laity in parish planning in own diocese

	%
Too fast	2.1
Too slow	76.3
About right	21.6
(Total of replies 3,014)	

67. Rate of change in rules for mixed marriage in own diocese

	%
Too fast	3.2
Too slow	43.6
About right	53.2
(Total of replies 3,008)	

68. Attitude on the Medicare Program

	%
Approve	82.6
Disapprove	6.4
Am neutral	11.0
(Total of replies 3,034)	

69. Attitude on Administration conduct of Vietnam war

	%
Approve	55.9
Disapprove	21.8
Am neutral	22.3
(Total of ·replies 3,002)	

70. Attitude on Negro Civil Rights Movement

	%
Approve	77.1
Disapprove	11.6
Am neutral	11.3
(Total of replies 3,022)	

71. Attitude on domestic war on poverty

	%
Approve	74.9
Disapprove	13.3
Am neutral	11.8
(Total of replies 3,019)	

72. Work expected of you in your current assignment is

	%
More than you can handle	10.6
Extending you just about to your capacity	43.9
Only partly challenging your abilities	34.0
Calling for little of your abilities	11.5
(Total of replies 3,025)	

73. Opinion of clergy conferences attended in past twelve months

	%
They were both informative and stimulating	17.6
More informative than stimulating	24.2
More stimulating than informative	4.3
Neither informative nor stimulating	53.9
(Total of replies 2,876)	

74. Opinion of last annual diocesan priests' retreat

	%
Well-conducted and spiritually refreshing	42.4
Well-conducted but not spiritually refreshing	18.2
Spiritually refreshing but not well conducted	11.5
Neither well-conducted nor spiritually refreshing	27.9
(Total of replies 2,877)	

75. Experience and arrangement for Day of Recollection during past year

	%
Yes, and made it on my weekly day off	17.0
Yes, and was given an extra day off to make it	12.4
No, did not make one during last twelve months	70.6
(Total of replies 2,966)	

76. Experience and arrangement for Institute or Study Week during past summer

	%
Yes, did it on my vacation	15.1
Yes, but was given time besides vacation	22.2
No, did not attend any such program	62.7
(Total of replies 3,010)	

77. Highest academic degree and intentions for further study

	%
Have no academic degree and will not get one	11.4
Have no academic degree but intend to get one	2.9
Bachelor's but will not go for Master's	40.9
Bachelor's and intend to get Master's	15.6
Master's but will not go for doctorate	19.7
Master's and intend to get doctorate	5.6
Have the doctoral degree	4.0
(Total of replies 3,025)	

78. Regional distribution of respondents

%

New England (Maine, New Hampshire, Vermont, Massachusetts, Rhode Island, Connecticut)   14.4

Middle Atlantic (New York, New Jersey, Pennsylvania)   29.7

South Atlantic (Delaware, Maryland, District of Columbia, Virginia, West Virginia, North Carolina, South Carolina, Georgia, Florida)   4.6

East North Central (Ohio, Indiana, Illinois, Michigan, Wisconsin)   26.0

East South Central (Kentucky, Tennessee, Alabama, Mississippi)   2.7

West North Central (Minnesota, Iowa, Missouri, North Dakota, South Dakota, Nebraska, Kansas)   9.6

West South Central (Arkansas, Louisiana, Oklahoma, Texas)   4.1

Mountain (Montana, Idaho, Wyoming, Colorado, New Mexico, Arizona, Utah, Nevada)   2.5

Pacific (Washington, Oregon, California, Alaska, Hawaii)   6.4

(Total of replies   3,048)

PRESCRIPT TO FURTHER RESEARCH

America's forgotten priests—these diocesan clergy of lowly position—are not the whole Catholic Church in this country, nor have we questioned them on everything that is pertinent to their life and ministry. Like some of the bishops at the Vatican Council who made "interventions" that were not voted upon, some of our respondents made suggestions about items that were not included in this survey. As a postscript to this report, and as a "prescript" to further research, we present here a series of suggestions roughly in the order of frequency with which they were mentioned.

1. *Spiritual Life of Priests.* Since priests are supposed to be holy men, what do they report about their personal piety and religious devotions? "We are called to be saints," says one curate, but another thinks that the concept of holiness needs redefinition in our day. It was suggested that we ask about the regularity and benefits of private prayer, Bible reading, meditation, examination of conscience, devotion to Mary, visits to the Blessed Sacrament, the weekly holy hour. The breviary came in for comments in that it should be revised, revitalized, read in English, and made optional. It was also asked whether the priest has a regular confessor or spiritual advisor.

2. *Problems of Morale.* What is the state of morale at the lower levels of the clergy, particularly as evidenced by work satisfaction or dissatisfaction? A priest in specialized work says that "research in large organization shows a close connection between high morale and competent management and that the former depends largely on the latter." The following kinds of questions should be probed: Are you happy in your

238

work? Do you find your life worthwhile? Do you feel that you are contributing to a better world? Are you wasting your time and talents on trivia? What are the sources of boredom and frustration in the diocesan priesthood? Are you pleased with the results of your work? Are you generally optimistic about developments in your diocese?

3. *Community Life of Priests.* To what extent is there a genuine fraternity, or fellowship, among the priests of the diocese? One of the youngest curates thinks that "there is too much autonomy for each pastor and each parish. We ought to have a central clergy house in each city that would provide companionship for those who need it." Research should be done on the relationship between assistants in the same rectory and with the priests from the neighboring parishes. What are the causes, the prevelance and effects of loneliness among diocesan priests? How frequently do the priests forgather, and are their gatherings more recreational than apostolic? Does close friendship with one's age peers frustrate the broader fellowship of the priesthood?

4. *Relations with the Laity.* To what extent have the diocesan priests developed apostolic communication and Christian relations with the laity? A noncurate wants to know "to what extent does the priest make an effort to visit all families in the parish? Is he willing to celebrate weekday Masses in the homes of parishioners?" Is the typical urban parish too large to allow meaningful contacts with the laity? Should it be subdivided into smaller "communities of worship"? The clergy has the mission of developing the Christian neighborhood and community. Do priests appreciate the Council's emphasis on the Church's service to the people rather than the people's service to the Church? Are they participating in civic organizations and social movements for community betterment rather than simply for parish improvement?

5. *Ecumenism Within the Church.* In what ways can the ecumenical movement be internalized to create harmony among the several factions within the Church itself? Some of the priests observe a "new and dangerous cleavage" that did not exist before the Council. One curate remarks that "there is much polemicizing, but little dialogue, between the traditionalists and the progressives about changes and innovations." The research problem is to investigate fruitful communication even while diversity is preserved. Some respondents deplore friction between diocesan clergy and religious order priests, between parish priests and the Sisters in schools and hospitals, between the specialists and the parish clergy. What are the causes of such disharmony and how can an "internal ecumenism" be promoted?

6. *Reform of Financial Administration.* What can be done to modernize the financial administration of the parish, the diocese, and other Church structures? "You failed to ask many questions regarding money," complained a concerned noncurate. There is wide agreement that efficient bookkeeping systems should be set up, and that qualified lay persons manage parochial and diocesan finances. To what extent are financial statements issued and made available by Catholic colleges, schools, hospitals, newspapers, seminaries, and other institutions? More immediate is the pressure from the Chancery to take up special collections in the parish, and also the question whether recognition from above, and perhaps promotion to a better parish, depends upon the priest's ability to send money to the Chancery. There is also the question whether parishes in the wealthy suburbs are willing to assist poor parishes in blighted urban areas.

7. *The Clergy's Standard of Living.* How does the material standard of living among the diocesan clergy measure against the norms of Christlike poverty? Some of the priests in the larger and more affluent parishes seem to have guilt feelings about the material advantages they enjoy compared to other diocesan priests who "barely make a living." This is a puzzling problem that asks for further research because it involves the whole style of life appropriate to cultured and educated men. Should the priest attempt to adapt himself to the social class of his parishioners, living in poverty in the lower-class parish and living well in the upper-class parish? What are their leisure-time activities? What are their reading habits? Do they appreciate the arts, drama, and music? Are they absorbed in television programs? What kind of vacations do they take? What make of automobile do they own? Are their visits to the homes of friends more convival than apostolic?

8. *The Housekeeper Problem.* To what extent does the "housekeeper problem" interfere with the living and working conditions of the curate? One curate remarks that "this is an indispensable question in your next survey of parish assistants," and several others say that the arrogance and "bossiness" of the housekeeper is a frequent source of the curate's unhappiness. To what extent does the housekeeper assume command when the pastor is absent? A number of suggestions were made: that "live-in" housekeepers should be replaced with part-time domestic help; that yearly conferences be given to housekeepers; that the diocese exercise disciplinary jurisdiction over them: that each priest in the rectory should make semi-annual reports about her behavior; that curates have the right to veto the employment of a particular housekeeper; that housekeepers,

interviewed, counseled and approved by a diocesan personnel committee, should periodically rotate parishes.

Conclusion. This series of eight "problem areas" suggested by these priests as worthy of further investigation points to the need of supplementary information about the lower-echelon diocesan clergy. The quest for data utilizable for the renewal of the Church is never finished. A scientifically designed research project limits itself to hypotheses formulated around specific problems and provides generalizations out of which action programs can be constructed. In making their interventions, the priests were not simply complaining about certain situations in which they live; they were suggesting that more knowledge should be obtained in order to improve these situations.

Overriding all these comments is a spirit of genuine loyalty to Christ and His Church. These men love the priesthood; they want to be "other Christs"; they are willing to sacrifice themselves for the cause of Christ. They recognize the frailty of their own humanity in trying to fulfill this high vocation, but they are also in anguish about the "system" which they feel helpless to change. They indicate confusion and lack of confidence in what the priestly role is supposed to be in the modern Church, but they frequently state their appreciation for the fact that "someone has finally asked us what we think."

INDEX OF NAMES

243

INDEX OF SUBJECTS

245